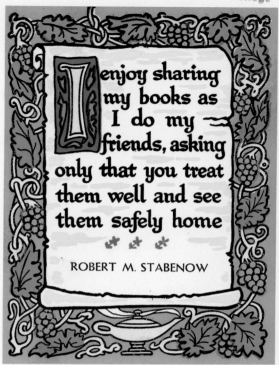

I enjoy sharing my books as I do my — friends, asking only that you treat them well and see them safely home

ROBERT M. STABENOW

GOD IS LIGHT

ALSO BY PROFESSOR DICKIE

Children's Addresses

One Year's Talks to Children
A Second Year's Talks to Children

For Youth

The Fellowship of Youth
—One Year's Addresses

Nonsense Stories

The Paper Boat
Mister Bannock
Psammyforshort

Translations from the German (Karl Heim)

The New Divine Order
Spirit and Truth
God Transcendent

Theology

Revelation and Response
The Obedience of a Christian Man

General

Scottish Life and Character
Ever in the Light
The Seven Words from the Cross
Normandy to Nijmegen

GOD IS LIGHT

STUDIES IN REVELATION AND
PERSONAL CONVICTION

By

EDGAR PRIMROSE DICKIE

PROFESSOR OF DIVINITY IN THE UNIVERSITY OF
ST. ANDREWS

NEW YORK

CHARLES SCRIBNER'S SONS

1954

"The light of the knowledge of the glory of
God in the face of Jesus Christ."

II Corinthians, iv. 6.

TO ISHBEL

There ys no solas under hevene
Of alle that a man may nevene
That shulde a man so moche glew
As a gode womman that loveth true

CONTENTS

ACKNOWLEDGMENT

The quotations from *God With Us* by S. L. Frank (1946) are made by kind permission of the author's executors and the publishers of the book, Messrs. Jonathan Cape.

INTRODUCTION

A FIGHTER-PILOT from an allied nation who served in the Royal Air Force while his own country was under enemy occupation has given a memorable description of the experience of flying at dawn and of the suddenness with which the light comes. He writes:[1]

> I climbed through the darkness embracing the earth towards the now luminous sky and the diminishing stars.
> Suddenly, without any transition, I plunged like a diver into full golden light. The wings of my Spitfire turned crimson. I was so dazzled that I had to lower my smoked glasses over my eyes. Beyond Holland, far away over there on the left, the sun emerged like a molten ingot from the inert leaden mass of the North Sea. . . . Moments such as these compensate for many a sacrifice and many a danger.

As the morning light came to Pierre Clostermann with the suddenness of a revelation, so we might say that revelation can come with the sharp impact of light. Revelation is to be counted, not as the answer to a problem, but as the unfolding of a mystery. There is, as it were, no answer at the end of the book for everyone to look up, to comprehend, and to quote with finality; but there is something that can be given only to those who are in a certain state of mind and soul. The organ of personal conviction is a spiritual organ. This does not mean that it dispenses with reason, but that it does not rest content with reason, and that it is never side-tracked into rationalism. God speaks to reason to say that which is above reason; and reason must be ready to be called upward. God speaks also through duty to say that which is beyond duty; and conscience must be open to enlightenment.

To enter a fresh claim for reason and for conscience in our present theological climate is to swim upstream, so that these chapters are offered as a few determined strokes against the current. They will try to say a good word for theological liberalism, in the belief that liberalism is far greater than all its greatest names, for in the first place we realise that much of

---

[1] In *The Big Show*, pp. 53-54.

its Continental theology which was translated into English represented the extreme wing. It said something unusual, or it was startling and stimulating, therefore it had an immediate appeal: and, secondly, we acknowledge that there was a vast company of Christian people who were profoundly influenced by the renewal of critical integrity fostered by this school, yet made their real contribution not through books but in the religious life of prayer and practice. In public worship, in the reading of the Bible, and in simple Christian goodness, they showed that they could combine a firm faith in criticism with a firm faith in God.

What we might call the Theology of Transcendence has lately occupied men's minds virtually to the exclusion of the Theology of Liberalism. The result has been sound and healthy, so far it has swept away the prolonged "traffic with the merely humanitarian", but it is already becoming clear that the truth must be sought in neither of these extremes, but in some Theology of Givenness and Growth; of Revelation and Response; of Mystery and Man. As schools of thought become known chiefly through their extremists, so it can be said of individual scholars that their startling utterances live after them, but their emendations are oft interred with their bones. Men like Fichte and Hegel may have modified many of their views in later years; Karl Barth may move a long way from his original centre by clarification or comment or even far-reaching alteration; but it is probable that the later theologian, like his predecessors, will be known to the history of theology by his earlier contributions. It is one of the ironies of controversy that amendments and alterations are apparently better done by others.

It has been said that a fatal step was taken when, because of a phrase of Augustine, God was identified with truth, the *aeterna veritas*. (*ubi enim inveni veritatem, ibi inveni Deum, ipsam veritatem*—Augustine, *Confessions* X. 24. See the discussion by Professor G. S. Hendry in *God the Creator*, Hodder and Stoughton, 1937, ch. iii.) Of course it cannot be maintained (as if this were the interpretation of Augustine's words) that when the philosopher has reached (if we can imagine him reaching) a complete system of true propositions, he has reached God; but we may on the other hand very well maintain that those who have been found of God have been brought to the eternal truth. God *is* Light. His grace is illumination as well as salvation. It would be a frail and inadequate form of salvation that did not give to a man new light on the mysteries of the universe. It is also a fact, too often forgotten, that the philosopher's integrity in the search of truth is blessed and his failure in integrity is sinful in the sight of God. False science, insincere philosophy—these are as despicable when they are due to the timidity of religion as when they are dictated by the rigidity of the Communist party-line.

The Theology of Transcendence has brought with it all the dangers of irrationalism and provoked the warning that the end of irrationalism is superstition. We must find a way out of this impasse. In particular we must seek a new stand-point over against Nature and History.

When St. Paul spoke of the revelation given to the Gentiles as sufficient to render them inexcusable in the sight of God, he was adopting a more hospitable view of natural theology than was customary with him. It is perhaps a truer view. Paul is at least willing to believe that pagan philosophy has been one form of preparation for the Christian revelation. (Cf. Eph. iii. 8-10.) His main contention is, however, (Rom. i. 18-32) that the Gentile argument from the nature of the universe to the existence of God has a value so considerable that the Gentiles must take the blame for their lapses into immorality and paganism, since these are crass betrayals of their own better thoughts and inspirations. It is, of course, customary to proceed by saying that Nature can never speak the word *Pardon,* but this perfectly valid discovery still leaves the further question open, whether *God through Nature* may speak that word to those who sincerely seek Him through Nature and have heard of no other way. To begin with Nature alone would indeed be an enterprise that could never bring us to God ; but we never do begin with Nature alone ; for in the first place we can set out only with the impact of Nature on our own minds, with a specific form of self-consciousness, possibly aesthetic experience ; and secondly, if we are brought to God by such an experience, it is because God was in it from the beginning. It may even be true that the revelation in Jesus could not come with saving power unless men had first learned of God in Nature. Nature cannot speak

of pardon; yet men have longed for pardon and believed it
was to be obtained if only they could discover the appropriate
medium. At a more advanced stage they acknowledge that the
medium must be prescribed by God, not invented by men.
Admittedly the longing and the subsequent acknowledgment
do not prove the reality of forgiveness; yet to us, in our Christian
setting, they show that the Spirit was at work, that there was
some glimpse of grace. It is therefore not true to say, simply,
that knowledge of God through Nature makes man inexcusable.
If the knowledge came through Nature alone, man might
legitimately say no more than that the world was meaningless,
or cruel, or capricious; for all these conclusions may be drawn
from Nature. Man need not blame himself unless—unless in
Nature he has also had a foretaste of grace.

The Christian attitude to History is bound up with the belief
in divine election and a covenant of grace. God is God of all
the earth. His elect people are His עַם־סְגֻלָּה, His "people of
special possession". His other people are, however, still His
people. The unfolding of history takes place according to His
will. His peculiar people were called and separated and
privileged; but His other nations too had been set in their place,
it may be all unconsciously and even through their rebelliousness, to serve His ends. The clue to all history is not given in
all strands of history, but only in the Biblical story; yet it does
not follow that other histories have made no contribution and
seen no light.

The mistake of Liberal Theology in dealing with such subjects as these lay in its claim to see in man's spiritual activities
converging lines, all leading in the end to God. What we have
in reality is better described as *radiating* lines. It is not a case
of rising from Nature up to Nature's God; or from duty up to
the divine Lawgiver. Rather we acknowledge that God was in
these spiritual activities from the beginning and in so far as
the Spirit was in them they were blessed. The theistic arguments are typical instances of such radiating lines. In so far as
they are valid spiritual activities of man they are discovering
in the world of nature, in philosophical speculation, in the moral
life, that which confirms what has come to men in the challenge
of God's presence and in the luminous moment. The thought
of God is progressively clarified and enlarged and with that the

interpretation of nature, of duty, of history, is clarified and enlarged also, until all is wholly luminous in Christ. All men do not begin with the same clarity, nor do all follow the same lines, yet these lines are not to be dismissed as mere discovery, but regarded as the elucidation of that which is being revealed. Of mysticism, moralism, and speculation, when these are honest, sincere activities of a dedicated heart, it can also be said, *sola gratia, sola fide, sola deo gloria.* They are not different human ways converging on God, but ways radiating from God. By them men have come to the Father because the Father was with them already; and, because no man cometh unto the Father save by Christ, we know that the Son also was with such seekers, though all unrecognised and unknown. Christian witness and evangelism will incessantly proclaim and set forth Him who is unwittingly acknowledged or falteringly invoked. Very different is the situation where pride or self-seeking or wilfulness have corrupted the mysticism, moralism, or speculation, so that these have become the ground of human self-sufficiency and boastfulness.

Thus in the historical Jesus of Nazareth, in His teaching and in His life and death and resurrection, we see, primarily, divine revelation initiated (for that which is said and done here is utterly new): we see also, secondarily, the fulfilment of that which was incomplete, the confirmation of that which was already in part revealed but timidly received, and the judgment of that which is inadequate or false. Few Christians can be happy about that tendency of theology which by a single stroke would excommunicate from the kingdom of truth and blessedness the reverent thinker, the earnest moralist, or the genuine and loyal adherent of an alien faith. The words of our Lord by which the exclusion is often justified are taken from St. John's Gospel (xiv. 6) " No man cometh unto the Father, but by Me ", yet if it is noticed that this passage begins with the saying " In My Father's house are many mansions ", it may be realised that the verse can be interpreted as saying, " Heaven is wider than you think. By whatever road men come to the Father, they come, it may be unwittingly, by the pre-existent Son of God, the eternal Way." Passages from the Synoptic Gospels such as Matthew xii. 30, " He that is not with Me is against Me ", can be balanced by others like Mark ix. 40, " He that is not against us is on our part ". Where it is said in John xiv that the *world* will not know the Spirit when He comes, the reference is, of course, not to the ethnic peoples of the earth but to the worldly-minded anywhere.

In dealing with the subject of certainty and with that of paradox, I have followed the lines of my articles in the *New Schaff Herzog Encyclopaedia of Religious Knowledge*, Baker Book House, Grand Rapids, Michigan ; and I have done so with the cordial permission of the publishers, for which I am most grateful.

For the reading of the typescript or parts of it I am greatly indebted to Professor Brand Blanshard, Yale University (the gifted and courteous Gifford lecturer in the University of St. Andrews for the sessions 1951-1952 and 1952-1953) ; Professor J. G. Riddell, the University of Glasgow; and the Reverend John B. Logan, minister of the Abbey Church, Coupar Angus (staunch colleague in Normandy with the British Liberation Army).

For careful typing of the manuscript I am very grateful to Miss Margaret Gordon and to my sister, Bertha.

CHAPTER I

REVELATION AND PERSONAL CONVICTION

"CONVICTION" is a word with many meanings. Indeed, the thing itself is frequently dismissed by the cynics, who delight to retell the story of the Scots lover who said, "Mary, I would go through flood and fire for you. And I'll be here again on Friday, if it's not raining." But the cynics are wrong. I well remember on a lovely midsummer evening in Normandy, shortly after we had landed on the beaches, seeing a young Norman peasant and his sweetheart walking along by the hedge-row oblivious to the devastation around them ; and my colleague aptly quoting from Thomas Hardy in *The Breaking of Nations*

> Yonder a maid and her wight
>   Come whispering by ;
> War's annals will cloud into night
>   Ere their story die.

Conviction is one of the inalienable factors in the life of the human spirit ; and when we further describe it as "personal conviction" we indicate another feature of it. It appears to be incommunicable, in the sense that it cannot be conclusively demonstrated as true to the satisfaction of other people. We can persuade others to share it only by bringing them to stand where we stand ; or, if the approach lies along the line of rational inference from reasonable evidence, there is always a moment when discontinuity appears. The chain of inference is broken, yet the strength of the conviction appears not to be impaired by the breach. It is as if we passed from one dimension to another, so that something which before was mysterious or opaque or even incredible becomes simple and clear and self-evident. When this happens it takes men to one of the supreme heights of human experience. The least inadequate description of the wonder of it is perhaps to be found in Browning's lines in Abt Vogler

> And I know not if, save in this, such gift be allowed to man,
> That out of three sounds he frame, not a fourth sound, but a star.

What form is taken by this experience of personal conviction when it occurs in the realm of religion? The most diverse answers are given by the many schools of thought which today discuss the question of revelation with special reference to its bearing on man's reason and the human capacity to receive revelation. It may be that authoritarian views are quite outmoded; for our generation acknowledges that it is illogical to fight tyrannies on earth while at the same time admitting dictatorial claims to divine jurisdiction made by the supposed delegates of heaven. At the other extreme, mystical schools of the Spirit, relying solely on private illumination, fail to satisfy, partly because they disagree fundamentally among themselves, but chiefly because they may easily lose touch with history and thus with the real and ultimate human situations; or with the Church, which is essential to a true doctrine of revelation, however hard it may be to state precisely where its place should be and what should be its significance; or with daily conduct and the inescapable claims of duty, which clearly cannot be separated from the witness of the Spirit.

THE PARADOX OF DOGMATISM

Protestant doctrine, in particular, tends to gravitate to one or other of two extremes. Either it hardens into orthodoxy, or it is softened into idealism. The danger of orthodoxy is gradually becoming clear. Professor D. M. Baillie has pointed out [1] that to the paradox of hedonism there must be added " the paradox of moralism "; that, even as the direct search for happiness defeats itself, so the quest of goodness, for its own sake and for nothing more, results, not in real goodness at all, but in Pharisaism. (It is so easy to forget that the first step in the search for goodness is the abnegation of spiritual pride.) It seems that we may add to these two " the paradox of dogmatism ". In seeking to be orthodox, to believe aright, to be invulnerable in faith, we may lose the real faith; it becomes pedantic, cold, sterile; we may be too much concerned to know *about* God. Faith can become a new form of mental security. Current Protestant orthodoxy tends to make true doctrine sacrosanct and so to lose the invaluable corrective of philosophy.

[1] *God Was in Christ*, p. 121.

It is true enough that doctrine has a strength and insight which are denied to philosophy; that doctrine may be less "of man" than philosophy is, but it is equally true that doctrine also is only man's expression of what God has revealed. Whereas the weakness of liberalism is pride in its own inventiveness, the fault of orthodoxy may be premature acquiescence. We must avoid the danger of supposing that our orthodoxy has exhausted God's richness.

On the other hand, Protestant idealism has constantly run into the danger of supposing that man can *discover* God. When Zophar asked (Job. xi. 7) "Canst thou by searching find out God?" he knew that the answer must be "No"; but this attitude is strongly contrasted with the Greek quest for knowledge which sets about its business with no intention of admitting limits to human discovery. It has been said [1] that the verse is "good Hebrew but bad Greek"; and it is abundantly clear that, if we have to choose, in the matter of revelation, the Hebrew has it. But do we need to choose? [2] The truth does not lie with either extreme. We ought to learn from orthodoxy the sense of abiding mystery. God has chosen certain ways in which to reveal Himself, and has left other experiences perplexing, or challenging, or condemning; *perplexing,* as in man's attitude to nature, when nature speaks, as it does, with two voices; *challenging,* as in man's reading of history, which may be ambiguous; *condemning,* as in morality, where man may be aware of the ultimate demand without consciousness of the final succour. These experiences are by no means annulled by the revelation in Christ, but we must realise that they are judged before they can be illumined. In this, orthodoxy is right. But we should learn also from idealism. To declare that we cannot by searching find out God may be "bad Greek" but the Greek impulse is not necessarily false, misleading, mischievous, arrogant. On the contrary, it is of God. The evil enters only when this is forgotten.

There are warning signs that we may be entering on a new period of Protestant scholasticism devoted more to right belief than to venturesome faith; that we ought to set about now trying to recapture the lost values of theological liberalism, which through all its vicissitudes sought to maintain a healthy sense of

[1] A. N. Whitehead, *Adventures of Ideas,* p. 132.   [2] See *infra,* p. 145.

the unity of divine truth, at the same time insisting that no doctrine formulated by man is final but leaves the field open for new vision. The task of recovering these emphases, now long obscured, is not wholly congenial to the theological outlook of today and will involve much swimming against the current; but, just as the insights of past generations have built up Christian doctrine, so there inevitably comes the point at which doctrine may begin to smother insight. We must avoid, above all things, the intolerance of the closed mind.

ATHENS AND JERUSALEM

On the other hand every parish minister is aware that the Greek view has too often come to dominate the minds of ordinary Christian people and church members. If they are reproached for not attending church they are apt to reply, not in all instances hypocritically, "We don't need to go to church ; we can find God in nature, in beauty, in art ". Or they may say, believing themselves in this to be showing commendable Christian tolerance, " All religions are ways to God. Why say that we have the only right one? " Hence the faithful preacher may be constrained always to give the Hebrew emphasis, knowing that only by so doing can he hope to counteract the tendencies that minister to man's pride. The average Christian, it would appear, has generally retained the weaker side of liberalism, accepting its tolerance towards other aspects of life but missing its characteristic of austere integrity in the face of truth.

The stimulating discussion between Barth and Brunner concerning natural theology has now run its course,[1] and each'side has learned much from the other.[2] Following upon these clarifications the time has come for theologians to take up the whole question afresh, not merely seeking some common ground in this or that circumscribed area where a point of contact can be discerned or safely acknowledged between the divine revelation and the human apprehension, but asking whether God's grace is not flooding in everywhere on human life, and whether

[1] See *Natural Theology*, comprising Brunner's *Nature and Grace* and Barth's reply " No! " in the translation by Peter Fraenkel, with an Introduction by Principal John Baillie, and the debate continued up to Brunner's *Revelation and Reason*.

[2] See Brunner's contribution to the *Scottish Journal of Theology*, June 1951, entitled " The New Barth ".

the absence of result does not lie in every case in man's sinful failure to accept and respond ; for we have forgotten that there may be grievously sinful failure in nature-mysticism, in the appreciation of beauty, in devotion to art, in the scientific quest, not because these are unworthy activities devoid of revelational significance, but because they have not been worthily followed, because there has been refusal to face the challenge presented by them—it may be a challenge to a life-long consecration. We have many instances of men and women who have gladly given precisely that dedication to their art or their science which is evoked by complete integrity, and these men and women, without doubt, will pass into the Kingdom of God before many others who are more obviously Christian believers. To take up the question afresh will mean returning on our tracks in order to recapture those values of theological liberalism which have been lost with the rejection of some of its theses.

THE PERMANENT CONTRIBUTION OF LIBERAL THEOLOGY

The strength of the liberal position lay in its insistence on two assertions, the first that reason is an ally of faith ; the second that freedom to apply rational methods of criticism is a religious principle. Its weakness lay in its uncritical acceptance of philosophical idealism.[1] Clearly, however, when that acceptance was uncritical it was made in opposition to the real character of liberalism. True liberalism took from philosophical idealism its integrity and, where it was true to itself as liberal *theology*, it departed from idealism in recognising, as the philosophy did not always recognise, the profundity of human sinfulness, a recognition which was manifest, much more than is commonly admitted, in its preaching, its worship, and its evangelism.

Liberal theology appears too often in caricature, being represented as no more than a system which traced the historical evolution of religion from primitive beginnings in animism or pre-animistic belief and practice, through the refinements of a sacrificial cult, to the moralism of the prophets and thus to Jesus, the Supreme Teacher who was found by his disciples to have the value of God and who taught a new morality of inwardness

---

[1] See, for example, the diagnosis by Dr. L. S. Thornton in *Revelation and the Modern World*, p. 44.

and divine forgiveness which outmoded sacrifice. In fact, theological liberalism has meant far more than this. (1) It has stood
for the oneness of the world; for the truth that creation and
redemption are acts of the same God, that creation is built on
redemption lines. (2) It has claimed that man's reason is therefore part of his endowment conferred on him by God's creative
act and made the fit medium of revelation. (3) It has indicated
that this reason evolved in the process of man's development
and with it man's grasp of divine truth; and it has affirmed
(4) that revelation is constantly proceeding and therefore (5) that
man's reason was not permitted to be wholly corrupted in man's
Fall. (6) It has maintained that man's response to revelation
in part determines the form which revelation will take and the
extent to which new truth can be revealed, and (7) that man's
response—in witness, in the formulation of belief, in the embodiment of the Christian life in Church and Society—is part of
revelation. (8) Behind all of this, it has maintained, is always
the mysterious activity of the one God, never to be wholly comprehended, yet never wholly beyond comprehension. (9) It
would always be wrong to imagine that we can precisely allocate
between man and God the parts played in religious knowledge
and in redemption; for we can say no more, according to liberal
theology, than that all is of God, yet man is not reduced to
the status of an automaton. Here we abide in mystery. (10) The
essential discipline of the religious life is seen when man faces
the divine challenge in finding himself confronted by God.
(11) This confrontation or encounter may take place anywhere,
at any time; but of special consequence is the Word of God.
(12) This Word is found most clearly in the Bible. (13) Creeds
and confessions make their contribution, since they are revelationary in so far as they are the testimony of converted people.
(14) The inner light of individual converted persons has its
contribution to make, though it is liable to be subjective, flicker-
ing, even eccentric. (15) The witness of the Church is essential,
though it is liable to corruption in a way which is not possible
with Scripture. Whereas Scripture can indeed be wrested
consciously or not to the private purposes of the interpreter, the
Church can go one worse; it can be guilty of actively promoting
the wrong interpretation.

THE INADEQUACIES OF LIBERALISM

Without doubt theological liberalism suffered from a tendency to believe in the goodness of man and to find justification for its belief in man's lofty ideals, ignoring the plain fact that man is incapable of carrying them out. There was a too facile readiness to be comforted by what man "aspired to be and was not". From that optimism there followed a simple trust in the inevitability of progress, not, let it be clear, through human efforts, but by the progressive realisation in this world of the Kingdom of God. Involved in this simple trust in the triumphant and inevitable march of divine events was the danger of misinterpreting the Person of Christ through employment of terms and ideas more appropriate to the realm of evolution than to that of revelation. This, as Reinhold Niebuhr has written [1] is "why liberal Christianity can give no satisfactory answer to the question why Christ, rather than some other 'good' character of history should be revered as divine, or how we can have the assurance that an evolutionary development may not produce a higher form of 'goodness' more worthy of our 'highest devotion'". Yet it must be said that the tentativeness of this school of thought can frequently be traced to a reverence for the truth, and it can be said of many of its adherents that they honoured the advice once given by Bishop Westcott to the boys at Harrow, to combine a firm faith in criticism with a firm faith in God.

The optimism of a past age contributed also to a defective view of human sin, and a tendency to look on it objectively. We realise more clearly today that it is not the outward spectator who sees sin in its true light, but the subject who is in its grip, and that the truest knowledge of it that man can have is that of one who has experienced, not only sin, but, in a full measure, the conquest of sin by grace. It is only from the experience of grace that the depth of sin opens up before us. All explanation of the fact is an explaining of it away. It is impossible, for example, to account for it by the opposition of spirit and matter, or of will and desire, or of understanding and volition; for the conflict of these is the *result* of sin. Nor may we account for it through the possibilities arising out of

[1] *Nature and Destiny of Man,* vol. II, p. 56.

freedom of choice, both evil and good, for these possibilities, with the apparent anarchy which they bring in their wake, are the *products* of sin.

Most of all does theological liberalism find itself in straits when seeking to establish and to expound the uniqueness of Christ. All other religions, prophetic and mystical, come to men with an Imperative; bidding them (as in two typical instances) to exercise themselves in the Buddhist submersion in order to arrive at Nirvana; or to fast and to pray and to keep the commandments so helping to bring in the Kingdom of God; but in contrast to all these Imperatives, demands and exercises which afflicted and tormented men, the message of the apostles came with quite another significance. It began with a Perfect Indicative. The Christian teaching about salvation takes its stand on a fact for ever accomplished. Thus arose the most difficult task of Christian Apologetics, to show how one event, occurring at an arbitrary point in human history, is nevertheless of absolute significance for all humanity; a task which must be approached, moreover, from the most practical of standpoints. The missionary in foreign lands knows that, in carrying the message of Christ, he is only doing harm unless Christianity is not merely the greatest religion so far evolved in the world, but the absolute religion; unless the Cross of Christ has absolute significance for the soul of every man. Jesus was not just the Euclid of religion, bringing to light ideas that were always true, but unknown till He spoke; nor the Copernicus or Columbus of religion. If we ask: [1] Without Christ would the love of God still be as bright, though we should see it only through a darkened window? we know that the answer must still be that of Paul and Luther, and quite unequivocal. The answer is that without Jesus man is altogether lost. Christ's life and death are of vital significance, not alone for this world, but for eternity. The words of Jesus Himself on the unique revelation of the Father in Him are, specially, those of Matthew xi. 27 and John xiv. 9: "All things are delivered unto Me of my Father; and no man knoweth the Son, but the Father; neither knoweth any

[1] See Heim, *Glaube und Leben*, pp. 181 ff.

man the Father, save the Son, and he to whomsoever the Son will reveal Him." "He that hath seen me hath seen the Father." But the uniqueness of His revelation of the Father is declared not so much in His words as in His acts. The announcement of salvation meant, at the same time, the bringing of salvation. Redemption, to be understood, has to be seen. Other truths can be declared and their truth established. The truth about divine grace has to be acted. Its proofs are not syllogisms, but the witness of one heart in touch with another. Every transcript of the Gospel in the heart of a Christian is a new argument to confirm it. Thus the uniqueness of Christ is to be understood only by understanding the meaning of His life and of His death ; and the core of that meaning is the claim of Jesus to forgive sins. The central thought of the tragic drama of all ages is the irrevocability of the past, the impossibility of taking guilt incurred and making it as if it had never been. Christ claims the power to liberate men from this tragedy. All titles that are given to Him are simply attempts to express this power to forgive sins. At the end of every discussion of the Person of Jesus we are compelled to say with Luther and Melanchthon, that every definition of the nature of Christ is no more than an unfolding of the truth of faith, that "He is our Lord and our Redeemer".

Liberalism's chief strength lay in the overcoming of the naive acceptance of the Biblical record as something mechanical or magical ; in the deliverance of religion from the dangers of superstition, since the earnestness and sincerity of its criticism, like that of good scientific thought, made it impossible for any form of faith but the best to survive; and in finding the criterion of interpretation in the right place, namely, the Person of Christ. Its main weakness lay in the difficulty it experienced of outlining the Person ; and the portrait of Jesus was painted too exclusively in the forms and colours of morality, idealism and reason. This weakness, however, was one which could be removed by following the very path which liberalism has signposted—unprejudiced and courageous exposure to truth. Thus liberalism, since this and not the too familiar caricature was its real nature, never became the idealistic ethical system which it is frequently supposed to be. It saw consistently in the light of the Bible the actual state of man, and by the same light it saw

what man could become in Christ. It promoted earnest study
of man's sin and God's forgiveness; and it recognised—though
it could not always expound it well—the uniqueness of Christ
for faith. Instead of withdrawing into the background, it ought
therefore to advance on two objectives. It should sharpen its
expression of the fact (indicated p. 12 *supra*) that encounter with
God is the sphere in which truth is apprehended. This question
has been handled recently by Rudolf Bultmann, but it was
earlier a major issue with Karl Heim. Secondly, new investigation should be made of the nature of Scripture as a human word
energised by God and the medium chosen by God for His
encounter with man. Here the dialectical theology has broken
fresh ground and greatly stimulated thought, but the truth has
also been conserved in an unbroken continuity in the practice
if not in the theory of theological liberalism, both in the manner
and pre-suppositions of its private reading of the Bible and in
the principles of its exposition of Scripture in public worship.
The two objectives are not disconnected.

PERSONAL ENCOUNTER AND THE SWAY OF AUTHORITY

There are many who feel that the requirement of nothing
more than personal encounter and revelationary event would
present faith as possibly little better than vague mysticism; that
something more authoritarian is needed; and that the stabilising
factor is the expression of truth in propositional form. This
suggestion is welcome in so far as it draws attention to a real
danger. What appears to be personal encounter may not necessarily be encounter with God. It may be no more than an uprush
from the unconscious self. And the only way in which the true
encounter can be identified as genuinely indicative of a divine
presence is by noting whether it is placed in a context of Church,
of Scripture, and even—remembering always that God is the
Lord of all these—of human history and of man's duty to his
neighbour. But the demand for some authoritarian element
contains within itself a new danger. To grant the demand
would easily bring us back to a rigid type of human orthodoxy.
We must indeed conserve a prominent place for the formulation
of Christian faith in the creeds of the Church, but without forgetting that the real authority is the Spirit, which shall lead

men into all truth—even into truth expressed in propositional form. In the Bible this appears to be a large part of the con- notation of the word "light"—not vague mystical experience but experience which can become the material for the expression of truth in terms sufficiently precise to bring others, even in distant ages and in very different circumstances, to the place in which personal apprehension, face to face with God, becomes a possibility; and definite enough to strike a chord of recog- nition in others who have had a similar experience. The expression of the truth in such precise and definite terms takes place primarily in the Bible, but notably also in every Christian circle, from the obscure household to the universal Church.

With reference to the second objective, that of fresh investi- gation of the nature of Scripture, we notice the link with the first objective; since the Bible itself grows out of a living religious community such as is seen in a humble family or a chosen nation; in a faithful remnant or a flourishing part of the universal Church. It is often supposed today that theological liberalism is ill fitted for such an investigation, and the reasons put forward, are in general, four in number. (1) It is alleged that this school of thought emphasises almost exclusively the human search for the divine; man's discovery rather than God's revelation. We are apt to forget, however, that many who were liberals in theology held as firmly as any to the dominant con- viction that the Scriptures were divine revelation. Their critical integrity did not diminish but rather illumined and purified their faith. (2) Too great a use, it is said, and too uncritical a use, was made of the concepts and principles of natural science; so that liberalism brought to its study of sacred documents certain prior constraints which were alien and so tended to warp the judgment and to influence interpretation subtly and perhaps imperceptibly. But, even if this were so, these theologians were setting their feet on a road which led straight out of the morass of verbal inerrancy and the multiple sense of Scripture, and were marking an important stage in the advance towards a right understanding of the Bible. (3) As a consequence of their un- critical acceptance of the categories of contemporary science, it is argued, the theological liberals became chary of accepting anything that could be regarded as infected with the super- natural. It is very true. Undoubtedly they were chary, frequently far too chary, of believing that which outsoared man's reason, but once again there was a fruitful consequence of this caution. Miracle had to authenticate itself. Even as one of the achievements of the scientific principles of our day in the service of religion has been to make untenable any faith but the best, so this critical outlook purged the faith of its magical and superstitious accretions. (4) Lastly, it is brought as a charge against liberal theology that in its interpretation of Scripture it was fettered and hampered by its complete surrender to the principle of evolution. Again, there is much truth in the accusation ; but it is hard to see how this could have been otherwise if the clear gains which followed from it were to be won. Undoubtedly, like the natural scientists themselves, the theologians of the period applied the category without sufficient analysis ; but it is scarcely possible even for theologians to be in advance of their time always and in everything. And the category did produce many true and lasting results which would otherwise have been unobtainable. It became clear to Christian believers that God leads His people gradually, inspiring their response to His revelation, and adapting His revelation to their response. Perhaps the liberals missed—but not all of them did —the discontinuity which underlies the process and at times disrupts it ; and, because of this consideration and others like it, the vital concern in every revival of liberal thought is not merely to hold fast to that integrity which gave the movement its vast importance, but to consolidate that integrity by every possible means and in every situation, particularly in that of Bible study, permitting the Scriptures to speak with their own message unhampered by the existence in the hearer's mind of presuppositions or indurated mental habits acquired from philosophical or other non-Biblical sources. It is, of course, impossible to begin from zero : presuppositions of some sort there must be : the important matter is that they should be made explicit and then submitted to the judgment of the Christian sources of religious knowledge. It has been suggested [1] that theological liberalism chose *conviction* instead of *revelation,* and the implication is that the two are incompatible. Surely they are not mutually exclusive alternatives. Revelation produces

[1] See L. S. Thornton, *Revelation and the Modern World*, ch. ii, and the references there quoted.

conviction and the conviction so produced may be characterised by the sense that all is of God ; that it is the divine truth itself which comes to the human heart to exercise a sway that cannot be challenged or gainsaid. Dr. T. W. Manson has summed up his suggestive treatment of the passages on light (Matt. v. 15 ; vi. 22 f. and Luke xi. 33-36) in these words : " So then we have the true and only sign from heaven, the light of God's revelation. This light shines in Jesus, and through Him in His followers. Its shining beacon is a guide to those who are in darkness. If they follow the light, they too will come to their desired haven."[1]

Liberalism has a vital contribution to make iŋ this realm. Humanist attitudes to the Bible have presented it as a superb literary document, but little more, a document which exhibits the remarkable development of a highly endowed segment of the human race in the progress of religion. Dialectical theology, on the other hand, has obliterated the fact of movement within the Biblical record and ironed out all to one consistency, leaving no room for a history of the divine dealings with man ; for Old Testament, like New Testament, must speak everywhere of the event of Christ. Where humanism has presented only natural growth, and dialectical theology has dwelt exclusively on givenness, the true liberal theology will hold consistently to the intricate interweaving of pattern and novelty, of growth and givenness.

God is not reached by right thinking, even by right thinking about God : nor yet is He to be reached by giving up thinking ; He is not to be attained through works : nor yet by abandoning works ; He is not to be apprehended through authority : nor yet by defying all authority ; but rather by following all of these, thought, works, authority, where they are worthy, and following them without pride in them knowing that where they are worthy they are of God and not of man.

THE QUEST FOR CERTAINTY

At the heart of the religious quest, sustaining it when the goal seems far off and unattainable, is that longing for certainty which is spoken of by the psalmist as the cry of heart and flesh for the living God.

[1] *The Sayings of Jesus,* p. 94.

Religious certainty is frequently identified with assurance of salvation or of the possession of divine grace (*certitudo salutis* or *certitudo gratiae*) and is usually connected with such passages as Isaiah xxxii. 17, "And the work of righteousness shall be peace ; and the effect of righteousness quietness and assurance for ever", or Hebrews x. 22, "Let us draw near with a true heart in full assurance of faith "; but it seems also to have attached to it constantly the underlying thought of *conviction* in the sense that the believer is sure of God's truth as well as of His redemptive grace ; and this is marked in the New Testament by the characteristic use of verbs of knowing.

If the certainty is to be genuine, not premature nor unexamined, but well-founded and lasting, ·one condition of its coming is the presence of *integrity*. In its insistence on this quality theological liberalism played a worthy part, which is reflected in the intellectual activity of its peak period, and in the biographies of its leaders. They had faith in the harmony of truth. With perfect confidence in their own creed, they believed also that it possessed that inalienable characteristic of truth, that quality which nothing else but truth possesses, that it can be reconciled with everything else that is true. Liberalism was strong also in its conviction that a belief which is once formulated in propositional terms must be submitted to the scrutiny of reason.

Integrity is one condition for the achievment of certainty ; but it is not the only one. There must also be *obedience*. And in this respect too liberalism has made its lasting contribution. It has held to the centrality of reason and the sovereignty of conscience ; it has acknowledged the supreme authority of the Word of God when free criticism has identified that Word and has set the Word free from narrow interpretations given to it by sectarian or dogmatical interests, and permitted it to bear its own convincing testimony ; and it has set in the forefront of its teaching the command to love God and to love your neighbour.

Something more is required, however, beyond integrity and prior to obedience. The creed of love to God and to one's neighbour may possibly be interpreted as sufficient in itself to bring salvation to man ; and man has to be reminded that most of all he requires *forgiveness*. Where theological liberalism was often content with a philosophical belief in God, immortality, and duty; and with the unquestioning acceptance of all the concepts of science concerning a closed universe governed by immutable laws from which not even the human mind might be exempted, we have learned to lay more and more stress on a living and acting God, One who confronts and challenges men; a Person who is not left powerless in the universe which He has made, Who does not only watch it spin or admire its evolution, but acts, wills, loves; One who is constantly revealing Himself; One who pleads, and punishes, and pardons.

Dr. Karl Heim, of Tübingen, has dealt notably with the historical development of the doctrine of Christian certainty in his book *Das Gewissheitsproblem in der systematischen Theologie bis zu Schleiermacher* (1911) and has given a very thorough philosophical and theological discussion of the theme in his *Glaubensgewissheit* (1923). Though neither of these has yet appeared in English dress the theme shines through all his work and is seen specially in two books which have been translated —*Spirit and Truth* and *God Transcendent*. Others, like F. R. Tennant, have underlined the distinction between certitude and certainty, the former as the convincedness of the believer, a state of mind; the latter as the objective character assigned to propositions dealing not with a mental act but with *credenda*.[1] Dr. R. H. Thouless has made a penetrating analysis of degrees of certainty founded on his own experimental research.[2] John Dewey urged the necessity of ending the false segregation of action and thought and maintained that certainty is a will-o'-the-wisp. At the most, he argues,[3] we can hope for a clarification of the possibilities of experience; and we should therefore give up the desire for certainty by cognitive means and turn instead to the search for security by practical means. He does not, however, always make it quite clear how this form of practical security escapes the difficulties which he believes to threaten the other. From another view-point both Marx and Lenin urged the combination of thought with action.[4] Revolutionary theory "loses its very essence if it is not connected with revolutionary practice". It is revolution which creates the situation propitious to

[1] Tennant, *Philosophical Theology*, I, p. 290.
[2] *The Tendency to Certainty in Religious Belief.* See *The British Journal of Psychology*, vol. xxvi, pt. 1, July 1935. [3] *The Quest for Certainty.*
[4] *Vide* Stalin, *Foundations of Leninism*, p. 26.

right thinking.[1] All these suggestions represent reaction from the tendency to see certainty only in the metric aspect of the universe in which the natural sciences are at home (where the more appropriate term would be *accuracy*) or in the fields of mathematics and physics where the certainty achieved is abstract, and concerned with form and not with content. The Christian truth in respect of the relation of action to belief is notably summarised in John vii. 17, "If any man will do His will, he shall know of the doctrine whether it be of God, or whether I speak of Myself".[2]

The idea of certainty has also been questioned in the sphere of morals, particularly by Oswald Spengler,[3] who applies current views on relativity to ethics in such a way as to suggest that the moral ideal may be exhausted of its meaning when the culture which gives rise to it has spent its force, and moral conviction may ultimately be no more than a parochial prejudice.

THE CERTAINTY OF PERSONAL ENCOUNTER

The Scriptural basis of a Christian doctrine of religious certainty may be found particularly in Romans viii. 15 ff. and Galatians iv. 6, where it is said that the divine Spirit bears witness within the spirit of man. The familiar term "full assurance" ($\pi\lambda\eta\rho\sigma\phi\sigma\rho\iota\alpha$) is found in Colossians ii. 2 ; 1 Thessalonians i. 5 ; Hebrews vi. 11 and Hebrews x. 22. What is here presented to us is not a rational certainty, but the certainty of encounter. We know and believe the love that God hath to us, but it is more than knowing *what* we believe. God is love. We know *whom* we have believed. (1 John iv. 16 and 2 Tim. i. 12.)

There is one kind of evidence which comes from human reason and is expounded in the logical syllogism ; and there is another kind that comes from personal encounter. It is the second that is present in religious certainty. God is not reached by inference from any given reality. Dilthey[4] did valuable work in stressing the difference between two modes of interpreting reality and, though he himself drew a negative conclusion when he came to consider the theological implications, that con-

---

1 Lenin, *Left Communism : an Infantile Disorder*, pp. 76-77. See *infra*, p. 105.   2 See *infra*, p. 103.   3 *The Decline of the West*.
4 See Hodges, *Wilhelm Dilthey* : An Introduction; and the same author's *The Philosophy of Wilhelm Dilthey*.

clusion by no means follows from his study. Contemporary Protestant thought emphasises that, so far from being subjective, the idea of encounter is utterly the reverse; for it implies that there is no help to be had from human analogies. God is always Subject. In strict accuracy we can speak of Him only in the second person. Moreover, as those who are born blind cannot make themselves see, so the work of redemption must be performed by Another. We either remain in the darkness of despair or we stand in gratitude before an immeasurable gift. This thought is developed powerfully by Heim throughout his book *God Transcendent*.[1] It is impossible for us by observation or by any thinking of our own to reach what God is and what He wills. We are thrown back on His own revelation. There are extensive differences in the mode of conceiving the impact of this revelation:—

CERTAINTY MAY BE BASED ON AN INNER LIGHT

The foundation of the certainty may be discovered in a moment of intense conviction, in some experience (perhaps incapable of analysis) which is overwhelmingly sure, and shines by its own light. The tendency is usually to adopt a subjective standard of certainty, though neglect or minimising of the value of Scripture and Church is not necessarily implied. When George Fox emerged from his spiritual struggles he believed that the Light from God which had visited his soul was available for all men: "Now the Lord opened to me by His invisible power that every man was enlightened by the Divine Light of Christ; and I saw it shine through all. . . . This I saw in the pure openings of the light, without the help of any man; neither did I then know where to find it in the Scriptures, though afterwards, searching the Scriptures, I found it."[2] He felt the call to "forsake all, young and old, to keep out of the way of all, and to be a stranger to all". When he began to attend meetings and divine services, it was often laid upon him to interrupt— especially when they were conducted by "professors" (that is, the opposite of the "profane") for he believed that the usual profession of the faith was formal. The divine origin of the

---

[1] English translation of *Glaube und Denken*, 3rd edn.
[2] *Journal*, Bicentenary edition, I, pp. 34-35.

Light appeared to be so unmistakable that the early members of
the Society of Friends shrank from regarding it as in any sense
a product of their human nature, with the inevitable outcome
that everything "human" was regarded with suspicion as
potentially inimical to the full freedom of the Spirit to move in
the hearts of men. For the same reason "good works" were
frowned upon: they were suspected as "creaturely activities".
The best that the creature could do was to wait for the Spirit to
move and inspire him. Nevertheless, the conviction that this
Divine Light was the prerogative of all men made of many
Quakers the most ardent philanthropists; and their chief service
to the world has been, paradoxically, their heroic efforts to sup-
press slavery, to put an end to wars, and to secure reforms in the
treatment of the criminal and the insane. So notable has their
contribution been to distressed humanity that it was not surprising to hear a small girl, caught in the aftermath of war in
Central Europe, when asked how she was being looked after,
reply "I'm being Quakered" (Ich werde gequäkert).

It is not to be denied that religious truths present themselves
often in startling fashion; yet it is not to be supposed that the
unaccountable nature of their appearance is sufficient to stamp
them as authentic revelation. On the other hand it must be
remembered that thought and speculation might never have
discovered them: they had to arrive as intuitions, revelations,
luminous experiences. As to the way in which they may be
verified by subsequent comparison with Scripture and with
Church pronouncement the case of the Friends has been fairly
stated by Robert Barclay, laird of Ury, the theologian of the
movement, in the Second Proposition of his *Apology*: "These
divine inward revelations . . . neither do nor can ever contradict the outward testimony of the Scriptures, or right and sound
reason. Yet from hence it will not follow, that these divine
revelations are to be subjected to the test, either of the outward
testimony of the Scriptures, or of the natural reason of man,
as to a more noble or certain rule and touchstone; for this
divine revelation and inward illumination, is that which is
evident and clear of itself."

The work of the Lutheran, Frank of Erlangen, is most
appropriately considered here, since he pointed[1] to the con-

[1] In his *System of Christian Certainty*.

vincingness of one particular inner experience, that of regeneration, which is beyond all questioning and free from all dubiety. Section 15 of Frank's book states: "The special moral experience which underlies the Christian certainty, is that of regeneration and conversion, a transformation of the man's moral state of life, accomplished by ethical impulses not proceeding from the subject himself, but yet willingly received by him; in virtue of which a new *I*, as innermost determining ground of his personal moral life, is henceforth distinguished from that hitherto prevailing, and in conflict with the same asserts its central, dominant position." Nevertheless, Frank did not rest in the subjective experience, for the consciousness of being reborn leads to other certainties—(1) the awareness of the nature of sin and of the new life; (2) awareness of the true God and of the redemption wrought by Christ; and (3) confidence in the Scriptures, the sacraments, and the Church, because they mediate between the first and the second of these awarenesses.

Doctrines of an inner Light raise their own problems and press first the question whether they can be so stated as to give the necessary truth contained in ideas of authority; since it must constantly be borne in mind that the inner Light itself has not developed in a vacuum but has been fostered through the vast contribution made by Church, by tradition, by fellowship with others, and above all by Scripture. Secondly, these doctrines do not always avoid the familiar danger of magnifying a little human candle till it appears like the sun in heaven. A very small illumination, simply because it seems to be our very own, can easily come to claim all our attention and, filling the mind to the exclusion of everything else, convey to us the impression that it is the essence of ultimate truth. Hence the importance of stressing the Protestant doctrine of the inner witness of the Holy Spirit, though not even that doctrine can always avoid the pitfall. The inner witness may come to be little more than human reason in disguise again. To secure a right objectivity, emphasis must constantly be laid on the second half of the phrase—the inner testimony *of the Holy Spirit*. The Spirit is that which is given without measure to Christ and dwells in Him fully, so that He alone is the criterion by which the measure of the Spirit's presence elsewhere can be reckoned.[1]

[1] Cf. Calvin's interpretation of John iii. 34.

Ultimately, as Augustine insisted, our light and peace are not "inner": they come to us from without.[1]

Authority, in religion, means Divine Authority. To rest one's faith on authority means that one believes divine truth to have been communicated to mankind unmistakably and through a reliable medium. Gwatkin has defined Authority as "all weight allowed to the beliefs of persons or the teachings of institutions beyond their reasonable value as personal testimony".[2] We accept many things because we are told, and we believe that we can trust our informants. We accept traditions because they embody wisdom. Authority can tell us what men in the past have thought and therefore can set before us the material with which we are concerned, both clearly and comprehensively; and authority can tell us what men in the past have felt, what have been their religious experiences, and so increase for us the realm of spiritual adventure of which we can take cognisance. When we come to ask ourselves what are the credentials by which we may recognise the trustworthy person and the trustworthy institution, we may feel that we are being drawn into a wide, but vicious, circle. We desire the authority to help us in determining when our judgment is right, and yet we must call in our judgment in order to decide which authority is reliable. Two contrasted types of credential are offered. The authority may claim miraculous powers. The prophet may cause an axe-head to swim, or may call down rain, or cure sickness, or bring calamity from heaven on his enemies or the enemies of his God. An institution like a church may make a similar claim. It may assert that it has a miraculous stability of doctrine, or an occult sanctity, or a mechanical infallibility transmitted down the centuries. This type of credential was explicitly rejected by Jesus, in His refusal to work miracles as proofs of His power and in the Temptation in the Wilderness. A miracle can prove nothing but itself.

There is a second way in which an authority can win trust for itself. It may do so by awakening a response in the hearts of men; and this appears to be the only manner in which an

---

[1] See later, chapters vi and vii.　　　　[2] *Knowledge of God*, I, p. 3.

authority can vindicate itself without doing violence to the spiritual character of man. It is of the essence of spirit that it cannot be coerced: it must be won through a conviction in which it co-operates. And from this it would seem that it is not what we are accustomed to call the "authority" which is in fact authoritative, but the truth itself revealed to, or embodied in, the "authority". Truth authenticates itself: authorities can only present or convey that truth. In the Commentary on St. John's Gospel (xxix. 6) Augustine makes use of the principle contained in the Septuagint version of Isaiah vii. 9, "Unless you believe you shall not understand", which in the Old Latin version appeared as *Nisi credideritis non intelligetis* and argues that many sluggish minds could have no certainty whatsoever save by trusting those who are more favoured. At one point [1] he even declares "I would not believe the Gospel unless the authority of the Catholic Church compelled me thereto". Concerning the last utterance it should be noticed that it was spoken in the heat of controversy; that it is an extreme statement nowhere else repeated; and that "authority" here means "testimony".[2] Even if the sentence were taken at its face value, it would still be necessary to go on to inquire, What is the Catholic Church? It is true that we make our first approach to Christ through those who have borne witness to Him in speech or in writing or in life; through parents, teachers, Old Testament prophets and historians, New Testament evangelists and missionaries; but certainty comes only when we find Christ confronting *us*, speaking to *us* by the Word. Yet neither must this be pressed too far. There are, it is true, lonely souls who have passed beyond all dubiety in their religious life and yet seem to owe little to the Church; but it is also true that it is unusual, in many cases impossible, to have certainty in isolation from the fellowship of Christian people.

To avoid the difficulties of these two schools of thought, that of the Inner Light and that of Authority, the foundation of certainty is placed in the Scriptures and the Holy Spirit. Two quotations will show how this is expressed in our own day. One is taken from the Reformed Church, the other from the Lutheran. First the Reformed writer, Professor Barnabas Nagy,

[1] *Contra Epistolam Manichaei quam vocant Fundamenti*, section 6.
[2] See Warfield, *Tertullian and Augustine* and J. H. S. Burleigh, *The City of God*, pp. 57 ff. Cf. *infra*, p. 164.

of the Theological Faculty, Sarospatak, Hungary [1]—" It is only
by obedience that the Church can have a real and valid authority
as compared with the Bible. The word of the Bible is God's
own Word, as the witness of those who themselves saw and
heard His revelation ; the word of the Church can only make
this claim at second-hand, relying on the word of the first witnesses. The position of these two authorities must never be
reversed, nor may they be put on the same level. No church
revelation may be set up side by side with the Bible as a source of
revelation. . . . In this connection the question is usually raised
whether the authority and correct interpretation of the Bible
does not depend on the witness of the Church. To this view
the Churches of the Reformation have opposed the doctrine of
the *testimonium spiritus sancti internum,* by which they
intended to maintain not any private judgment but simply the
absolute authority of God's Word and the relative authority of
the Church." In the same composite work, Dr. Regin Prenter,
Professor of Dogmatic Theology in the University of Aarhus, in
Denmark, sums up his conclusion (p. 111): "The testimony of
the Holy Spirit is the way in which God helps a Church which
has the courage to preach the message of God's revelation without possessing an infallible Bible and an infallible interpretation
of the Bible. The testimony of the Holy Spirit is the divine
miracle by which the message can be heard here and now, in
divine truth, in spite of human relativity and insincerity. Firm
confidence in the testimony of the Holy Spirit is the only thing
which can give the Church courage to embark upon the adventure of preaching the message of God's revelation in every age."
Luther put the testimony of the Holy Spirit in the forefront of
his teaching first as guarantor of Scripture and second as
guarantor of personal certainty. Thus he broke through the
long error of the Christian Church by which it had sought for
premature certainty by the way of doctrine declared on authority
to be infallible. No authority can provide such a guarantee :
certainty can come only through a more than human source.
Calvin developed the doctrine of the *testimonium Spiritus sancti
internum* in *The Institutes,* book III, and in chapter xxiv he
anchored the doctrine in election and God's hidden decree. The
special election " which otherwise would remain hidden in God,

[1] *Biblical Authority for Today,* S.C.M. Press, 1951, pp. 89-90.

He at length manifests by His calling ". When men are called, " the enjoyment of their election is in some measure communicated to them " and the Spirit by His testimony " confirms and seals the certainty of future adoption on their hearts ".[1]

If a man once ask what proof he has of his election, the thought " keeps him perpetually miserable, subjects him to dire torment, or throws him into a state of complete stupor ". Thus it is important to rest not in man but in God, " to begin with the calling of God and to end with it ". We cannot find the certainty of our election in ourselves, nor even in God the Father if we look at Him apart from the Son but " if we are in communion with Christ, we have proof sufficiently clear and strong that we are written in the Book of Life ".[2]

Many Calvinists are conscious that there is the suggestion of a circular movement in the argument at this stage. Man cannot have assurance until he has—assurance. And not all have been able to feel this security. Nor has it always been evil deeds and thoughts, lack of faith or failure in brotherliness, disobedience to the divine commands or sloth in devotion which have brought them to this pass, where they are in doubt. Frequently they have come there through humility, a sense of the greatness of God and of their littleness before Him. If a man has not this assurance yet believes as Calvin believes, the result will be to place him in a state which is worse than his first condition. It may bring him to despair. Thus the assurance which might at one time count as part of the blessedness of the system loses its conviction ; and it is seen that there is as much room for doubt and despair as in certain aspects of the Roman system. In both, men may rest in doubt rather than in assurance, in one case because there is ambiguity in our interpretation of the eternal divine decree ; in the other because the final decision seems to lie in the power of the Church in its aspect of a human organisation taking to itself a rôle as the earthly dispenser of divine grace. In fact, the emphasis in each case is at the wrong point. Christian assurance should mean, not " I know that I am going to Heaven ", but " I know that the love of God is to be trusted in life and in death, everywhere and always ". " Though He slay me, yet will I trust in

---

[1] *Eorum cordibus futurae adoptionis certitudinem suo testimonio stabilit et obsignat.*   [2] III xxiv. 5.

30 God is Light

Him." If it is of this kind, then assurance is not presumption, nor is it a scarcely attainable goal in the future, but a present fact. It is grounded in the words of the Lord and in His abiding promise.[1]

In all forms of the interpretation of religious certainty we come to a stage at which the luminous moment is central, and it is therefore important to examine its nature. Frequently the Bible indicates the nature of revelation under the symbolism of *light*. This is perhaps the most natural of all symbols and it is widely employed. Beginning with Plato in his Seventh Letter, the mystics have seen their illumination as a kind of "leaping spark". Christian baptism is an "enlightenment". Zoroastrianism is full of the struggle between light and darkness. Christians find in the Logos a reflection of the glory of the Father. The Wisdom of Solomon had already described Wisdom as " An effulgence of everlasting Light, and an unspotted mirror of the energy of God " (ἀπαύγασμα φωτὸς ἀϊδίου, καὶ εἰσόπτρον ἀκηλίδωτον τῆς τοῦ Θεοῦ ἐνεργείας) (Wisdom vii: 26). And the writer to the Hebrews seizes upon this metaphor and boldly applies it to Christ as the "effulgence of God's glory and the impress of His substance " (ἀπαύγασμα τῆς δόξης καὶ χαρακτὴρ τῆς ὑποστάσεως αὐτοῦ) (Heb. i. 3). In the First Epistle of St. John we find it declared that "God is Light, and in Him is no darkness at all". The source of light is a mystery (Job xxxviii. 19). ("Where is the way where light dwelleth? and as for darkness, where is the place thereof?") It was the first thing to be shaped by God, before sun and moon and stars; only later it was located in them. (Gen. i. 3). Light was created before "the lights of the firmament". Poets like Wordsworth and artists like van Gogh have experienced the ecstasy of a world "apparell'd in celestial light", echoing the cry of the psalmist praising God Who has covered Himself with light as

[1] See also a passage from Calvin's *Commentary on Hebrews*, xi. 6, quoted by Professor T. F. Torrance in *Calvin's Doctrine of Man*, p. 177, "No one, except he be blinded by presumption, and fascinated by self-love can feel assured that God will be a rewarder of his merits. Hence this confidence of which we speak relies not on works, not on man's worthiness, but on the grace of God alone; and as grace is nowhere found but in Christ, it is on Him alone that faith ought to be fixed ".

with a garment (Ps. civ. 2). Among the prophets Ezekiel is conspicuous in his imagery. He visualises the heavenly beings as like coals of fire (i. 13) and he sees in the brightness the glory of Yahweh (i. 28). "The numinous" says Edwyn Bevan "is essentially the luminous".[1]

The symbol is, of course, employed also of human qualities. Light indicates single-mindedness, the generous spirit, sincerity of soul, the rejection of every temptation to reconcile God and worldliness. It speaks also of Christian influence on others and the activity of evangelism. The lamp is not to be placed under a bushel. The light is to shine before men. But most of all in the Bible the metaphor takes us into the sphere of revelation, so that, passing over the use of the word in the everyday sense and its employment in the familiar simile, we may concentrate on this special sense.

The remainder of this introductory chapter may now be given to marking out the ground; spitlocking rather than digging.

"God is Light." If we take the metaphor seriously, it means that God is for all, without exception. His revelation is universal. Or did He blind some?—presumably by excluding them from the number of the elect. There is immediately pressed upon us the problem of the pre-Christian religious man and of the ethnic faiths. St. Paul (Acts xiv. 15-17) speaks of the living God who made heaven and earth and the sea, and all things that are therein; who suffered all nations to walk in their own ways; but nevertheless left not Himself without witness, in that He did good, and gave rain from heaven, and fruitful seasons. It cannot be that the ethnic faiths are of none effect. When we ask, What is the value of the values of the non-Christian religions? our answer must be that others are valuable only as they point to Christ, the fulfilment of all that is pure in them. The impure is not of God but of men; God does not deceive when He comes to men. He is the Light. It is arguable that there is no such thing as "natural theology": that it is only a human product and is to be described as a philosophy of some sort; but it would be dangerous to press this too far; for Christian theology itself is a largely human product and very fallible. If we are strict with terms and decide to reject "natural

[1] *Symbolism and Belief*, p. 130. See also Inge, *Christian Mysticism*, p. 85.

theology " we must go further and remind ourselves that there is no such thing as "revealed theology".

There are three types of conviction which raise discussion. The arguments for the existence of God are not reckoned in this number, partly because the assurance which emerges from them is not the kind of personal conviction which is here under consideration, but chiefly because they are not, for the moment at least, an arena of keen debate among theologians. It is clear to the believer that his conviction does not arise from such arguments, nor would it be removed even if the arguments were shattered. Principal John Baillie has pointed out[1] that the tendency of Western philosophy to regard the existence of God as the conclusion of a sustained argument is derived from Plato's eagerness to meet the Sophists on their own ground and, where they sought to demonstrate that the new science ruled out God, to show that, on the contrary, it established His existence on the surest foundations. The other tendency has, however, been happily preserved. It is that which is derived from the Scriptures ; which know God not as an inference but as a Presence. And Dr. Baillie adds : "The knowledge of God of which the New Testament speaks is a knowledge for which the best argument were but a sorry substitute and to which it were but a superfluous addition."[2]

The three forms of conviction to which special attention has been directed in recent discussion are—that which belongs to the realm of conscience ; that which is present in aesthetic experience particularly in the appreciation of Nature ; and that which is expressed by insight into human history. Are these three of God? Or are they only human productions?

CONSCIENCE, NATURE, HISTORY

It is extremely difficult to believe that the conviction which is present when we know what our duty is ; or when we are overwhelmed by the wonder and beauty and mystery of nature ; or when we are solemnised by the workings of history—it is hard to believe that this conviction is altogether different in kind from that which comes from Scripture ; that it has nothing whatsoever to do with revelation ; that it concerns our salvation

---

[1] *Our Knowledge of God*, ch. iii.   [2] p. 126.

not at all. In any one of these experiences men have been known to come very near to their redemption; and that should not surprise us, when it is the same God who is at work on the soul, the Father of our Lord Jesus Christ. What we need to notice carefully is that each of these experiences can more readily be twisted to our own use and our own interpretation than can our meeting with Christ crucified and risen. God's revelation is never deceptive; the human response may well be. The nerve of the problem is to determine which forms of human response are in greatest danger of erring; and the safest criterion is the adequacy of the response in the matter of man's sin. Does even our utmost faithfulness to the ethical demands of life convince us of our deficiency in power and our need of pardon, or does it leave us complacent and well satisfied? Does the mystery of nature make man aware of his sinfulness and does it indicate the direction from which succour will come? Does the sense of the numinous convince man of—not his finitude; that goes without saying, but—his sin; or is his experience only an aesthetic one? Does our insight rescue human history from its ambiguity, or are we merely deceived by our own presuppositions, as is the case in the Marxist interpretation?

These problems will receive a fuller treatment in a later chapter (pp. 135 ff.). In the meantime, there is one possible danger that must be considered.

THE SYMBOLISM OF LIGHT

It may be that the symbol of light suggests that the source of revelation is impersonal or supra-personal. Rudolf Otto argues[1] that the use by St. Paul and St. John of the terms "Light" and "Life" underline the supra-personal aspect of the divine; yet without indicating any sudden irruption into religion of a wholly novel and alien element. This simply represents the complete realisation of what was all the time potentially present in the character of Yahweh in his essence as a numen. Otto applies this thought to his analysis of some Christian hymns—"'Third person' hymns . . . are not necessarily less, but under certain conditions may even be more genuine and

---

[1] *The Idea of the Holy*, Appendix on "The Supra-Personal in the Numinous".

first hand utterances than those which address God as 'Thou'.
There is a further consequence. It is often thought that the
designations of deity in impersonal, neuter terms ('It') rather
than in terms of person and masculine pronoun ('He', 'Thou'),
are too poor and too pale to gain a place in our Christian thought
of God. But this is not always correct. Frequently such terms
indicate the mysterious overplus of the non-rational and numinous, that cannot enter our 'concepts' because it is too great and
too alien to them ; and in this sense they are quite indispensable.
even in hymns and prayers." Here, I believe, Otto is saying
something that is quite stimulating and suggestive. "Light"
is not a personal term or attribute ; but so far from directing
attention to the more material realm of thought, as it may have
done for the Hebrews so that they were careful to show that
God created the light but was never identified with it, in the
New Testament it is rather a safeguard against conceptions
which are all-too-human. It has the connotation of that which
is pure spirit ; of the "sheer abounding overplus of the non-
rational element in religion". This is a sound conclusion, but
it should not be pressed further than it can endure ; for manifestly both prayers and hymns of the saints can make use of
the concept of Light in expressing penitence in the presence
of God the Father of Jesus ; that is, in the most personal of all
contexts. We think, perhaps of St. Bernard's hymn (version of
1632 Breviary): *Lux alma Jesu mentium—*

> Light of the anxious heart,
> Jesus Thou dost appear,
> To bid the gloom of guilt depart,
> And shed Thy sweetness here.

He is the *dulce lumen patriae,* "Sweet Light of our eternal
home" and He is *Splendor paternae gloriae,* "Brightness of God
above". Or, nearer our own day, we may turn to Thomas
Binney's lines at the end of his hymn "Eternal Light! Eternal
Light!"—

> The sons of ignorance and night
> May dwell in the eternal Light,
> Through the Eternal Love!

or the late Latin hymn *Aeterna lux, Divinitas* "O Light eternal,
God most high".

If we were hesitant in drawing out the full significance of the metaphor of light lest it give an impersonal view of God, we may have still stronger qualms in the fear that we may be left in the position of the gnostics, treasuring (and being proud of) special illumination, and paying little heed to the moral demands of the Christian life. It is here that contemporary schools of Christian existentialism have contributed richly. Revelation comes to man in his particular situation, and it is the outcome of his being placed in a situation of challenge and decision, where his whole destiny is manifestly in hazard. That new emphasis was urgently required, and it came with refreshing timeliness through Kierkegaard, Buber, Heim, Barth, Brunner, Marcel, Berdyaev, and a host of others.[1] The fault which sometimes becomes apparent in existentialism is that which the symbol of light is specially suited to retrieve, namely, the tendency to assume that *spiritual* wrestling is not part of the staking of the soul. The cry for more light may be as worthy as the cry for more action. The challenge may be that presented by the truth ; the decision may be that of the mind for sincerity of thought.

In the second series of his Gifford Lectures delivered in Aberdeen in 1950,[2] Gabriel Marcel indicates his view that " conviction " comes midway between " opinion " and " faith " (p. 75). Opinion operates, as it were, at a distance ; we do not " hold opinions " of our closest friends or of artists and writers and musicians whose work we really cherish. And opinion can be highly aggressive ; it represents the passage of " it would appear " into " I claim ". The less the knowledge, the stronger and the more pugnacious is the assertiveness. " Conviction " has far more information, but it too puts up a barrier to further investigation, in the determination not to allow anything to modify the way of thought which has been chosen. " Belief ", on the other hand, escapes the tragedy of the closed mind. The assurance which it brings is not a conviction ; it goes beyond what has been given to us ; it is a leap of faith ; it is, Marcel says (I do not like the phrase though great writers have used it) " a bet—and, like all bets, it can be lost " (p. 79). But it

---

[1] " There are as many Existentialisms as there are Existentialist philosophers " says Paul Foulquié in his *Existentialism*—quoted by James Mathers in his article " Existentialism in France " in *The Scottish Journal of Theology,* June 1951.   [2] *The Mystery of Being,* II: *Faith and Reality*

adds "an existential index". We *rally* to our beliefs; they
involve all we are; they call out all that we have to give; we
stand by them to the end. It would seem to follow from his
discussion that "conviction" has to do only with statements
of truth; with the formulation of beliefs in syllogistic and dis-
cursive form. We are convinced *that* ——. It is true that we
often say "I believe *that* ——". But in such cases the word has
deteriorated in meaning and may imply only a vague opinion—
"I am told that ——". What we are concerned with is the
word "belief" in its true sense and there, as Marcel rightly
says, it is better represented by the phrase "I believe *in* ——".
It is directed towards a person.

The point I wish to make here is simply this, that Marcel
has carried the contrast too far. Men *do* rally to the defence
of their convictions. They *do* follow them, sometimes to the
end. "The way to live with God", said Florence Nightingale,
"is to live with Ideas—not merely to think about Ideas but to
do and suffer for them." Men may "die for their convictions"
as men may die for their faith. Integrity attaches also to conviction as well as to belief and for the same reason, that it is
not concerned only with facts, but with values. Conviction too,
like belief, belongs to the realm represented in Marcel's helpful
illustrations by the mother and her son, and not to the realm
of the banker and his client. Should we inquire whether
religious conviction involves an I-It or an I-Thou relation, we
should point to the first if we emphasised the factor of the precise
formulation of belief and we should point to the second if we
underline the whole spiritual setting of the conviction. It is
in this second sense that I am interpreting "conviction". God
has *given* light which bears its own assurance because it is a
direct and divine gift.

When the Bible speaks of conviction it is in reference to
sin. The New Testament term is ἐλέγχω or one of its com-
pounds. The meaning is therefore "convicted" rather than
"convinced" but it is with the latter that we are here concerned.

In contemporary speech (apart from the special realms of
logic and mathematics) there appear to be four types of conviction. (1) Conviction which is *emotional*. It can easily lead
to fanaticism and persecution, and it may be very far away from

the truth.   (2) Conviction which is *conventional*, arising from beliefs that are prevalent in our environment.   (3) Conviction which is *rational*.   Its beginnings and its roots may be emotional or conventional, but it has also been submitted to the processes of sincere reasoning and to Reason, moreover, considered not simply as intellectual judgment but as that property of the self which decides on values as well as on means to realise them, and is the principle of harmonious development of the soul.[1]   (4) Conviction which arises *from the coercive element in reality*. We believe because we must, and we also believe that the coercion comes from God.   Our conviction will only be strengthened through being submitted to the sincere processes of Reason, but its compelling urgency will not depend on the success of Reason in substantiating it, since the conviction in the first instance was reached by avenues other than those of the Reason.   It would be wrong to speak of this simply as Inner Light for indeed it is more Outer than Inner.

The more obvious symbol for revelation—the Word—appears to have all the appropriateness, since it is prominent in Scripture, full of significance in both Old Testament and New Testament ; and leads to a right conception of the Biblical record as central and definitive and ultimate.   Moreover, it conserves the truth that revelation is rational, in that its appeal is not to the ecstatic in man, but to man " in his senses " ; and it indicates that, under the promised guidance of the Spirit, doctrine can be formulated in a way that will not be misleading, but will serve the purposes of evangelism and Christian education.   The term " Word " has moreover the advantage that, as the Greek *Logos* in the Fourth Gospel, it takes to itself some of the connotation of the Hebrew *dabar*, which could mean *act* as well as speech ;   and reaches back to that climate of thought in which words once uttered became, as it were, materialised, taking independent power to themselves.[2]   Therefore the symbol has rightly been adopted in Christian teaching and given the most prominent place.   Yet it has its disadvantages.   The special use of *Logos* in the Fourth Gospel is confined to the Prologue, where the *Logos* is the eternal divine Person, the Son of God who was made man in Jesus ;   and it may draw upon a Logos-

[1] See J. G. McKenzie, *Nervous Disorders and Religion*, p. 50.
[2] Cf. Isaiah lv. 10-11 ;   Mark i. 45 ;   Luke ix. 28 ;   Acts viii. 21 and xi. 22.

hymn which was not originally Christian at all.[1]   When the
writer of the Fourth Gospel calls Jesus the Logos he is seeking
to explain the extraordinary fact of his Lord not by Greek
notions primarily but "by reference to the Hebrew notion of
the effective word of God, which is God Himself in action, and
which is powerful in proportion as this word is the word of God
Himself ".[2]   A constantly recurring danger has been that of supposing that the Word not only became flesh, but became Scripture, so that the Word of God becomes identified with the text
of the Bible.   A further danger is, oddly, the reverse of what
might be expected.   As we saw, one of the values of this symbol
is its conservation of the rational significance of revelation ; but
in fact the concept of the Word has been too often employed
in our time to support the claim of irrationality.   The Word
has become an utterance which has no conceivable analogies
in the nature and thought and activities of men.   Hence it is
essential to preserve the contribution made by other symbols
hallowed by the use of our Lord.   Outstanding among these
others is that of Light.

The symbol of light is saved from wrong interpretation in
the sense of intellectualism by the clear fact that it stands, not
for propositions concerning God, but for illumination.   It is
inevitable, as Professor Leonard Hodgson has pointed out, that
the Bible comes to us with propositions, because it is only statements in that form which could open the eyes of future generations to see what had been evident to those who bear the record ;
but it is not these propositions which are the "revelatum".
"They bear record of the ' revelatum ', but as the ages go by they
can only continue to mediate the revelation in so far as in each
generation men's eyes are opened to see for themselves the significance of the revelatory acts of God to which they bear witness".[3]   The same thought has been expressed by using the
other symbol, that of life.   Christianity is not the handing down
of doctrine by uniform repetition ; it is a question of life again
and again kindled afresh.   Where men bear witness to Christ
in the power of the Spirit, there God gives a revelation of Himself which is self-authenticating.   And we need not be afraid of

[1] See Professor J. Y. Campbell in *A Theological Word Book of the Bible*,
sub voce "Word".
[2] See the late Professor Macnicol in *The Scottish Journal of Theology*,
vol. v, pt. 3, p. 247.   [3] *The Doctrine of the Trinity*, p. 35.

the term self-authenticating, αὐτόπιστος, as if it were a question-begging word. It is not. It is essential in all philosophy too. Our ultimate convictions, in reason as in religion, are not inductions from experience: they are insights into experience. The *testimonium Spiritus sancti internum* should thus be closely associated with the encounter of the soul with God, the challenge which comes when God meets with it. Religious knowledge is not propositional, but, as we constantly say, a contact of the soul with God. It is not knowledge which can be set down in statements, but illumination of experiences which otherwise would be opaque, or superficial, or obscure, or liable to misinterpretation. The different levels of religious knowledge, of " natural theology " and Christian theology, are marked by their liability to lead to misunderstanding. It is much easier to misunderstand nature than conscience; and much easier to misunderstand conscience than Scripture. The Incarnation itself can be misunderstood and can suggest the birth only of a great and good man; the death of Christ can be misinterpreted as. the sacrifice of a noble martyr. We are on the wrong lines if we conceive the Incarnation and Atonement and the Resurrection as problems; we are confusing two things which are quite distinct, namely, a problem and a mystery. A problem can be solved by applying the correct technique, so that an answer can be produced which is available to all, irrespective of their spiritual state. A mystery has no answer " at the end of the book "; the resolution of it comes, not by demonstrations in propositional form, but by faith which is communion with God.

Light is a symbol of the self-communicating, self-authenticating goodness of God.

"The darkness is past, and the true light now shineth."

CHAPTER II

FROM DARKNESS TO LIGHT

In the Old Testament, Light signifies release from error, deliverance from wrong thoughts of God and of our fellowmen ; release from anxiety and from sin with its guilt and power: it is regarded as conferring certainty in the making of moral choices, and giving peace in spite of all the turmoil and disharmony of human circumstance. By the Rabbis, the designation "Light" was employed as a name of the Messiah. Light is frequently associated with life, as in the story of the Creation and in later Jewish writings where the terms "light" and "life" are used to indicate the consequences of obedience to the Will of God as it is given in the Mosaic Law.

In the New Testament, human obedience is replaced by the divine grace revealed in Jesus ; and in the Gospel of St. John we find Jesus, the Life of the world, raising Lazarus from the dead (ch. xi) and, as the Light of the world, healing the man born blind (ch. ix).[1] In the preface to the story of the latter miracle, Jesus says to His disciples, "As long as I am in the world, I am the light of the world " (ix. 5), and the theme of the healed man's thanksgiving is (ix. 25) "One thing I know, that, whereas I was blind, now I see ". Light is the New Testament symbol for all religious certainty, conviction, peace, confidence ; that which cannot be shaken by argument, because it has not been reached by argument. Fundamentally, the Greek idea of deliverance appears, in contrast to this, to affirm that the root cause is not religion, but reason ; yet it is arguable that Plato and Aristotle were really drawing out the rational content from the religious rites and beliefs of earlier generations, or perhaps simply forcing a rational meaning upon those rites and beliefs.

Greek philosophy made too sharp the distinction between the practical reason (which is useful in solving the day to day problems of living) and the speculative reason (which dwells on the metaphysical heights)—the first, as A. N. Whitehead says,

[1] See Sir Edwyn Hoskyns, *The Fourth Gospel*, revised edn., p. 143.

we share " with the foxes ", the second we share " with the gods ". The importance of the first, developed along its own appropriate human lines, is recovered by Wilhelm Dilthey.

TWO WAYS OF EXPLORING THE WORLD

There are, broadly speaking, two contrasted ways of exploring the world. It may be looked on with cold, critical, impersonal eyes, on the natural assumption that it is alien to men's minds ; or it may be interrogated by methods which arise out of a belief that, ultimately at least, the world and man's spirit are akin. The contrasting methods may be roughly indicated as (1) sense and (2) sympathy. For very long, it had been assumed that the first way alone can give accurate and unprejudiced knowledge of reality. Here there was no personal equation to come as a hindrance to truth ; no bias : all was disinterested inquiry. Now it is being argued by some, and particularly by the followers of Dilthey, that the very opposite is the case.[1] The methods of the senses, it is declared, are wholly inadequate for the examination of reality : if knowledge is possible, it must come through the method of sympathy. The first is the province of the physical sciences—which proceed by accurate measurement, but are appropriate only to that portion of the world which is amenable to measurement, the metric part of existence ; the second is the province of the human studies (*Geisteswissenschaften*), where the object of study is the spirit of man. And man is the proper study of mankind.

By sympathy—or by empathy—we " go through it all " with another person. This is specially noticeable when there is a relationship of deep affection or loyalty between the two persons concerned. The anxious friend in the audience may go through sympathetic travail when the orator rises to his peroration. And through sympathy with the speaker the conveying of meaning is accelerated. As we listen, we fill in the blanks without being aware that we are adding anything ourselves. (A mild form of this is the tendency from which we all suffer in conversation, either as agents or as victims, of supplying the last word of a sentence for the speaker.)

---

[1] See the excellent summary and comment by Professor H. A. Hodges, *Wilhelm Dilthey : An Introduction*, the same author *The Philosophy of Wilhelm Dilthey* ; and Leslie Paul, *The Meaning of Human Existence*.

Dilthey gave a real impetus to the reformation of psychology —a study, he said, which has been half-baked and has misunderstood its own function. It need not be cold-shouldered or abandoned; but it must be reformed. Under Karl Jaspers (one of Dilthey's pupils, a psychologist and psychiatrist) and a succession of like-minded writers, there has been outlined a psychology of understanding, not aimed at being a natural science, but depending more on poetry and philosophy for guidance in its interpretations. Dilthey's philosophical battle-cry was therefore: "We *explain* nature: but the human spirit we *understand*."[1] We cannot *know* nature. Dilthey adds that neither can we know God and he quotes with appreciation the words of Pope,

The proper study of mankind is man.

On the one hand, positively, this means that the human mind and all its works are intensely interesting and are amenable to understanding. On the other hand, negatively, it means for Dilthey that neither in the physical world nor in the transcendent sphere of religion is it possible for man to know what it is that confronts him.

Dilthey speaks of the element of genius necessary in the interpretation of character and of human action, such genius as is possessed by poets, dramatists and historians, and by men of action whose leadership depends on accurate judgment of others. (It has been said of one such leader that he had the old soldier's gift of knowing his man after a few minutes' talk.) This touch of genius—let me for convenience refer to it as the "hunch" (*Ahnung*)—is present in all penetrating investigation even in the province of the natural sciences. It is needed, for example, in the formulation of hypotheses which are to guide research, and in the final leap to a conclusion, which in many cases is not arrived at as the close of an intricate piece of reasoning, but is the reward of patient research *plus* imaginative intuition. The hunch is not perhaps so conspicuous in the realm of the natural sciences, and so its presence is not always suspected and very seldom admitted; and it is, of course, amenable here as it is not in the human sciences to verification by measurement and the repetition of experiments. When, however, we hear it charged against the

[1] *Die Natur erklären wir : das Seelenleben verstehen wir.*

sympathetic method of interrogating the world that it consists
too much of hunches and is therefore subjective, unreliable, in-
accurate and unscientific; when we hear it accused of judging
without evidence, we ought to realise that the hunch is part of
the evidence and of the most reliable kind, because it is direct
insight into the nature of what is happening. (Is it possible
even that the hunch of the scientific kind is in the end dependent
on the type which is apparent in the sympathetic approach?)

In the province of the human studies, Dilthey is not prepared to find any trace of ultimate principles. The philosophy
of history looks for a meaning in the process and professes to
find one in a governing purpose. Dilthey cannot agree. He
recognises no superhuman purpose in history, whether in a
transcendent God or in an immanent Absolute or world-spirit.
There are no purposes in history, he bluntly declares, except
human purposes, the purposes of actual historical agents.

To us, I think, this reads a little like a begging of the question; since those who believe strongly in the presence of a
divine purpose in the world are not ruled out from believing that
this purpose is achieved normally through the overruling of
human activities or the employment of human agents to work
out the divine will. Specifically of morals, Dilthey insists that
the search for absolute ethical principles is the pursuit of a will-
o'-the-wisp. There are no absolute principles for him, but only
those which arise from time to time in the course of history.
Ethics ought therefore to cease this search and should confine
itself to the description of those principles which have in fact
been *regarded* as absolute from time to time.[1]

When Dilthey goes on to say that no ultimate principle is
to be discerned in history; what finally confronts us is the
human situation as a whole; there is nothing permanent save
the structure of man;—when he says all this we realise at once
that two things at least have to be added to make Dilthey's
world-picture credible. One is the permanent nature of the
stimuli given to the basic structure of man, in virtue of which
the characteristic reaction takes place. The other is, of course,

---

[1] This, it will be seen, leads straight up to the programme of Westermarck
in his *Origin and Development of the Moral Ideas*, and on the other hand
to Oswald Spengler, who wrote of the relativity of all ethical systems. This
kind of thing also prompts Rudolf Otto's rejoinder " ' Ought ' is a primary and
unique meaning, as little derivable from another as blue from bitter ".

the abiding nature of God. This, therefore, is the point at which criticism of Dilthey naturally begins. It cannot be developed here, but it may suffice to indicate that he lays far too much stress on the "structure of the individual mind" and far too little on the stimuli. Thus art and religion are lumped together ; and he speaks too often as if the reaction were predetermined by the basic structure of man. A criticism which Kierkegaard made of Hegel is relevant here and may fairly be levelled against Dilthey. Life offers, not syntheses, but *choices*. Dilthey has never carried sufficiently far his own insistence that man must be considered, not in any single aspect, but in his whole personality. Clearly, one of the most vital aspects of human life is that in which a man is called on to stake all on his decision. There are questions here which may very fruitfully be pressed much further than has been done by Dilthey. He began the intensive study of man's knowledge of other persons, which has played so important a part in our day. Kierkegaard had broken ground in the same line of research, and writers such as Buber and Heim have followed.

SOME NEGLECTED FACTORS

Some of the factors which, I believe, have commonly been overlooked by these writers may here be briefly noted. When we come to know the mind of another through sympathy and imaginatively, we ought to take notice that we may in fact be seeing far more than the mind of that other as it actually exists at the moment. We also see in it *the ideal character* after which it is as yet only striving. It means, next, that we have *faith in the other and in his attaining* what he has not yet attained. There is, third, *knowledge of ourselves* given through knowledge of the other ; for we see *him* reacting in ways unthought of by us, thus revealing unsuspected possibilities in ourselves.

Professor Brand Blanshard has pointed out to me the major difficulty, in the eyes of a philosopher, of all theories of "knowledge through sympathy". Even if we admit the existence of sympathetic—as opposed to rational—knowledge, and not all would be ready to admit it, we should still be compelled to say that such insight is supplementary to our knowledge of the more ordinary kind and not a substitute for it. When we are introduced to a new acquaintance and after a time come to understand him and love him, this sympathetic knowledge is verified in many ways through his speech and behaviour; but suppose we had never met this other man, and yet said that we had this sympathetic knowledge of him; suppose that to someone else who doubted his existence, this knowledge were offered in evidence: standing by itself it would probably be rejected. Thus the thoroughly sceptical person will feel the same way about the sympathetic knowledge of God, and will incline to say, "Granted that behind the screen of nature there *is* a personal mind, I am prepared to believe that such knowledge can give us some report of it; but until that prior matter is settled by other means, the claim to this knowledge involves a begging of the question".

This clear statement of the fundamental difficulty drives home the essential point, namely, that the knowledge which comes through sympathy is in its essence the illumination of that which is already known. All these features, attributes, characteristics, with which we have long been familiar in an acquaintance are suddenly polarised; they belong now to *this man* who, by a word spoken or an interest shared, has in a flash been illumined for me. Whereas up to now he was a kind of geometrical pattern in two dimensions, subject to precise laws, he has now acquired depth. He has passed beyond the state in which his attributes are measurable and his attitudes are predictable, and we recognise that now he can no longer be explained but only understood. Now we are constantly on the watch for actions which we should never have expected before, and which therefore we overlooked or misinterpreted. Up to this moment he was conventional; we thought we knew all about him; he would never surprise us: now we see him as creative; he may do the startling thing and yet it will be seen as quite in accordance with his character as now we know it. Pressing the analogy as far as it is legitimate to press it, we realise that true knowledge in religion comes through expecting great things from God; comes when we pass from theory to worship, from theology to prayer. These are all expressions in terms of human activity, but the change is one that is brought about by an illumination not achieved by man.

FROM KNOWLEDGE OF MAN TO KNOWLEDGE OF GOD

When, however, we ask whether this way of sympathy really throws any light on our knowledge of God, the answer might appear immediately to be negative, since the familiar presuppositions of right knowledge of God are such things as humility, obedience, repentance, forgiveness ; and God does not have these experiences ; these moods in ourselves cannot be echoes of similar moods in God and therefore sympathy might seem to be completely ruled out ; but it would be wrong to dismiss the possibility so quickly ; for humility, obedience, repentance, forgiveness, as we know them in the Christian experience, would have little significance and no content were they not related to the Word of God for us. They have their correlatives in God. This is not to say that we can go with Professor Urban in *Humanity and Deity* (pp. 49 ff.) where he claims that "Humanity and Deity, like the inside and the outside of the curve, like the mountain and the valley, are apart from each other unthinkable". Such a thought can be helpful, if at all, only when we realise that the likeness, the *imago*, the analogy, are solely of God's contrivance and not of man's (and this alone casts doubt on the metaphor of the inside and the outside of the curve) and further that the likeness, the imago, the analogy, are sustained solely by God, because the constant endeavour of rebellious man is, by claiming them in pride, to destroy them in actuality. Nevertheless, with all due care to avoid anthropomorphism, many believe that in the experience of man's love to God we are dealing with that which is of the same texture as God's love to man, since both alike are motions of the Spirit. They can be regarded as homogeneous, "univocal". The extreme Calvinist ought to be the last to deny this for he must hold that man cannot love God except in so far as God enables him so to do ; that is, so far as God's love inspires him. St. Bernard and his biographer, William of Thierry, have lighted up this avenue of thought and have done so without suggesting that there need be any conflation of that which is proper to the creature and that which belongs to the Creator. The witness of religious experience enables the identification to be made without endangering the essential element of transcendence in our thought of God.[1]

1 See de Burgh, *Morality to Religion*, ch. v, and Heim, *Glaube und Denken*.

The witness of the believer has been joyously summed up in the words of Samuel Rutherford, taken from *Canticles* ii. 16; vi. 3 and wrought into the fabric of our hymn—" I am my Beloved's And my Belov'd is mine ". The love which man experiences for God Who has created and redeemed him is not something alien to the divine nature; but, in the providence and mercy of God, is of the same texture.

Are we not, then, in danger of minimising the difference between the human and the divine? Is it not evident that the vital thing in the relation of man to his God is not love but faith? Not satisfied, perhaps, with the other extreme of *totaliter aliter,* we may yet hesitate to affirm that the love which flows upward from man to God is of the same quality as that which comes down from above. This danger is averted if we constantly remember that we are speaking of *caritas infusa;* of the love which has been inspired and called forth by God's grace and by no other thing. Faith is the rightful *attitude* of creaturely, sinful man; but love is the outcome of it. Faith believes where it cannot prove: love is the beginning of proof, for it is the beginning of sight, the light in which vision is made possible and we can see God as He is.[1]

FAITH AND INTUITION

It has been said that both in religion and in metaphysics we begin with the answer. A light shines in us, and we trust it.[2] Let us ask, Is this trust legitimate?

The answer to that question involves an examination of the nature of faith and of intuition. We may confidently affirm that faith and intuition are both avenues to the truth; we might even proceed to say that, if they are genuine faith and genuine intuition, they are infallible guides to the truth. But who can tell when this is the case? Man is sinful and prone to error: his faith and his intuition are not the ultimately authoritative guides. They are not revelation, but response. Therefore they should be patient of whatever form of verification is available, so that the misleading and distorted manifestations of faith and intuition may be eliminated. Religion has nothing

[1] See further, pp. 90 ff.
[2] Cf. Professor E. T. Ramsdell, *The Christian Perspective,* pp. 36-37.

to fear from the scrutiny of reason, experience, history, since God's hand is also in all of these.

VERIFICATION

The word "verification" has been used. Does this mean that religion is reduced to the prosaic level dictated by reason? Is it in danger of losing what William James once called "the exceedingness of the possible over the real"? Is it to canalise the broad flow and sweep of faith within the exact but unexciting boundaries of rationality?

Indeed it is not. In the first place, we have noted that God is in all of those other spheres from which verification is reasonably sought. Secondly, the purpose of these examinations is not to oust faith from its regnant position, but to liberate the real faith by removing the crudities and the irrational prejudices which fallible man carries around with him in mind and heart. And, thirdly, reason, which is the medium most nearly concerned in the available processes of verification, is itself indebted for its development and its purification to religion. There is, it is true, a natural opposition between reason and religion, because the first is jealous of its rights and suspicious of all external authority, and because the second is concerned with realms of experience which transcend the province of reason; but it is equally true that the two cannot be separated. Religion fosters—perhaps even creates—reason. Philosophy of religion is not external to faith; not, at least, if it is vision and not merely argumentation. All reasoning is someone's reasoning— mine, yours, X. Y's—never just reasoning in the abstract. We believe that our rational experience is reliable and objective, but this is a belief, not the conclusion of a syllogism. "A thinker may abstract from his experience what he regards as universally significant and ignore the rest, but it is just such a judgment that is inescapably personal." [1] And the other man's experience is understood only when we somehow occupy his perspective view-point sympathetically. Reason, even in the lower sense of argumentation, syllogistic discussion, *dianoia*, is probably indebted much more profoundly than we usually imagine to religion, which gives sincerity, balance, judgment, health of

---

[1] E. T. Ramsdell, *The Christian Perspective*, p. 31.

mind, clarity of thought ; but we are more concerned with the higher sense of reason—insight, vision, *nous*—and here the indebtedness is inescapable. Faith not only gives to the philosophy of religion the psychological facts that are to be examined ; but also purifies, illumines and stimulates the reason which is to examine them. Our decisions on those things which are worth while, our value-judgments—these are the heart of the religious attitude. Each time we make use of these concepts we are saying "I believe", and the belief is one which, ultimately, depends on the God in Whom we believe.

One of the clearest features of thought is the sharp distinction and indeed the tension between intuition on the one hand and patient reasoning on the other. We cannot explain the functioning of intuition, but, while acknowledging that patient reasoning is at every step dependent on intuition for its convincingness, we nevertheless believe, and justifiably, that we do know something of the rational process and of the conditions under which alone reasoning can be legitimately pursued. Let us discover, if we can, what part it has to play in that transition from darkness to light which takes place where there is revelation.

1. *Light as the symbol of Wisdom and Insight.* Russian Orthodox theology has developed to a notable degree the study of the divine *Sophia*. Berdyaev, for example, claims that Orthodoxy has been fortunate to escape both Reformation and counter-Reformation, thus avoiding the subtleties, the over-definition, and the provocative forms of doctrinal statement which are the fruits of those two movements ; and thus achieving a valuable freedom of thought. He suggests as an instance of the injurious effect of controversy on doctrine that Protestantism has been driven to demand for every individual Christian what the Papacy has secured for itself, recognition as the ultimate court of appeal in questions of faith and authority. Over against this Berdyaev sets his interpretation of the nature of tradition. Authority, he writes,[1] is not a category appropriate to the spiritual world but only to the natural world of division and hatred. In the spiritual world, if it has any meaning at all, it stands for a certain humility and submission which precede freedom. Thus "Tradition is not

[1] *Freedom and the Spirit*, p. 331.

4

authority ; it is the creative life of the spirit ". And, if we point
out that there are traditions which are good, but others which
are manifestly unhealthy, his reply is that it is the whole body
of the Church that decides which is healthy and which is in
error. Though the teaching office belongs to the ecclesiastical
hierarchy, infallibility rests with the Church as a whole. He is
acutely aware of the danger of the concept of Wisdom being
misapplied. Theosophy is a perilous road. " The spirit of Mme.
Blavatsky or Mrs. Besant differs considerably from that of
Heraclitus, Plotinus, Origen. . . ."[1] But his writings are a valuable contribution to the theme of revelation in its double aspect
of *givenness and growth.* Divine revelation is not directed to
pure passivity. It is not like the rattling of hailstones on a roof
of corrugated iron : it is deep calling unto deep, involving on
man's part a spiritual activity of his whole self. Nor is God to
be conceived as unchanging and impassible. If the capacity of
love is in God then the capacity for suffering must also be
ascribed to Him. It is the immobile, static God of theological
thought that is imperfect.[2] Dramatic movement and tragedy
arise out of the fulness not out of the poverty of life. There is
a divine spark in man ; and there is humanity in God. Often
it seems indeed that Berdyaev is removing all barriers between
man and God. " It is a mistake " he says [3] " to regard the relation
between God who reveals and man, to whom the revelation is
made, as being of a transcendent character. God cannot reveal
Himself to the man who will not come to Him. Revelation presupposes faith in man and in his higher nature which renders
possible that religious upheaval which we call revelation, the
birth of God in man, and the meeting of man with God. This
means that revelation implies the immanence of the divine
within the human spirit—not of course within the human soul.
In revelation the transcendent becomes immanent. The denial
of a higher spiritual nature in man which renders him God-like
is tantamount to a denial of the very possibility of revelation

[1] *Op. cit.* p. 271.
[2] " People are afraid to ascribe movement to God, because movement
indicates the lack of something, or the need for something which is not there.
But it may equally well be said that immobility is an imperfection, for it
implies a lack of the dynamic quality of life. Tragic conflict in the life
of the Deity is a sign of the perfection, and not of the imperfection, of the
divine life "—Berdyaev, *The Destiny of Man* (Bles, 1937), p. 38.
[3] *Freedom and the Spirit*, p. 94.

for there would be nothing to which such a revelation could be made. . . . This is the reason why both theology and philosophy must refuse to take either God or man as their starting-point, but must rather begin with the God-Man whose theandric nature is beyond and above this antithesis." Nevertheless, God remains God and man, man ; but the quotations which Berdyaev cites elsewhere [1] and with approval, make it difficult to believe that the distinction is still preserved. (Eckhart: "I was my own first cause and that of all other things. I desire that neither I myself nor they should be non-existent. But if I did not exist neither would God." Angelus Silesius: "I must be the Word in the Word, God in God." "I am as great as God, He as small as I." "Every Christian must be Christ Himself." "He who wants God must become God.") The consequences of his view are awkward, but Berdyaev accepts them.[2] What can come out of a man's freedom when it meets God's grace? God Himself does not know, for that is precisely the mystery of the dark uncreated abyss of the non-being into which even divine eyes cannot probe.[3]

"Freedom", Berdyaev writes [4] "is not determined by God ; it is part of the nothing out of which God created the world. The opposition between God the Creator and freedom is secondary: in the primeval mystery of the Divine Nothing this opposition is transcended for both God and freedom are manifested out of the *Ungrund*. . . . God the Creator is all-powerful over being, over the created world, but He has no power over non-being, over the uncreated freedom which is impenetrable to Him."

It is the question of this contrast between givenness and growth which the metaphor of light brings sharply to notice.

[1] *Op. cit.* pp. 244 ff.

[2] See especially his treatment of the *Ungrund* in *The Destiny of Man*, pt. 1, ch. ii, and of *The Ethics of Creativeness*, pt. 2, ch iii.

[3] Cf. also *Freedom and the Spirit*, pp. 117 ff. It is the old, old problem whether the products of man's creative genius, inspired by God Himself, come as a surprise to God. A minister of the Church of Scotland, gently challenged by some members of his Kirk Session because he appeared not to be giving his full strength to the pastoral care of the congregation, defended himself on two grounds ; the first that he was responsible, not to the Kirk Session but to the Presbytery ; and indeed claimed to answer for the employment of his time to no man, but to the Creator of all men ; the second that he had not been wasting his time, but could point to the three books which he had lately published. One of the elders then inquired, " But, moderator, you canna surely expect the Almighty to read them? "

[4] *The Destiny of Man*, p. 33 f.

There is the flash of light like that which came to St. Paul on the Damascus road, the insight, the sudden glimpse of the "depth of the riches both of the wisdom and knowledge of God"; but there is also the abiding light which shines unceasingly on men: and Scripture has a place for both, for grace coming by what seems a miracle, wholly unconnected with all that has gone before (though we now know that the process is not quite as it might appear, and studies in the psychology of the unconscious have penetrated to some of the deeper workings of the mind) and on the other hand grace coming by steady growth on a level which, if not entirely conscious, is largely observable. The familiar contrast between the sudden and the gradual is well known in religious conversion: it is perhaps equally marked in human friendship and love. The affection which inspires the "beautiful friendship, tried by sun and wind, durable from the daily dust of life" and the cry [1]

> One must go first, Ah, God! one must go first:
> After so long one blow for both were good

or drew from Vaughan the lament for friends departed

> They are all gone into the world of light!
> And I alone sit ling'ring here;
> Their very memory is fair and bright,
> And my sad thoughts doth clear

may have begun, we do not know, with "love at first sight", or may have grown with the sure gradualness of flowers reaching up to the waxing heat of the sun through spring and early summer.

The characteristic of non-continuity is found in many other spheres of man's experience. In art, we find William Blake crying "It is not mine! It is not mine!" In scientific research we meet with the bold, imaginative hypothesis, by no means following from the previous findings, yet leading to the desired solution. "It was given to me" Helmholtz said of one of his discoveries. In morals we notice the conventional pattern of behaviour combined, often with far-reaching results for good, with the creative decision which follows by no ordinary process

---

1 Stephen Philipps, *Marpessa*.

of thought from the premisses.[1] H. A. Prichard used to point out to us—anticipating by a decade some of the findings of the existentialists—that there is available to the man who is faced by the challenge to make a decision, evidence which is withheld from one who views the situation merely as a spectator. The spectator has only the conventional pattern of conduct to go by; the man who is challenged is, in virtue of the challenge, in a position to make a creative decision. In the experience of the mystic, the characteristic of non-continuity is frequently indicated by this same symbol, of light. Professor E. W. Lyman quotes the experience of Margaret Prescott Montague [2] who said " Once out of all the gray days of my life I have looked into the heart of reality ". The experience was not the culmination of any course of discipline; it was not the outcome of any particular doctrine of religion or system of philosophy. It did not recur. It was an experience of illumination, of swift vision, in which Reality was revealed in the aspect of Beauty. " I cannot say what the mysterious change was. I saw no new thing, but I saw all the usual things in a miraculous new light—in what I believe is their true light." [3]

In examining the phenomenon of discontinuity it is interesting and important to notice that the pedestrian plodding and the flash of insight may both be essential parts of the experience. There may be apparent severance, yet real dependence. The flash of insight cannot come if the pedestrian plodding is spurned.

In the same way we can affirm that belief in God is not derived from the facts of the world or the events of history, yet it gives coherence to these facts and significance to these events. Man cannot take the leap of faith himself: there is discontinuity; God Himself must bring man over the gap. Even when we look back from the side of faith and the new life which is brought by conversion, the hiatus does not disappear. There is still, there is always, the miracle of grace. We may not see how the new grows out of the old. But one must hasten to add that we may indeed see, and it is our blessedness to see, that in a very real sense the new is not discontinuous, since it is

[1] Professor Brand Blanshard in *The Nature of Thought*, vol. ɪɪ (ch. xxiv on " The Sub-Conscious in Invention ") has collected an imposing array of instances from literary and scientific fields.   [2] *Twenty Minutes of Reality*.
[3] *Vide* Lyman, *The Meaning and Truth of Religion*, p. 106.

all of the same pattern with God's goodness. We might, we say, have known to expect such graciousness from Him—though we could never have expected it to emerge from the old situation. Hence when we go on to make a plea for courtesy towards the ethnic faiths or towards nature mysticism, it is not because of their intrinsic worth, but because the grace of God has been made known to us in all His dealings. We affirm that there is none other name given among men for men's salvation save the name of Christ the Lord; and therefore concerning the good pagan, or the lonely mystic outside the Church, or the sincere thinker before the coming of Christ, or the faithful adherent of an alien creed, we can say only that, while we cannot explain how they may be saved, yet we ought not to be taken by surprise if through the grace of God their salvation should be accomplished.

2. *The Uncreated Light.* This familiar phrase of mystic writings will at one time indicate the Absolute with which union has been achieved; at another it is the Abyss of the God-head, the light in which the universe is bathed; often its nature is so far beyond expression that it can best be described as darkness. The paradox appears in Vaughan's lines

> There is in God, some say
> A deep but dazzling darkness.[1]

It is *lux vivens;* it is Dante's *somma luce;* and Augustine said that it is above the intellect but known to him who loves.[2]

The idea, obviously, must be handled with care, and I suspect that to all but his fanatical admirers, Berdyaev's treatment of his favourite theme of the *Ungrund,* which is akin to the Uncreated Light, is less satisfactory than other parts of his theological contribution.[3] The term *Ungrund* (taken from Boehme, who wrote of the Eternal Abyss of the divine nature, the Nothing of unrevealed godhead, which, in Still Rest and as pure Will, contains all things potentially) means, literally, "falseness" and the adjective "groundless". In Berdyaev's use of it, it means either too little or too much. If connected with τὸ μὴ ὄν it seems at most to indicate the unlimited possibilities open to God in creating the universe. If pressed, it may mean

---

[1] *Dear night, the stop to busy fools.*   [2] *Confessions,* VII. ch. x.
[3] Cf. also *Freedom and the Spirit,* ch. vi.

much more, namely something over which God has no real control.

In the account of Creation in *Genesis,* light exists before the creation of our sun, moon and stars ; but we have to remember that in *Genesis* we do not read that " God is Light " : we read that God created Light. It is in the Babylonian myths that God is Light, the sun-god ; just as in Persia the Light is eternal and uncreated. We are on safer ground when we notice how St. Paul uses the passage from *Genesis.* He acknowledges joyfully that his own conversion has been like another act of divine creation. (" If any man be in Christ, he is a new creation " καινὴ κτίσις— 2 Cor. v. 17).

Creation is closely connected with the Word of God. He spake and it was done. Hence there is no separation of God in creation from God in Scripture. Creation is built on redemption lines. The basic theme of the Bible is not the divine Trinity —a doctrine which owes something to Greek speculation—but the unity of creation and redemption. We cannot visualise creation ; but we *do* experience creatureliness, and in the consciousness of our limitation lie open to the Word of the Creator and are made aware that His work shall be consummated only in the creation of creators. It is not to be contended that the realms of creation and of grace are identical, but that they are acts of the one God and thus organically related. Nature, says Philo, is the language in which God speaks, with this difference that " While the human voice is made to be *heard,* the voice of God is made to be *seen* ".[1] St. Paul, however, records that which is still more wonderful. Whereas in the beginning God brought forth the light into being through His command, in redemption God has come Himself. " God who commanded the light to shine out of darkness, hath shined in our hearts, to give the light of the knowledge of the glory of God in the face of Jesus Christ " (2 Cor. iv. 6).

3. *The bearing of the symbol of Light on divine Guidance.* We might, with Kierkegaard, adopt the direct and simple way of affirming that the command of God is clear but incapable of analysis ; overwhelming in its authority, but discontinuous with all that has preceded it in a man's thoughtful application of himself to the moral problems of his life. Kierkegaard's favourite

[1] *De Decem Orac.* 11.

illustration is taken from the incident which is known in Jewish literature as the Binding of Isaac. The command which Abraham received to slay his son is clearly to us as it was to Abraham's subsequent reflection one that involved a morally wrong act. Even at the time there must have been in the mind of Abraham a hesitancy which was not solely due to his grief over the contemplated sacrifice of Isaac. There must have been an agonised questioning whether the act was right. He prepared to obey, not because he believed the act to be ethically justified or demanded but because of his personal relationship to God. Kierkegaard speaks of the "teleological suspension of the ethical". Faith for him is wholly opaque and irrational: it is something given to us, something done for us without any inter-relationship with the ethical or the rational.

The question is raised of the way in which God can speak to His servants apart from the reason. How was it that there came to Abraham the command to slay Isaac? How did he recognise it as a command of God? And how did he come to realise that God was carrying him farther along the road of revelation? Kierkegaard, by the solution which he offers, is launched on a path which has no end, if he refuses to admit reason at any point whatsoever. There is a danger here, which is familiar in all irrational theologies, that the door may be opened to every kind of nonsense as possessing a claim to be divine revelation. Its irrationality, so far from being a hindrance to its acceptance, becomes a recommendation. That is a danger in many ways, but particularly may it be a snare when the powers of the unconscious can, as we know now, exercise so compelling an influence in commending a belief, a conviction, or a course of action. For Kierkegaard, faith rests on discontinuity. It is not reached, as we all must agree, at the end of a continuous piece of ratiocination; nor is it the natural continuation of a process initiated and developed by human reason. Somewhere there is the irruption of the divine, somewhere the qualitative leap. It could not be otherwise if we believe with Kierkegaard that, between the divine and the human there is an infinitive qualitative difference. Here also, however, a *caveat* must be entered. This infinite qualitative difference between time and eternity, if it truly exists also between man and God, must, in the severe method in which Kierkegaard applies it, lead to a conclusion in which Christianity cannot long be content to rest. If it is pressed logically it means that we can accept no human analogy whatsoever for divine things. Human life at its highest ethical achievement can have nothing to say concerning the divine will. Every anthropomorphic phrase must be scrutinised with the gravest suspicion. The result is inevitable. Almost invariably, Kierkegaard, in his anxiety not to be too majestical towards God, must characterise the divine in negative terms. God is the absolute Unknown, the Limit of the known, the sheerly unqualified Being.

As we shall see later,[1] the Scripture passage is misinterpreted by Kierkegaard, and the scheme of blind, unquestioning obedience which he propounds is false to the facts. The evidence which convinces us from time to time that we are certainly confronted by the Word of God, in the form of a divine command, is *rational* evidence. It is not magical, not a writing in the sky, not a communication out of all relation with the remainder of our reasonable and moral life. When the commandments were given on Sinai, they came as the clarification of that which God has given to every man in his conscience. "Every man's heart is a Sinai."[2] The command of God is not a tyrant's *Diktat*.

In *The Way to Wisdom* (pp. 67 ff.) Karl Jaspers states very clearly the problem of conscience. In the unconditional imperative we see an intimation of God's guidance ; but since God is not corporeal, since there is no unmistakable form in which He exists as God, we are faced with the perplexing question, "If God lends guidance, how does man know what God wills? Is there an encounter between man and God? And if so, how does it occur?" We desire to do God's will : we believe that in conscience we learn what that will is ; but we know that conscience is often fallible, its pronouncements misleading, its light distorted. Thus we seek confirmation from others, and especially from those others whom we most respect for their integrity and moral uprightness. Here is the highest confirmation we can have in this world, yet, says Jaspers, it can never be decisive. Man's judgment is liable to error from the beginning if we expect to find in it God's final word. " We must mercilessly unmask the self-will that lies in our moral self-

---

[1] Ch. vii, p. 196 f.   [2] Joseph Hall, *Works*, 1837, 1 : 109.

satisfaction and self-righteousness." Only the judgment of God can be decisive, yet it is never definitive and always equivocal (p. 68). In all lucidity, therefore, we may be choosing a wrong road. God's guidance carries no certainty; it cannot be made into a possession. His speech can become historically clear only in the existential situation and cannot be generalised (p. 82). The voice of God can be heard only in sublime moments.

It is in the last words of this paragraph that we have the positive truth to set over against the negative analysis. For the sublime moments do occur; the existential situations do arise, and God does indicate when He is "making a special announcement". He may do it through special clarity in the soul and we speak of vision; or through His prophets, and we look on them as inspired; or by the testimony of His Church, or by His word in Scripture speaking with inescapable force. It is still true that we must avoid pride and the overweening claim that we have found that which is absolute; we must seek all the evidence that is available, from other believers whose judgment we value; from authority, so far as it is honest and unprejudiced; and from history where it can be reliably interpreted; yet amid all these testimonies the supreme evidence is that of the luminous moment when the Holy Spirit bears witness in the soul. It is not *hybris* to trust the revelation which God has given for a special purpose and with overruling convincingness. The witness of the luminous moment will be found to coincide with the evidence received from sound authority and tradition; from Bible, Church and Christian fellowship; and that coincidence will provide the highest form of religious conviction that man can have.

Conscience is mysterious enough as it is. (Heaven help us if we try to make it more mysterious, as is the aim of some contemporary "guidance" groups.) Yet, again, though mysterious, it is never magical. There will always be the familiar tension— the human appreciation and the divine illumination: the achievement of integrity by conscientious plodding and by miracles of grace: advance towards the sonship of God by gradual growth and by marvellous redemption. Thus, frequently, the figure of Light stands pre-eminently for the conscience which God has illuminated; and the source of the quality is said to be like the quality itself.

Eternal Light! Eternal Light!
　How pure the soul must be,
When, placed within Thy searching sight,
It shrinks not, but, with calm delight,
　Can live and look on Thee! . . .

O how shall I, whose native sphere
　Is dark, whose mind is dim,
Before the Ineffable appear,
And on my native spirit bear
　The uncreated beam? [1]

"So different is His light that made the sun and moon", says Augustine, "from the light of the sun and moon".[2] Can we have any inkling of the nature of it? We cannot conceive eternal light, but we do have experience of human goodness. The connotation of "the pure in heart" includes sincerity, integrity, single-mindedness. It is something positive. The mystics who think of purification as the emptying of the mind of all objects and images of the senses are very much further away from the truth than such a close observer of men as we have in, for example, Lord Moran, whose *Anatomy of Courage* contains a penetrating analysis of the quality of single-mindedness.

A true emphasis on conscience is particularly important in this age when there appears to be a revival of vague and spineless nature-worship. Every pastor has probably heard the plea, "I have no need to come to Church: I can worship God in Nature". Perhaps once in a thousand times the remark is made in sincerity. (We are not, I think, asked to believe that the stream of traffic which crowds the roads on Sunday morning and evening is all carrying devout people out of town with the object of worshipping God in Nature.) Let us suppose we have found a case where the claim is honestly made, "I can worship God as well under the canopy of His heaven, as in a stuffy church". We recognise that in this cult of the blue-domers we are dealing with a mind which is a little old-fashioned; and one which cannot afford to smile indulgently at the idolatries, say, of Central Africa. For it is every bit as sensible to bow down to a spirit of the jungle as it is to bow down before the spirit that made the trees and the stars and

---

[1] Thomas Binney.　　　　　　[2] *De Civ. Dei*, bk. v, ch. xvii.

the flowers. Both are worshipping a god whom they do not
know. Suppose, then that our interlocutor acknowledges himself a pagan three thousand years out of fashion, is there anything we can say to help in bringing him up to date? Very
important is certainly the emphasis on conscience. Of all the
world's religions nature-worship is perhaps the most selfish ; it
does not cost a man anything, nor suggest that he should do
anything to help his fellow-men or to care for the weaker and
the less fortunate. On the contrary, if he learns from Nature
alone, he will learn to fight only for himself. He may indeed
see some kindness shown by animals to their own young, and
so reach the conviction that he is right in showing every kind
of savagery in protecting his own brood, but that does not carry
him very far in the scale of civilisation for, in general, Nature
will not ask him to protect the weak or to care for the suffering.
(Nature never built a hospital.) The religion of Nature will
make few demands on his time and his pocket and his
conscience. It will not ask him to do justly and to love mercy.
Should he deal his bread to the hungry or sacrifice himself in
any way for others, then he is breaking the rules of Nature.
He is a rebel. If he is a loyal worshipper at this shrine, he will
give no mercy nor expect any. The light of nature is discredited : it is shown to be the gloom of ignorance. The starry
heavens above are dangerous guides when divorced from the
moral law within. A true appreciation of Nature requires much
more than is suggested by most people who would claim to be
"lovers of Nature". It implies the raising of ultimate questions
concerning creation and divine immanence, and concerning the
appeal of natural beauty and the shock of Nature's cruelty ; it
involves the humbling of man's pride and the acknowledgment
of intellectual bafflement in the face of mysterious events and
inscrutable power.

Since we are moving towards a conclusion which involves
a high estimate of reason and of conscience, and since therefore
we are at variance with other theological trends of the time, it
may be opportune to indicate that there need be no fear that such
a conclusion is at variance with evangelical religion. It is true
that, in the New Testament, faith is explicitly opposed to Greek
speculation on the one hand and to Jewish works of the law on
the other ; and it is a constant feature of Christianity that the

Word of the Cross will be to the Jews a stumbling-block and to the Greeks foolishness. Reliance on man's search for truth, and human pride in good deeds are both condemned; but it is necessary to distinguish. It is the reliance and it is the pride which are judged, not the search for truth, and not the good deeds. Indeed the same warning against misplaced confidence must often be given concerning faith itself; for it also can be all too human. There is the overweening assurance that our form of faith is ultimate and alone genuine. And there is the indulgent attitude of those who are at ease in Zion—as Madame Guyon discovered when she confessed that she had been too much taken up by the interior joys of the religious life, "basking like a pious tabby cat", says Miss Underhill "in the beams of the Uncreated Light".[1] Moreover, the same dubiety concerning the part played by man's freedom is present in the analysis of faith as it is in the sphere of the search for truth and the doing of good works.

4. No account of the transition from darkness to light would be adequate that did not emphasise the *note of Joy*. The flame of revelation should not merely burn: it should illuminate; but, further, it should warm. There are theologies which proceed as if only the first were true. The gloomy prophet may not only announce coming disaster: he may by his gloom contribute to it. The Old Testament Prophets were never dismal without cause. Certainly, men must rejoice in the right things, or joy is feeble and ephemeral; and only gratitude to the Redeemer of the world can give that release which brings true and lasting joy. But God has given joy also to His other children, still outside the fold; and it ill becomes the believer to want only to quench it.

The connection of the symbol of Light with the manifestation of Joy is not so clear as is the case with Wisdom and Guidance. This is surprising, since there is a natural relation in the physical world. Most of us acknowledge a rise of spirits and an increase of bodily elation when the sun shines—so long at least as we reside in a temperate zone. Proverbs xv. 30 may be an instance of this—"The light of the sun brings joy to the heart, like the coming of good news". In Job the sunless life of the wicked (xviii. 5-6) is in striking contrast with the happy

[1] *Mysticism*, p. 247.

lot of the righteous (xxii. 26-28) "Yea, the light of the wicked
shall be put out, and the spark of his fire shall not shine. The
light shall be dark in his tabernacle, and his candle shall be
put out with him." "Thou shalt have thy delight in the
Almighty, and shalt lift up thy face unto God. Thou shalt
make thy prayer unto Him, and He shall hear thee, and thou
shalt pay thy vows. Thou shalt also decree a thing, and it
shall be established unto thee: and the light shall shine upon
thy ways". In Psalm iv. 6-7, the joy of the believer is associated
with the light of God's countenance. "Lord, lift Thou up the
light of Thy countenance upon us. Thou hast put gladness in
my heart, more than in the time that their corn and their wine
increased."

The symbol of Light and the sense of Joy are indeed
explicitly associated in some passages. Esther viii. 16—"The
Jews had light, and gladness, and joy, and honour". The two
are parallel in Psalm xcvii. 11, "Light is sown for the righteous,
and gladness for the upright in heart". In Isaiah ix. 2-3 the
association is obscured by conflict of readings, but it is clear
that the passage is one of rejoicing. "The people that walked
in darkness have seen a great light: they that dwell in the land
of the shadow of death, upon them hath the light shined."
"Thou hast multiplied the nation" (so it goes on according to
one reading) "and increased its joy: they joy before thee
according to the joy in harvest, and as men rejoice when they
divide the spoil." (Cf. 2 Sam. xxiii. 4, "And he shall be as the
light of the morning, when the sun riseth, even a morning
without clouds; as the tender grass springing out of the earth
by clear shining after rain", and Matt. v. 16 where the passage
from Isaiah is freely quoted in describing the coming delivery
from joylessness and misery which are like the very home and
shadow of death.)

More frequently the connection of Light and Joy is only
implied. The New Testament often connects Joy, as is natural,
with the consummation of the Kingdom of Heaven. (Phil.
iv. 4; Rom. xiv. 17 and xv. 13.) Deliverance from sin and
anticipation of the perfect life in the presence of God are the
believer's grounds for rejoicing; and there is joy in Heaven
itself over the repentant sinner. Christ Himself is the Light of
the world and the Joy of the believer; and this theme is caught

up in early Christian hymns, outstanding among which is the
one known as the "Candlelight Hymn" because it was sung
in the ancient Church at the Lighting of the Lamps (the
Epiluchnion or *Lucernarium*). It is still used as the Vesper
Hymn by the Greek Orthodox Church and is familiar to us
chiefly in Keble's translation ("Hail! gladdening Light, of His
pure glory poured").

Φῶς ἱλαρὸν ἁγίας δόξης
Ἀθανάτου Πατρὸς οὐρανίου

Among the mystics, the element of joy sometimes appears
as forced, artificial brightness, sometimes even boisterousness;
and sometimes all too human, as in the transference to adoration
of the playfulness of lovers with their shared, secret fun. Nevertheless, it is good that they should have what Miss Underhill
called "a horror of solemnity", which they thought to be "only
fit for hypocrites".[1] They "fly, they run, they rejoice".[2]

5. There are other passages which remind us of that which
should be constantly in mind, *the Glory of the Lord,* "Who
only hath immortality dwelling in the light which no man can
approach unto; whom no man hath seen nor can see: to whom
be honour and power everlasting" (1 Tim. vi. 15-16). The divine
glory has its aspect of awesomeness. None other than God has
eternal life as his essential property; and this He has accorded
to the Son, "For as the Father hath life in Himself; so hath
He given to the Son to have life in Himself" (John v. 26). Or
again, "The city had no need of the sun, neither of the moon,
to shine in it; for the glory of God did lighten it, and the
Lamb is the light thereof" (Rev. xxi. 23).

The reminder is wholesome, since in studying religious conviction we must always recognise the danger of supposing that
we are examining some human experience, some human activity.
Nevertheless, we must not fall into the opposite error of supposing that human reason and human speculation are ruled out.
The process of elucidating and scrutinising religious experience
is not to be scorned, as if it were somehow irreligious; for it is
precisely this method which we adopt every time we dismiss
an experience as spurious because it has no commensurate results
in character and morality, or on other rational and ethical

[1] *Mysticism*, p. 440.   [2] *De Imitatione Christi*, III, v.

grounds. In the end, however, and with all that can be said on verification in mind, it must be firmly stated that revelation needs none to vouch for it. It is self-authenticating. God is His own best evidence. "Do we need any means to behold this material sun beside the sun itself ? " asks Philo. "Do we behold the stars by any light beside that of the stars themselves? In general, do we not perceive light by light? In the same fashion, God, being His own illumination, is beheld by means of Himself alone." [1] All elucidation, all theorising and defining and explaining are secondary and ancillary to religion. Real faith begins when the dictionary is put down. Dogma, says Buber, can become "the most exalted form of invulnerability against revelation ".[2] The right starting-point is neither God nor man. If we try to begin with God, we arrive in deism ; if with man, we end in idealism. Religion begins with Incarnation, with the God-Man. "It pleased God to reveal His Son in me." The right way to knowledge is not by proofs but by worship, by communion, by obedience. Without these the knowledge cannot come. And the right way to certitude is neither autonomous nor heteronomous ; but theonomous. There is no criterion of God except God. We are incurably rational ; we always return to demand proofs, but in the end we learn that better than having proofs is having—God. The believer is like the poet and like the child, desiring above all not to explain but to experience.

Was it wrong and sacrilegious when Kepler gave thanks that he was permitted to think God's thoughts after Him? Is that attitude in complete contradiction to the plain words of the Bible, "My thoughts are not your thoughts, neither are your ways my ways, saith the Lord. For as the heavens are higher than the earth, so are my ways higher than your ways, and my thoughts than your thoughts " (Is. lv. 8-9) ? Possibly the verses in Isaiah refer to the plans and purposes of God : these indeed are far above man's understanding, especially when, as the first verses suggest, man is immersed in the sordid things of the market ; and this may leave us free to say that, whenever we grasp the truth, God is moving in *our* thoughts.

Reason, Logos, is in One alone, and in others only in so far as they are one with Him. What we face, therefore, is not a conflict of faith and reason, but a distinction between two

[1] *De Praem.* xlv. 46. [2] *Between Man and Man,* p. 18.

possible illuminations of the *whole* person; or a distinction of the various possible faiths which a man may hold so vigorously that they dominate his life. The irreligious man may be as dogmatic a believer as any Christian, but his faith is in something other than the divine. Lord Lister used to assert his faith in carbolic acid; and that, so far as it goes, is excellent. The scientist ought to be dogmatic about his technique, when he has proved it to be right; but not so as to close his mind to all else. We may quote Lister's own words "I desire to correct a mistake into which I fell when investigating the fermentation of milk some years ago; for next to the promulgation of new truth, the best thing, I conceive, that a man can do, is the recantation of published error".[1] Every man lives by faith, and the object of his faith is determined by that which in his heart of hearts he holds to be most significant. The scientist is in duty bound to proclaim his scientific certainties for the welfare and instruction of mankind, but if he is wise (if, indeed, he is a good scientist) he will realise that a sceptical attitude to other realms of truth is at best a belief, and may be a prejudice. Speaking of the "logical positivists" E. T. Ramsdell in an admirable study of the relation of faith and reason writes:[2] "There is something almost amusing about the way in which the logical positivist prides himself on being objective and free from all subjective evaluation even as he asserts the value judgment that sensuous propositions alone can be significant." The spirit of wisdom is *given* to man when the eyes of the understanding are enlightened. (Eph. i. 17-18.)

To the believer, reality is both other than himself and yet one with himself. God is Light and in Him is no darkness at all (1 John i. 5); it seems impossible for man to have any part in His glory; but in the divine mercy knowledge of Himself is imparted. "He that doeth truth cometh to the light" (John iii. 21). By the Incarnation we learn that the Beyond is both *within* man and *akin to* man.

There are three special ways in which the figure of Light assists us in grasping something of the divine nature.

Light is a familiar symbol of the presence of God; but it is also more than a symbol. Many have reported that there is

---

[1] *Trans. Pathological Society of London*, vol. **XXIX**, 1878.
[2] *The Christian Perspective*, p. 28.

actual experience of a radiance, a flooding of the personality with light.[1]

Light is shed on all other things because of the inner experience of illumination.[2] Quite apart from the clearer vision of the poet which is very frequently expressed in vaguely poetic language in terms of light, there is an enhanced radiance in the world which is the special privilege of the mystic.

There is, I believe, a third element, a clarity of intellectual vision, which also can best be described as Light. It has affinities with the first, because it is recognised as coming through encounter with the divine; and it has associations with the second, because it sheds light on all experience. Yet it is separate from both. It has to do with knowledge, not feeling—knowledge of the nature of God. The Light within us is not merely a symbol but a contact. It gives reliable knowledge (indeed the most reliable that can ever be possessed) of ultimate reality. Yet have we this treasure in earthen vessels, "that the excellency of the power may be of God, and not of us".

---

[1] See Evelyn Underhill, *Mysticism*, ch. iv.　　　　　　[2] *Ibid.* p. 254.

CHAPTER III

THE NATURE OF MAN

WE may now follow out the implications of the symbol of light in its *anthropological* significance.

Light commonly indicates moral excellence, as in Proverbs iv. 18, "The path of the just is as the shining light, that shineth more and more unto the perfect day"; or Matthew vi. 22, "The light of the body is the eye: if therefore thine eye be single, thy whole body shall be full of light". Special caution is needed here lest we fall into the "paradox of morality". Principal Oman used to think that many of the mystics would have been "very ill to live with, as good people ought not to be".[1] An arranged scheme of self-deliverance from evil may use the forms of self-sacrifice, but still be only an arranged scheme of self-exaltation. The lessons of life can be learned only by looking with the open eye at all its situations and facing all its challenges.

Light indicates spiritual knowledge, as in Luke xi. 34-36. In this connection Richard Kroner suggests that the vehicle of God's Word to man should be regarded as the imagination, and certainly that function is intimately linked with man's worship. The word has perhaps been debased in meaning, as if it indicated the realm of fancy; and we may note that when Jeanne d'Arc was rebuked because of her visions on the ground that they were in her imagination, she replied that it was precisely in her imagination that they came to her.

Light may imply influence on others, as in Matthew v. 16, "Let your light so shine before men, that they may see your good works" and Ephesians v. 8, "Walk as children of light ... and have no fellowship with the unfruitful works of darkness".

The word has also a wider and more general significance. In all ages when the nature of man became an urgent theme of inquiry, the symbol of light has seemed the appropriate one to express the paradoxical thought of a being who is other than

[1] *Vide The Natural and the Supernatural,* p. 500.

God and yet one with God. The beam of light is derived from the luminous body in a unique way without, it was supposed, diminishing the source or losing its oneness with its origin. More critical appreciation of the nature of the case found it necessary to raise the question, Wherein shall we say that human nature is akin to the divine? and to answer, perhaps, that man retains his likeness to God in virtue of his reason, his conscience, his capacity of loving, and so forth. In particular, there are two features which have been emphasised. They are to be observed, it is said, even in natural man. One is responsibility, the other autonomy. "Sinful man", says Dr. Emil Brunner,[1] "can no longer understand anything about his origin save this, that he is responsible to a divine law, and thus that he must fulfil this law. With this consciousness of legal responsibility, which is the central point of our 'natural' consciousness of personality, there is combined that of autonomy. The 'natural man' cannot help thinking that what he ought to do he can do, and what he can do he thinks, 'Well, at bottom that is what I am like'. This is why he reacts so violently against the doctrine of original sin. . . . The message of Jesus Christ is to him, necessarily, a folly and a scandal."

If man were ever wholly "natural", it would clearly be absurd to speak of him as retaining any of the divine likeness. It would mean that God had cut him off; that there was now no longer any communication between him and his source. Does this situation ever arise in our experience? Or is it the limiting case, to which the Gospel continually directs attention as the inevitable end of rebellious ways, without indicating any instances in which that end has been reached? Does the love of God ever abandon a man to final excommunication from Himself? There is possibly no clear answer given in the Bible either with reference to this world or in connection with the world to come; but we are always confronted by men who are finite over against the Infinite; creatures over against the Creator; sinners over against the Saviour; and all we can say is that man, because of God's unwearying and unconquerable love for him, has the potentiality of the infinite; has the chance of overcoming his creaturehood; has the hope of losing for ever his sinful status.

[1] *Revelation and Reason*, p. 173.

SELF-RESPECT

Reflection on the Christian doctrine of man brings inevitably to my own mind a haunting incident connected with the tramp-poet of Galloway and the Borders, Roger Quin ("a true poet, if not a great one" it was said lately when the centenary of his birth was celebrated).[1] I can just remember him, when he was already an old man, still living in Dirk Hatterick's Cave on the shore of the Solway Firth during the summer and in an old people's residence in Dumfries during the winter. It was very touching to find him writing a poem on *A Skylark Singing Above the Poor-House*. He sometimes made a little money by travelling on the local railway, selling note-books and pencils. One who was new to the district and had learned nothing of his background told me how Quin came along the corridor to his compartment, saying, "Pencils, twopence each, or a penny if you're poor". A little impatiently, my friend handed him sixpence, saying that he didn't wish a pencil in return. The old poet drew himself up with splendid dignity and said, "I don't want your charity. Do you know where I slept last night? I climbed over the railings of St. Michael's Churchyard and slept by the grave of Robert Burns. I don't want your charity." It is a lesson in giving. It can easily become cold and impersonal, and then it ceases to be Christian charity. The gift without the giver is bare. And it throws light on the inner thoughts of the tramp-poet. He knew that charity could be purchased at too heavy a price. Self-respect is a great treasure. Take that from a man and you do him grave injury.

Is this in accordance with New Testament teaching on man? Indeed it is; it is the New Testament which gives this conception all its strength and its convincingness. At some period of his life probably everyone is persuaded that he is the most important person in the whole world. We do not entirely outgrow that conviction when we cease to be children: we are merely a little more skilful in concealing it. It lies at the heart of the worst selfishness; and yet it is also the outcome of a deep, essential human instinct. It *may* lead to the "Watch me!" complex, or, as Gabriel Marcel describes it, "Here am I! What

---

[1] I realise that I have given this reminiscence elsewhere, in *The Obedience of a Christian Man*, but as that book is out of print I venture to recur to it.

luck!" but on the other hand the teaching of Christianity is that the instinct, rightly interpreted, is profoundly true. Each man *is* of supreme importance in the eyes of God. That truth is pressed home in the parables of the lost coin, the lost sheep, the prodigal son. Seen from the fixed stars, man *is* no more than the fraction of an atom. But God does not regard His children in that way. What is man that He taketh knowledge of him? The answer is that He made each one for Himself. For each one Christ died.

MAN IN COMMUNITY

On the other side we are at once aware that men are dependent on one another. They must co-operate or perish. They cannot reach the heights of spiritual life except in the company of others. A Robinson Crusoe must live a circumscribed and stunted life, even spiritually. Karl Barth has scoffed at the absurd idea of "Humanity without neighbour", the fantastic notion of egocentric man, which must be eradicated from Christian anthropology. And of course St. Paul has expressed it notably and with finality by saying "We are members one of another". The community in which we live is like a second body. Apart from it each one of us is like a finger cut off, a limb amputated. Others in our own day, secularising this thought and carrying it to its extreme, have argued that religion is no longer required, since we have replaced it by the lofty ideal of the community. We should live, not for the private blessedness of faith, but for the common good of all mankind. Unfortunately for this secular theory, history has already uncovered the snag. Wherever the common good of man has been exalted above the worship of God, there has grown up a crude worship of the State, a veiled idolatry. Religions of humanity have ended in the degradation of man. Before we can see anything noble in man, we must first have faith in God.

In His teaching, Jesus exalted the value of the individual. His action reinforced His words. He liked to avoid the crowds. He constantly sought to be alone with individual people who were in need or in distress. Perhaps in every generation of the

Christian Church, the real work of evangelism is done soul by soul.

> " There is no expeditious road
> To pack and label men for God
> And save them by the barrel-load." [1]

Is it paradoxical that His message, *because* it is for the individual, is for all men and for all time? That sounds contradictory: it is really good sense. Had His teaching concerned the community, it must have been a message for the Jewish people in Palestine about the year A.D.30. But, being addressed to the individual, with his needs and desires and hopes and fears, it is for all individuals and for all ages. [2]

THE INDIVIDUAL WITHIN THE COMMUNITY

There are two far-reaching consequences of this emphasis on the individual. (1) If we regard man as a child of God, we must see in him *a person who is responsible*. His decisions are his own; others may advise him and offer examples from the lives of those who have faced similar problems before; but in the end a man must decide for himself. As a child of God he is a responsible agent. He may not shelter behind the state, or the law, or the family, or public opinion, or tradition, or convention. He must decide, and stand by his decision. (2) *His decision is of eternal consequence.* He must render account at the last before God. We have it in the parables—that of the Talents; and that of the Last Judgment, when the sheep and the goats are separated. These parables raise very acutely, and sometimes in the young mind with urgent perplexity, the question whether the Christian teaching does not appear to lay overmuch stress on reward and punishment. We may have a feeling that St. Theresa was right when she said in longing, " Oh that there were neither Heaven nor Hell; that I might serve God for Himself alone ", and Calvin when he wrote that it is not the fear of punishment that keeps man from sin; but, loving God as his Father and honouring Him as his Master, although there were no Hell, he would revolt at the idea of offending Him; [3] or Thomas à Kempis when he wrote—but he

---

[1] Francis Thompson: Epilogue to *A Judgement in Heaven.*
[2] See Dr. E. F. Scott's illuminating study, *Man and Society in the New Testament*, published in New York in 1946.
[3] *Institutes*, bk. I, ch. ii, *sub. fin.*

erased it from his manuscript—"Better to be with Christ in Hell than to be without Him in Heaven". With a right instinct we have altered the hymn which once ran

> Whatever, Lord, we lend to Thee,
> Repaid a thousand-fold will be:
> Then gladly will we give to Thee,
> Who givest all.

Dean Inge pardonably felt that it was like the prospectus of a new commercial company, promising a rich and certain dividend. That reaction is sound and healthy ; but the fact remains that the aspect of reward cannot be left out of account in the Christian doctrine of man. Man is bound to carry with him beyond this life his moral character, his real self. Of course the Christian resolution of the paradox is well known. This attainment, this character—these are not man's own doing ; they are of the grace of God. Man's whole worth depends on the fact that he is the child of God—the lost and prodigal son, it is true, yet His son still, because the grace of God is tireless. If man professes to discover values within himself, that is mere presumption and pride. He is like the young brother of Marshal Foch, running home from school and calling, "I am the cleverest boy in the class! " and being gently rebuked by his mother in words which he never forgot, "Cleverness that needs to be mentioned does not exist". The worth of man is all of grace. All comes from God. Man's only true value is that which can never be *discovered;* it must be *revealed.* For men are not only beset by temptations in the fierce conflicts of life : they are also burdened by sins. Christ had to deal with both evils. Man was held down by fear. Yet God's ancient promise was not annulled. Man stood in the face of a destiny unattained, yet unrevoked : a destiny which he could not reach by himself (experience had proved that) yet could not abandon as beyond hope. So in the Incarnation of Christ we see human nature consecrated by His sharing of it. He came to the help, not of the angels but of the race of mankind. So He was made like His brethren, that He might be tempted as they are, yet without sin ; might suffer and die for them, and rise again to reign for ever. That will suffice for the greatest sinner : and for the man who feels himself the greatest failure, that will be enough. When

Jesus discovers the first spark of faith, He can see in it already all its unfoldings in this life and beyond. He can see a Church arising because one man confesses Him: in a dying thief can see a companion with whom to cross the threshold of the unseen world. For the great sinner, for the manifest failure, the Son of God did not disdain to die. To the age-old question, "Lord, what is man, that Thou art mindful of him?" we have the answer, "A thing of price is a man, because for him Christ died".

THE COMMUNITY AND CONSCIENCE

So far we have been deliberately abstracting, in order to recover that emphasis on the individual which has often been obscured in this age, causing a grave misinterpretation of Christian teaching. Now we must turn from the individual to the community; and we can link them together most fruitfully by examining the nature of moral endeavour, where the two spheres meet. When a conference of Christian youth was convened in Oslo in 1947, one of the questions set for study was "Who decides what is good and what is evil?" Let us address ourselves to that inquiry. Could the answer be "Ourselves"? The first reply that comes to hand is, probably, "Our conscience"; and indeed conscience can scarcely be given too high a place. Its importance must never be minimised in this day of many attempts to establish the totalitarian state and to control the individual's life and liberty. Again, if a man loses his faith and yet clings to duty, he will in the end almost certainly come back to faith; and his return will be by this path, the path of conscience. Yet many have been wondering (the time is not yet come to make a reliable estimate) how far the children of the occupied countries of Europe have been affected by the moral conditions of their war-time life. They were taught—and it was in the best homes that this teaching was most competently given—that a high form of ethical conduct was to steal and to tell lies, so long as the victims were the soldiers of the German army. In Holland, some of the children were instructed in methods of decoying the enemy into manholes and canals, often, I understand, with considerable success. What is likely to be the lasting effect of this *legalised lawlessness* on the moral character of the child? Is he going to be able to distinguish between theft and falsehood directed to an enemy and dishonesties of all kinds in normal existence? I put the matter to a friend in the French Resistance movement who after suffering severe torture at the hands of the Gestapo had escaped and was already renowned for the large number of trains which he had managed to steal from the Germans for the use of the F.F.I. in south-western France. He promised to consider the problem when he had more leisure. He is now a medical student and his answer was given when he visited me in my home in St. Andrews. "Since the war ended, Professor, I haven't stolen a single train." But of course we realised that his case was different, since he was about sixteen years of age when he first served with the Resistance, and able to discriminate. The conditioning of young children remains an unsolved problem. Is the moral law so deeply embedded in the heart of the child that the unhampered compass-needle will always swing back to its right place? We may not just take it for granted. But there is interesting confirmation of the profound penetration of the moral law in another illustration from the experience of the Resistance. Captain Savouret, who was playing an extremely dangerous rôle within the counsels of the enemy, was at last suspected and delated. Being suddenly confronted with those who had shared the danger, he found it an almost unbearable strain to deny his knowledge of them. Even in that moment when all of them realised that their lives depended on bold denials, emotions of loyalty, trust, comradeship reinforced the moral obligation to speak the truth in a way which made the moment particularly painful.

We mark the importance of conscience by calling it "the voice of God"; but it may not always justify that high title. It is fallible. The conscience may be "the conscience of a fool". Worse than that: it must be acknowledged as the conscience of a sinner. In none of us is it a pure and sensitive instrument for recording God's will. Many in fact will not agree that God is to be brought in at all. Duty, they think, becomes artificial if it is done because it is "the will of God"; and it needs no divine sanction to guarantee its authenticity.

We must acknowledge that there *is* such a thing as non-religious morality. Christian people are frequently put to shame (or ought to be) by the courage, the kindness, the loyalty, the self-sacrifice of those who are not only altogether outside the realm of organised religion, but would reject with complete decisiveness the epithet "religious". It is perfectly true that this non-religious morality may often be like the tree whose roots are severed. It will go on flourishing for some time. The leaves may put on even more glorious colours than hitherto; but they are the colours of decay. The tree is doomed. Goodness without God is parasitic: it is living on the spiritual capital of the past. It owes much to religion that it does not acknowledge. Perhaps we seem to have an exception in Confucianism to the rule that sound morality stems from religion; for Confucianism appears to be much more accurately described as a moral system than as a religion. It is interesting to read in a report on juvenile delinquency in New York that the Chinese citizens have an excellent record, due to their steady moral teaching, to their strong family life, and to their habit of punishing recalcitrant children not so much by chastisement as by sensible deprivation. But we must also remember that the Chinese *do* depend on religion, in their reverence for Confucius and for T'ien; and that their morality is said, by those who have studied it, to emphasise only the narrower family loyalties, at home or in the family business concern, and in so far to be circumscribed. Thus, the chief thing to say about non-religious morality is this (it is a double criticism): (1) It lacks dynamic. It *may* be able to discern what is right: it certainly cannot offer the power to put it into practice. (2) The system has nothing to offer to the man who fails to keep faith with the demands of duty. It cannot speak the word "pardon". Forgiveness is not "ethical", but a breach of the ethical; since strict morality demands justice not pardon. (See *infra*, p. 108.)

There is another difficulty. Non-religious morality can give no account of why it is "right to do right". We may ask, perhaps, Can *we*? And the answer is, No. I do not believe that we *can* give a final account. But we come nearer to it, because we, as believers, are concerned with the realm of personal relations. Men are to be treated as brothers, because we are all children of God. Therefore if a man is good without having faith; when he reflects on duty and its consequences, he is making the universe appear more mysterious than it need be. He is obscurantist. The religious view-point is here the more scientific.

THE STATE

It is not possible to hold that the individual self is the legislator, deciding what is good and what is evil. Conscience may be the conscience of a foolish, it certainly is the conscience of a sinful, person. Something wider is sought; and strong claims have been put forward on behalf of the State. It must be acknowledged that there is a much larger measure of agreement as to what is good and what is evil than is sometimes supposed. Ethical beliefs have certainly varied enormously in different ages, and this might be quoted as an argument against tracing them to a source in the State, which, from the tribal stage onwards, might be supposed to have fundamentally similar needs, leading to similar moral codes; but in fact the variation has not been by any means so vast as earlier observers believed. The differences in moral practice in primitive peoples concern means rather than ends. All early societies appear, in fact, to be going in the same direction towards the same goal, the satisfaction of the whole of their human nature.[1] Moreover, in the same periods of time far wider variations have taken place in man's scientific conceptions than in his ethical ideas. Compare primitive man's notions about the stars or about the cure of disease with those of a physicist and a doctor today, and we realise that the gulf is much less wide in ethics. But the claim of the State to be the arbiter in morality is untenable. The State, if it stood alone, could legislate only for expediency. What the State has decreed, the State can revoke. Our own time has seen the full fruition of this doctrine that the State determines what is right and what is wrong. For Fascism and Nazi-ism and the like, *what the State decides* is the very same thing as *what is right;* and we know what this led to—the whim of one man; the concentration-camp and the gas-chamber; disaster and nemesis. There is always the right and

[1] See Professor Alexander Macbeath's Gifford Lectures, *Experiments in Living*, Macmillan 1952, where he examines the findings of Westermarck and other writers of the beginning of this century and the theories of contemporary anthropologists who hold to the view that primitive societies may be " travelling along different roads in pursuit of different ends "—the opinion advanced by Miss Benedict in her *Patterns of Culture*.

the duty of rebellion. The individual is above the State; but both individual and state are answerable to moral laws. They are subject, not sovereign.

THE MORAL EMPIRE

Can the ultimate be this system of moral laws? the Kingdom of ends? the grand moral principles in their vast, coercive, convincing power? Fichte, Nicolai Hartmann and many others have argued this case eloquently. Dante called the law of righteousness the bridle directing man's wayward steps to God; but there are many who believe in the system of laws without finding it necessary to go forward on this next step, to belief in God. Is there a law or a principle to determine what is good and what is evil? We recall the insistence of Kant on the "moral law within". Can conduct be reduced to a code? It is almost a *reductio ad absurdum* of his ethics to read Kant's essay "On a Supposed Right to Tell Lies from Benevolent Motives"; and his defence of his words "To tell a falsehood to a murderer who asked us whether our friend, of whom he was in pursuit, had not taken refuge in our house, would be a crime". The truth is, of course, that God does not want just obedience to a set of rules, but rather people of a particular sort; not pedantic adherence to a code, but character. Perhaps, then, ultimately, it *is* we who decide what is good and what is evil; but *we* are now no longer the fallible, bewildered, erring people of whom we spoke earlier, but men and women who are living under grace, inspired, guided, strengthened by God.

IT IS GOD WHO DECIDES

Inevitably we come back to the Christian conviction that it is God who decides what is good and what is evil. And then the perplexing philosophical problem, which has been awaiting its opportunity, swoops down on us. Is a thing good because God has commanded it? Or does God command it because it is good? The question is connected, historically, with the name of Duns Scotus, scholastic philosopher. Will, he said, dominates intellect. Intellect may present the evidence to the will, the material on which will must make its decision; but in the end

will decides, and does so in complete freedom. This analysis
holds good also, he believes, in God. *His* will is not determined
by intellect either ; that is to say, it is not determined by God's
own wisdom. And it is often said that Duns Scotus went further
and taught that we call a thing "right" because it is commanded by God. It is true that some followers of his taught
this doctrine ; but Duns Scotus never went so far. He said,
indeed, that God *could* have given a different nature to everything He has created ; and thus a different nature even to man ;
in which case, the laws of morality might have been quite other
than they are ; but there is no sign that Duns Scotus believed
that, *human nature being what it is,* God could have changed
the nature of morality. If we ask the question, "Is a thing
good because God has commanded it? or has God commanded
it because it is good?" we are not going to get a satisfactory
answer, because the question is wrongly posed. If you say that
a thing is good, and therefore God commands it, you are im-
plying that there is something over God and superior to God,
namely the moral law. But if you change round and say that
God commands a thing and therefore it is good, you are making
God too like an Oriental tyrant, who can decree that to be
right which he wishes to bring about, acknowledging no obligation other than his own arbitrary caprice. The truth seems to
be that the two are inseparable, like the two sides of the same
lens. *God is goodness.* But what, once again, of non-religious
morality? Was that courage shown in war-time by men and
women, who were not Christian, but pagan, really just pagan
virtue? Surely not. Even the non-religious European is steeped
in the influence of Christianity. "Pagan" virtue is not really
pagan : it is the grace of God flowing into a man. The pagan
who is morally upright argues that duty is simply the right
response to the total environment. And with that humanistic
explanation we can in fact agree, if it is made quite clear what
we mean by "environment". Man's total environment is God.
The end and aim and purpose of life is to worship. And, when
we go on to discover the ethical consequences of this worship,
the results in moral life and in duty of this fellowship with
God, we do not abandon the starting-place, as if it were only
a spring-board. It affects, and may affect profoundly, the quality
of our conduct. In particular, it may affect our conduct in

the treatment of the weak and of the criminal. Forgiveness will enter in, because all men are seen as children of God, and our communion with the Father makes us realise that we have desperate need of forgiveness.

There is another consideration. Hastings Rashdall wrote:[1] "If the existence of God is not a postulate of all morality, it is a postulate of a sound morality." Superficially, indeed, it may appear that precisely the same virtues are cultivated by humanism and by faith, but in the former case they are soon discovered to be brittle and precarious. The secular person, if he is sincere in his search, and even although he regards the Bible as merely a handbook of moral instruction, will assuredly not fail to find much light in Scriptures. It is scandalous to deny this. But in seeking unselfishness and humility apart from belief and worship, the humanist may easily end by becoming *odiously* unselfish and *repulsively* humble. Trust in God seems to be the only recipe for unselfishness and humility which are *true* and the genuine basis of sound judgment and legitimate self-reliance. To be conscious of a divine call to a great task is the one way to self-confidence of the right sort.

On the other hand you have the "religious" person who is *not* ethical. In an old "Moocher's Map" passed from hand to hand a century ago, with its conventional signs to indicate the nature of the reception likely to meet the tramp at various doors, there is one mark which appears only occasionally. Its interpretation, given by the vagrant composer, is *religious but kind*. There is a world of criticism in the "but". The picture of a soulless piety is, of course, a caricature of religion, as is also the person who is kind because it is a religious duty to be kind—and how you hate to be shown *dutiful kindness*. It is said that ladies of the Victorian period sometimes went visiting in the poorer quarters of the city not for Christian love of the inhabitants, but because they regarded "slumming" as a religious duty. It is told of one lady who "got" religion that she wanted to spend the rest of her life in "doing good to people", and found that people do not want to be done good to. This type of thing may and does appear in many Christians, but it is not to be regarded as a right interpretation of Christian teaching. It is reminiscent rather of the *megalopsuchos* of Aristotle, who

[1] In *The Theory of Good and Evil*, vol. ii, pp. 212-213.

always strikes one as quite insufferable. The Christian, knowing himself to be under judgment, is humble before God and therefore is patronising to no one. Dr. C. S. Lewis finds a response in us all with his sound Christian psychology: "When a man is getting better, he understands more and more clearly the evil that is still left in him. When a man is getting worse, he understands his own badness less and less. A moderately bad man know he's not very good: a thoroughly bad man thinks he's all right. This is commonsense really. You understand sleep when you're awake, not while you're sleeping. You can see mistakes in arithmetic when your mind is working properly: while you're making them you can't see them. Good people know good *and* evil: bad people don't know about either." [1]

THE BROTHERHOOD OF MEN

The philosophers of Greece had sometimes proclaimed in lofty fashion the brotherhood of men. They founded their conviction on the nature of *man*. Jesus began with the nature of *God*. There is something in man, the Greeks argued, which makes him of one substance with all mankind. There is love in God, Jesus said, which will look on all men as His sons, even when they are the most sinful and rebellious. Begin with the Fatherhood of God, and you cannot help believing that all men are your brothers. Begin only with the nature of man, and you may not be able to retain long your belief in man's brotherhood. "Man's inhumanity to man makes countless thousands mourn." In the Old Testament teaching, far too often, national loyalties had imposed their narrow vision on the idea of brotherhood. "Brother" meant "fellow-Hebrew". It is true that the best of Old Testament teaching transcended this narrow nationalism. We notice it, in fact, chiefly because it contradicted the noblest words of the prophets, because in this narrowness Judaism was untrue to itself. But the narrowness was there. Jonah represents the attitude—as if God could have nothing to do with other nations, except to punish them for idolatry. Jesus corrects it in the parable of the Good Samaritan. "Who is my neighbour?" The kindness is shown by the hated and despised Samaritan, and shown, we realise

[1] *Christian Behaviour*, p. 26.

from the story, at a moment when there were no spectators but God.

It has often been thrown against Christianity as a gibe that it takes no sufficient account of social questions. It has long been a charge that religion is the opium of the people, an accusation first made by a clergyman of the Anglican Church (Charles-Kingsley) long before it was adopted by Karl Marx and his followers.[1] And that suggests two points that are most relevant in connection with this familiar and rather superficial criticism. (1) The Church has always been on the look-out to rebuke itself, and to chastise itself for becoming concerned wholly with the life of contemplation. It has sought rigorously to keep its members sensitive to the needs of the poor and the down-trodden and the under-privileged; and, in fact, it has been the Church which has held the highest laurels in the work of social amelioration. Dictators have never found the Church an easy means of keeping the people quiet. They incline to strike at it immediately and strongly, since it stands for the opposite of all their dreams and plans. So far from being dope, the Christian Gospel has been in the nature rather of dynamite. (2) It is the Church which has itself supplied the standard by which it is criticised. Had it not kept true Christian faith alive there would be today no sensitiveness about harsh conditions in the life of some men and women. If we are not Christians; if, at least, we do not believe in the Fatherhood of God, we cannot find any reason for protecting man from exploitation. Once you throw religion overboard, there is no foundation remaining for belief in the equality of men. There is nothing left but unbridled exploitation. The strong will trample on the weak until the weak gather strength enough to rise in rebellion. When that has been said, we ought to ask how it is that this superficial criticism has gained the plausibility which it appears to command in our day. (i) It may be that Christianity is regarded as being conservative. It certainly has endured for a long time: there must be something eternal about it. And it is also true that it conserves many values which

---

[1] See *Kritik der Hegelschen Rechtsphilosophie*, Introduction—" Die Religion . . . ist das Opium des Volkes ". Is there another point of contact between these two? Cf. Marx, *Critique of the Gotha Programme*, " From each according to his ability, to each according to his needs " with Kingsley's famous hymn, " From Thee all skill and science flow "—" And part them Lord to each and all, As each and all have need ".

would otherwise be lost to the world, but it is, I think, just not true to go on to argue that the Church is also conservative in the political sense of the word. It counts among its members those of all political parties and of none. It unchurches no one for political opinions and if it is wise it attaches itself officially to no political party and to no political expedient. It is no part of the Church's duty to carry out any political programme: it is its duty, on the other hand, to train as Christians those people who will have the responsibility of thinking out those programmes. (ii) It is supposed by some of the critics that the Church is always on the side of established government—and therefore, presumably, that it is against the people who are exploited by the government. That idea has been shattered for ever, one trusts, by the experience of war. The most courageous opposition to dictatorships came from Christian people. The criticism was pressed particularly against the Church of Rome, on the ground that it too readily identified itself with power politics in Italy—but that Church also had its courageous fighters for truth in Germany and some of the occupied territories. From the ranks of Protestant Christianity we think of Bishop Berggrav in Norway, Pierre Maury in France, Bonhoeffer in Germany, and countless others whose names have never been recorded. (iii) Probably the chief reason for the criticism appearing plausible is the lack of knowledge concerning the Church of Christ and its work. The Church has been very modest, perhaps unduly modest, in speaking of its vast work among the under-privileged. The tendency has been for the ordinary man to hear much about the government and little about the Gospel.

EARLY CHRISTIAN COMMUNISM

In the Acts of the Apostles we read of the close and harmonious relations of the early Church. They had all things in common. In our time, when political Communism rears its head, it is well to have a true picture of this early Christian communism. So many people say, lightly and unthinkingly, "After all I suppose that the first Christian Church practised communism". The truth, of course, is that the Communism of today is a political creed, following on the theories of Karl

Marx, believing that there is no freedom in history, but only inevitable working-out of certain forces; believing in materialism; in class-warfare; proclaiming and practising an atheistic attitude to life. It is fanatical in its beliefs, so that it has come to appear as a new religion—faith in God with the negative sign. How far this is from the kind of thing described in the New Testament we can easily detect. The two are poles apart. It is enough to notice about the particular incident in Acts that there was no compulsion in sharing possessions. (1) Ananias and Sapphira were blamed and punished, not for keeping something back, but for lying about it. (2) The action of Barnabas in voluntarily surrendering all his wealth for the common good of the community is specially singled out for praise. There was therefore no obligation to contribute, and no one was rebuked for remaining apart from the scheme. (3) Simon Peter in his rebuke of Ananias and Sapphira makes it quite plain that it is all voluntary; that there are still all the ancient rights of property. "Whiles it remained was it not thine own? And after it was sold, was it not in thine own power? why hast thou conceived this thing in thine heart? thou hast not lied unto men, but unto God" (Acts v. 4).

But the ideal was to have all things in common, for it was an age in which there was no social welfare system to help out the poor and the sick. Christians naturally desire to help one another to the limit of their ability, and in the unusual circumstances of the early Church, this Christian solidarity was very necessary. In visualising the bettering of the social structure the New Testament does not advocate social movements. Indeed it did not speak out against slavery, nor against tyrannical government, though both must have been, to enlightened minds, obvious scandals. It was to be Christianity that in the end was to fight these abuses most devotedly, but the writers of our early Christian documents knew quite well that improvement waits, not on revolution or re-organisation so much as on conversion. "They saw that the evil lay much deeper than any one surmised. There could be no real improvement in the world's condition without a new attitude to God, a new conception of the meaning of man's life. The social question, as they saw it, was a religious one." [1] "Jesus Himself had been

[1] E. F. Scott, *Man and Society in the New Testament*, p. 168.

tempted to come forward as a king, and correct all evils swiftly by his sovereign edict. But He had perceived the snare and avoided it, and had chosen the toilsome road of bringing a new life to the souls of men."[1] The human heart is the key to the whole problem. If it is right, all is right.

How is the human heart made right? It is not in human power adequately to analyse the process of conversion ; for, if a man is himself the subject of it, his experience transcends expression, and, if he is only an observer, he has not yet known its depths. When we speak of revelation, the divinely appointed medium by which conversion is brought about, the same is true, but only partially true. It is impossible to reduce revelation to rational terms, but it is not impossible to unfold the rational elements within it. Revelation will always be mysterious, but it is never magic.

It is right and proper to guard ourselves against that presumption which would "find out the Almighty unto perfection ", but there is one kind of *hybris* which is always legitimate, and we have it in the same book of Job. To some it may seem like questioning God, but it is really questioning the inadequate, unsatisfying views of God which men have been holding, when by God's grace we know, deep down, that He must be different. God cannot reveal Himself, it has been said, to an irreligious mind ; and part of religion—a large part—is sincerity of mind. No man will be great who is constantly digging at the roots of his faith to see whether all is sound ; but neither will he be noble if he is prepared to leave unexamined that of which he is not convinced.

CONDITIONS FOR MAN'S RESPONSE : REPENTANCE

There are conditions governing, not revelation, but the human response to revelation. One of these is *Repentance*. And far more important than to know whether man's sin has dimmed and distorted his reason so as to make him incapable of straight thinking, is to inquire whether man is wholly incapable of repentance. This is the real and tragic frailty of man's fallen condition. When repentance comes, it is certainly mysterious. Is it a magic? Assuredly, there is the false semblance of it, in

[1] E. F. Scott, *Man and Society in the New Testament*, p. 169.

remorse. At its best, this is merely aversion, only a barren pain with little moral value ; at its worst only the emotion of disgust at some offence formerly cherished. Judas is said to " repent himself ". (Matt. xxvii. 3 μεταμεληθείς.) True repentance is a godly sorrow, and it involves the whole man, intellect, emotion, and will. It brings emotional release, liberation of the will, and hence, inevitably, illumination. In *The Republic* Plato has the image of light as symbolising the turning of the inhabitants of the cave from the darkness and the shadows of error to the illumination of the real world. (Bk. vii. 514.) In the religious life, faith and repentance are closely intertwined ; for if there is no faith there cannot be true repentance, and until there is true repentance there cannot be real faith. In Hosea (ii. 19) the order seems to be—the knowledge of God ; repentance ; response ; restoration. Amos (iv. 6 ff.) has the refrain, " Yet have ye not returned unto me, saith the Lord ". And Ezekiel (xxxvi. 25-27) insists that the initiative lies with God alone, " A new heart also will I give you, and a new spirit will I put within you : and I will take away the stony heart out of your flesh, and I will give you an heart of flesh ". More typical of Jewish thought in general is the view of man repenting and God relenting ; and this is developed in later teaching : but the rabbis could say some very beautiful things about repentance. " ' Open for Me ', says God, ' a gateway of repentance as big as a needle's eye, and I will open for you gates wide enough for horses and chariots '." [1]

In the Sermon on the Mount and in many of the parables we have studies in that profound change in the heart of man μετάνοια ; and in many instances (for example, Peter in Luke v. 8 ; Zacchaeus ; the dying thief) that change is the natural outcome of direct contact with the Person of Jesus. Outwardly there may be no spectacular indications ; but there is the mysterious crisis of the inner life. The Spirit of God has secured entrance : our sin and our Saviour are made manifest simultaneously. Illumination is one result, and the light gives new knowledge of God and new self-knowledge at one and the same time. There is an illustration of this in the familiar and lovely incident of the visitor to Scotland in the seventeenth century.

[1] See the article by C. G. Montefiore in the *Jewish Quarterly Review*, vol. xvi, pp. 209-257 entitled " Rabbinic Conceptions of Repentance ".

What news of Scotland? he was asked; and he replied "Good
news! Good news! for when I went to St. Andrews I heard a
sweet, majestic-looking man, and he showed me the majesty of
God. After him I heard a little fair man, and he showed me
the loveliness of Christ. I then went to Irvine, where I heard
a well-favoured, proper old man with a long beard, and that man
showed me all my own heart." The merchant was clearly a
connoisseur of sermons. From David Dickson of Irvine, he
learned to see all his own heart. From Blair of St. Andrews he
heard of the majesty of God. And Samuel Rutherford showed
him the loveliness of Christ. When some preacher, some Scripture, or some accident shows us all our heart, it may be that we
are able to clear ourselves of many of the charges that the world
would bring against us unjustly, but it is only to fall into a
worse condition; to be accused by ourselves or by God. The
words at the beginning of St. Luke's Gospel might be a brief
description of us—"son of Adam, son of God". On the one
side we are astonished by the wonder of the human heart as
it comes from the hand of God, with a natural desire for that
which is pure and that which is good. We seem to respond
readily to the appeal of heroism and sacrifice. We witness some
brave, chivalrous action, and we are prepared again to believe
that God has really made man in His own image, and is not
ashamed of His work. But we are terribly conscious of the
other side of the picture. Though we feel that our proper home
is with God, we know that our roots are in the human past.
Both good and evil have been handed down to us as children of
Adam. Our heart shows the traces of God's creative act, but
it shows far more than traces of an ancestral taint. At times
it shows a lurking, secret, miserable hankering after evil and
not good. To be shown all our own heart would be an unbearable revelation. Nor should we be in better case if the second
theme, the majesty of God, alone were pressed upon us; for
we should see it in holiness and in judgment. It is not with
celestial good nature that we have to deal. The naked human
heart and the divine majesty will not bear the encounter unless
the third theme, the loveliness of Christ, is justified. It is He
in His coming and in His redemptive love who makes it possible
for man to deal with his own heart and to endure the majesty of
God; for Christ came not to show the lofty heights that man

has forfeited, but to reveal the lovely thing he may yet become. There are people who need most to be warned away from evil, and there are others who need most of all to be drawn by the attractiveness of good. In Jesus, God offers both ways. Men need not be afraid of the stern character of God, for it is all one with the character of Jesus; if they have seen the loveliness of Christ aright, they have seen the loveliness of God. He will win men to repentance and forgiveness, to make them good and even to make them lovable.

CAN REASON BE PENITENT?

Can we speak of such a thing as repentance in the sphere of Reason? Professor Tillich discovered that the principle of justification through faith refers not only to the religious-ethical side of man but also to his religious-intellectual life. "There is faith in every serious doubt, namely, the faith in the truth as such, even if the only truth we can express is the lack of truth."[1] And the allegory of the Cave in the seventh book of *The Republic* seems to indicate something very like a turning of the whole mind in a different direction, which might possibly come under the head of repentance. Recently Professor Reinhold Niebuhr has suggested that "The negative task of exploring the limits of human knowledge and the fragmentary character of all forms of human virtue is a procedure not unrelated to the experience of repentance".[2] A somewhat similar suggestion is put forward by supporters of traditional theism in order to claim that the Thomist arguments are not so coldly metaphysical as is generally supposed. In extenuation, it is claimed that a considerable measure of *moral activity* is involved in formulating them, understanding them, and accepting them. There must first be diligence in investigation; second, definite humility in recognising the data, since the implications of finite existence are not understood unless we recognise finitude in ourselves; third, courage in acting on the conviction when it is acquired (not, at this stage, the moral consequences in conduct of belief in God, but the acceptance of this realisation of our finitude, insufficiency and dependence); fourth, a child-like simplicity which is ready to sit down before facts and learn

[1] *The Protestant Era*, p. xxix. [2] *Faith and History*, p. 172.

from them. To me it is doubtful whether these four considerations are really helpful. They are applicable to all sincere inquiry. They do not contribute much to lift the "proofs" out of the arid metaphysical realm towards the sphere of religion. The truth seems rather to be that, in the Bible at least, it is not the reason that is sinful and in need of repentance, but the heart, the moral and religious personality. Reason is indeed involved in repentance, since that is a change of the whole man, but to speak of Reason experiencing repentance would be to make the mistake of segregating it and reverting to the erroneous view of it as an isolated faculty, whereas it is in fact the instrument of the whole person, used for good or for bad purposes and changing as it is used.

Man's own nature, consisting mainly of reason, was so designed that it might receive the Word; and, if creation is not only built on redemption lines, but also continuous, it means that God is coming upon us in two ways, first by Word and historical event and personal encounter; second, by the fostering, restoration, and even redemption of our reason, that it may receive the Word; and therefore the criterion by which the Word of God is discerned and identified in the words of men is a double criterion, first the numinous quality of the words themselves and secondly the response of the soul. And God is on both sides of the experience.

Reason is at the service of the Word of God. If it is affirmed as an objection that the prophets of the Old Testament are anti-humanist in their proclamations, it must be remembered that our estimate will depend on our interpretation of the term "humanist". Is it detrimental to the worth of man to lay stress on his proneness to disobedience and rebellion? The opposite may be true. Berdyaev, for instance, insists that the Biblical doctrine of sin is the most profound affirmation of the dignity of man. The prophets were really trying to lead their people from a sense of *grievance* to a sense of *guilt*. The people were constantly complaining about God's treatment of His own nation; and this sense of grievance always distorted their view of God. The prophets showed them that they ought to feel, rather, a sense of guilt. The fault was all theirs. On the contrary it has been suggested (for example, by the late Canon Quick) that the real defect in Hebrew prophecy lies in this, that the prophets appear to assume that man *could* perform God's will if only he desired it. Their message appears to be "Pelagian" in so far as it assumed that man had the power within himself to bring about the change. (Quick: *Gospel of the New World*, ch. iii, and *Doctrine of the Creed*, pp. 216 ff.) But, as is pointed out by Dr. N. H. Snaith (*Distinctive Ideas of the Old Testament,* p. 66), when the prophets assume that a man can change his way of life if he will, they also realise that man does not so will. If there is ever to be any turning, then God Himself must turn them (Jer. xxxi. 18). Men are fast bound by their deeds, so that they cannot turn (Hos. xi. 7). ("Surely" says Dr. Snaith in a footnote, "this is the very antithesis of Pelagianism. It equals anything in Augustine.") If passages such as Micah vi. 6-8 appear to assume that the responsibility rests wholly on man himself to change his ways and that he has the power to bring about the change, the corrective is given also in Ezekiel xxxvi. 26 and in the penitential psalms, especially Psalm li. The continuance of the sacrificial theory in one form or another conserved indeed the thoughts that God has taken the initiative and that, by the ordinances which He has decreed, immediate succour may be had from the defilement of sin; but we see from its subsequent history how easy it was for the sacrificial theory to deteriorate. The transgressions with which it could deal were mainly non-ethical, and in particular those which involved ceremonial uncleanness. Sacrifice brought no deliverance from "sins with a high hand". For them the priest could not offer mercy, though the theory no doubt was that repentance combined with the scapegoat ceremony of the Day of Atonement would save from them also. The campaign of John the Baptist was a revolt against outward observances as means of salvation and a call to true penitence; and the Galilean mission of Jesus (Mark i. 14-15) called on men to "repent and believe", thus indicating how repentance and faith are interlocked. "Now after that John was put in prison, Jesus came into Galilee, preaching the gospel of the kingdom of God, And saying, The time is fulfilled, and the kingdom of God is at hand: repent ye and believe the Gospel."

CONDITIONS FOR MAN'S RESPONSE : LOVE

A second condition governing the human response to revelation is found in *Love,* man's love for God and his love for his fellowmen as the children of God. The verses in 1 Corinthians ii. 9-10, are frequently confined, in quotation, to a reference in the world beyond; but they are clearly intended by St. Paul to indicate the divine truths which are conveyed in this life to those who love God. "Eye hath not seen, nor ear heard, neither have entered into the heart of man, the things which God hath prepared for them that love Him. But God hath revealed them unto us by His Spirit."

Love of man for his fellow-creatures, when it is true love, is a response to the love which God shows for all His children, and it is so spoken of regularly in the New Testament. "Beloved, if God so loved us, we ought also to love one another" (1 John iv. 11). Above all, it is of the first importance that Christians should be charitable towards one another, and the New Testament gives prominent place to the love which must lead to Christian oneness in the life of the Church. It is not, of course, any legitimate difference in practice that is the sinful thing about disunity, but the bitterness and intolerance which may accompany disagreement. (Cf. Eph. iv. 1 ff.; 1 Cor. 11.)

The earlier writers of the Old Testament seem hesitant about ascribing love to God, either, it has been suggested, because there might be confusion with the ideas of ancient fertility-cults, or because the ascription of what might seem a purely human faculty to God would tend to reduce that sharp distinction between God and man which is characteristic of Hebrew thought.[1] Dominated by the idea of a Covenant and of a Covenant too frequently interpreted in a legal fashion, they failed to develop fully the theme of divine love. There lurked in the minds of the writers a suspicion that it is improper to ascribe to God any such creaturely emotion, and a refuge was found in the translation of love into the more legalistic terms of righteousness, judgment, mercy. The same perplexity must have faced St. Augustine, for, when he uses the term *Amor Dei* or its equivalent, he is always referring to man's love for God, "I am at a loss", he says, "to discover in what way God

[1] Cf. C. E. B. Cranfield in *A Theological Word Book of the Bible,* p. 131.

can love us". And, as Professor Burleigh has pointed out,[1] when St. Augustine, in his verse-by-verse commentary on the Fourth Gospel, comes to the 16th verse of the 3rd chapter, he simply passes it over.[2] The prophet Hosea was central in the development of the theme. He sees in the sin of Israel a transgression, not simply against the righteousness of God, but against His love. He compares their apostasy to the unfaithfulness of a wife. There is no formal account of Hosea's "call" to the prophetic ministry as there is in the case of others; and perhaps this incident in his own personal history constitutes his call. Brooding over his own tragic experience, he saw Israel's treatment of Yahweh in the same light. "God chose Israel and made her His bride, and, as a man brings his wife home, God brought Israel to Palestine. . . . But, when God looked for the response which He had the right to expect, He did not find it. When love claimed loyalty Israel had failed. She took the gifts of the new land and squandered them on Baalim (ii. 8). She heartily desired His gifts, but she wanted them apart from Him."[3] Israel must suffer banishment from the land, which is no longer her home; yet penalty is not the end. Even when Gomer failed him, Hosea found that he had not been able to go on and forget her. Because God had once redeemed, He would still redeem.[4] Two features of the divine love, emphasised more and more as revelation unfolds, are already plain in this prophet. First, God's relation to His people is not that of a natural bond, theirs by right of inheritance or descent; but a bond forged by Himself in adopting the people whom He chose to be His own peculiar possession. Secondly, men are chosen, not for their lovable qualities, but in spite of their moral

---

[1] *The City of God*, p. 130.

[2] This odd omission is in part compensated for by the references made elsewhere by Augustine in the same Homilies on St. John's Gospel. God's Love is incomprehensible and immutable; in all His creatures he loves His handiwork, loving His elect even when they are as yet unreconciled and at enmity (Tractate cx on John xvii. 21-23). To love God is the gift of God. He it was that gave the grace to love Him, who loved while still unloved. Even when displeasing Him we were loved, that there might be that in us whereby we should become pleasing in His sight. "We love Him because He first loved us". (Tractate cii on John xvi, 23-28). And it is God's Love alone which can bring about our obedience. It is not that we endeavour to keep His commandments in order to awaken His love for us; but that, unless He loves us, we cannot keep His commandments. (Tractate lxxxii on John xv. 8-10).

[3] A. C. Welch, *Preparation for Christ in the Old Testament*, pp. 105, 106.

[4] A. C. Welch, *Kings and Prophets of Israel* (1952), ch. v.

and spiritual unloveliness. The Gospel parable of the workers in the vineyard (Matt. xx. 1-16) stands as the permanent correction of the view that men have deserts before God, or that His relations to them are amenable to precise calculation.

We must raise particularly the question whether the love of man for God is of the same stuff as the love of God for man. In the first [1] do we have analogy with the second, or real identity of essence? Is the first only grateful response, a feature which could not be attributed to divine love? Is it significant that St. Paul uses the term *agape* of God's love for us, and avoids it as a description of our love for God? The avoidance, as it happens, is not absolute; and Nygren, who examines this matter closely, admits the instances of its use in Romans viii. 28; 1 Corinthians ii. 9 and viii. 3; Ephesians vi. 24.

Is there here, may we believe, the sole instance in which we have not analogy but identity of nature in an activity that is both God's and man's? Is the response of the same kind as the revelation? Is Love univocal? The danger in an affirmative answer would be that of falling into anthropomorphism; a danger which, as a matter of fact, is not necessarily avoided by remaining in the sphere of analogy; for by emphasising the similarities between man's love for God and God's love for man, it is certainly possible for analogy also to run to the extreme of anthropomorphism, whereas, on the contrary, by emphasising the unlikenesses, we may easily run into the opposite excess and end in the *via remotionis*. The former danger is, however, avoided if we bear constantly in mind that revelation is mediated by the Holy Spirit and response is mediated by the same Holy Spirit. Grace is at work in both; there is room for the word "univocal". Other types of human love are, it is true, very well known; types in which there is nothing of the characteristic quality of *agape,* that it endures even when the object on which it is bestowed is worthless and unlovable; and St. Bernard has indicated the four stages of love [2]—the first that of fleshly love in which man loves himself; the second a love of God which is selfish; the third love of God for His own sake; the fourth in which man wholly forgets himself and becomes one spirit with God. It may be that the

---

[1] See Brunner, *Divine-Human Encounter*, p. 63.
[2] *De Diligendo Deo*—Migne PL., clxxxii, cols. 974 ff.

cleavage between *eros* and *agape* has been too sharply made. Within certain limits, it has been pointed out,[1] *eros* yields to secular conditioning and training. "The stress in child nurture upon living, playing, and working together is demonstrably fruitful. In higher education scientific discovery, the philosophic quest for the true and the good, and the love of the beautiful may all afford control over aggressive self-seeking." Yet it is a kind of education which never reaches to the centre of life ; for "when *eros* remains at the centre of man's life, his deepest potentialities are blocked ; when it yields to *Agape* his energies are profoundly unified and released ".[2] Surely we are not wrong to employ the same word when we speak of love, whatever the form of its manifestation, provided that it is a sincere, genuine emotion and activity of the human spirit. In mother-love, filial love, marital love, it is not with a different thing we are confronted each time. Though, naturally, human affections are complex, and love in consequence is mingled almost inextricably with other emotions like pity, protectiveness, remorse, gratitude, reverence, trust, faith ; nevertheless in its pure essence it is the same attitude of mind. Even in the human sphere, and especially in the relations of close friends and of married partners, we know that love does not take account of dependence or gratitude. Though these may have been very real factors in bringing two people together and may continue to play their part, they are wholly subordinate to the affectionate relation of love, which rejects the lore of nicely-calculated less or more.

Augustine[3] brings all the cardinal virtues under the category of love : "I would not hesitate to define these four virtues which make such an impression upon our minds that they are in every man's mouth : temperance is love surrendering itself wholly to Him who is its object ; courage is love bearing all things gladly for the sake of Him who is its object ; justice is love serving only Him who is its object, and therefore rightly ruling ; prudence is love making wise distinctions between what hinders and what helps itself."

The study of Love by Gottfried Quell and Ethelbert Stauffer[4] shows that there are four particular respects in which Nygren's

[1] E. T. Ramsdell, *The Christian Perspective*, p. 193.
[2] *Ibid.* [3] *de Moribus*, i. 15 (25).
[4] Translated from Gerhard Kittel's *Theologisches Wörterbuch zum Neuen Testament* by J. R. Coates, A. and C. Black, 1949.

thesis cannot readily be reconciled with New Testament usage. (1) ἀγάπη is *not* used in the Synoptic Gospels of God's love towards men. The dominant thought is that of ἀφέσις. God's love is *pardoning love*. (2) There is the other kind of divine love, *preferential love*, bestowed on Jesus alone, who is the beloved son, υἱὸς ἀγαπητός; a love therefore which is *not* directed only to the sinful and the loveless. (3) St. Paul, it is true, speaks very infrequently of love to God, since he is much more concerned with man's love to his neighbour; but in his greatest passages on this theme (Rom. viii), as Nygren frankly acknowledges, it *is* the word ἀγάπη that he employs. (4) St. John regularly makes use of the verb without a direct object (1 John iii. 14; iii. 18; iv. 7; iv. 19), thus indicating his view that love is " a movement of life, a form of existence, a realisation of God in this world ".[1] All of these writers of course agree that this love of men for God has its only source in God Himself and His love for men. Though it may appear to spring from the very depths of man's being, it is in the end the work of God alone.

The proper attitude of man towards God, says Nygren, is not love but faith, not *Agape* but *Pistis;* and here he loses something of great value. Man's love towards God can be spontaneous, desiring no privilege, expecting nothing from God save God Himself; hoping that all men, even the worst sinners, may be brought to Him too. Such love is indeed a response; not a means of winning God's favour; not one of the good works that might appear to contribute to salvation, but that which arises out of gratitude, yet is not only gratitude. St. Paul, Nygren believes, " sets our love for our neighbour in direct relation, not with our love to God, but with God's love to us; and both this, and his unwillingness to speak of man as having *Agape* towards God, are the direct consequence of the root-idea of *Agape* as he sets it forth. For if *Agape* is a love so utterly spontaneous and uncaused as the love which is manifested in the Cross of Christ, then the name *Agape* cannot fittingly be used to denote man's attitude towards God. In relation to God, man is never fully ' spontaneous '. Man's self-giving to God is no more than a response; at its best and highest, it is but a reflection of God's own love. It lacks all the essential marks of *Agape*;

---

[1] Quell and Stauffer, *op. cit.* p. 63.

it is not spontaneous and it is not creative. It requires, therefore, a different name: not ἀγάπη, but πίστις ".[1]

The difficulty in such an interpretation is, of course, that Jesus spoke without embarrassment of man's love towards God, and one cannot help feeling that the better way is to begin with the word in the Gospels rather than to try to explain it away. There is no need to qualify it by calling it "faith": it is sufficiently differentiated already by the fact that it is man's love towards God. In the same way "love of child towards mother" is not identical with "love of mother to child", but there is a quality in the love which is the same, and merits the same word to describe it. When Nygren speaks of St. John running into the danger of weakening *Agape* down, we feel rather that there is here an aspect of Jesus' teaching which went past St. Paul, the former persecutor, but was apprehended by the beloved disciple. Both aspects are needed in a full interpretation of the Gospel. And where St. John admonishes "Love not the world" he is saying in effect, "Do not transfer that love which you should have for God to any unworthy object". In our time we have learned (from militant Communism, for instance), that there can be emotions of religious quality devoted to evil. *Agape* is that love which can be characterised as *devotion*, which brings Christian people to say, like their Lord, "Father, for their sakes I sanctify myself". Unhappily such consecration *can* be offered to tyrants and dictators and brutal causes. Nygren's argument that the Fourth Gospel weakens *Agape* is his own weakness; for he is led to explain away what is essential evidence. It is untrue to say that God loves, not the good man, but the sinner. God *does* love the good man—how Jesus loved him when He saw him!—but His love is more needed by the sinner. In coming to seek and to save the lost Jesus did not pass by those who were earnestly striving. Often our writers speak as if the just man had no possible chance of being saved. That is a parody of Christianity, and in the very form given to it by Celsus. It is not man's justice that stands in his way, but his pretending to have justice when he knows that he has not; not man's righteousness that hinders his salvation, but his *confidence* in his own righteousness.

There is thus a love of man for God which is not simply

[1] *Agape and Eros* I, p. 92.

the equivalent of faith; a love which, through the divine grace,
need take no account of the·rift between the majesty of God
and the littleness of men; not even of the gulf that separates
the Holy One from man the sinner. For the wonder of it is
that, when man truly loves God, that separation is overcome.
Nor is this the delusion of mere superficial, humanistic
mysticism; for it is God who is acknowledged as overcoming
the separation.

The extension of *Agape*, God's love for us, to our love for
our fellow-men gives one more instance of that feature of man's
spiritual life which we have noticed already, the interlocking
of pattern and novelty. There is a law of love; its action can be
predicted within certain limits; but it is also the nature of real
love to be creative, to reveal initiative, to spring surprises on
the onlooker, and suddenly to enlarge the horizons beyond
our dreams. It walks in the well-trodden ways of faithful service; and yet it is to be looked for upon a peak in Darien. The
abiding element runs like a pattern through its activity; yet the
outcome of its operation is often a new, creative solution. Moreover, it does not necessarily follow that the characteristic of *agape*
which most profoundly impresses the mind, its quality of endur-
ing the rebuffs of the unlovable object of it, is exhaustive of its
whole nature. The father's love for the rebellious child continues when the child is good again; and the love seems still to
be of the same quality and nature. There is therefore nothing
inherently absurd in asking whether the same term may be
applied to the love of man for God as is appropriate for the
love of God towards His rebellious children. When right love
for God is shown by man, it is a miracle that has happened
(cf. Deut. xxx. 6) and one that could happen only through God's
gracious action on the soul of man. "We love Him, because
He first loved us" (1 John iv. 19). If we ask whether we are
not tending to confuse the distinction of Creator and creature,
the answer might be in the words of St. Bernard. In the unity
of spirit which this miracle has brought about, "love knows
not reverence".[1] It is a bold sentence; but not unjustified.
In the analogy of the love that exists between husband and
wife we have a relation which is not (as, for example, that of
son and father is) one of dependence. Though each, no doubt,

[1] *In Cant.*, LXXXIII.

is dependent on the other in many enriching ways, dependence is not the essence of the relation. Nor is it one of deference, as that of pupil and teacher. It is, rather, that which has been indicated by the appropriate metaphor, " I am my Beloved's and my Belov'd is mine ". We recall, of course, that the hymn, founded by Mrs. Cousin on the words of Samuel Rutherford and going back to St. Bernard's Sermons on *Canticles*, continues with the lines

> He brings a poor, vile sinner
> Into His house of wine.

The consciousness of sin far more than the consciousness of creatureliness makes us pause when we are on the point of identifying the essence of man's love for God with God's love for him. The divine love towards us is seen first and foremost in reconciliation. When man has carried to the very limit his rebelliousness and self-will, God withholds His hand from striking, He refuses to destroy, for the very reason that He is God and not man. (Hos. xi. 9.) The darkness of sin obscures the light, but God's love is not darkened: it is everlasting. Where can we find human love like that? It is never put to the supreme test, as the divine love is put to the test ; and, if it were, it would fail. Can we dare then, to ascribe to man love of the same quality towards His Redeemer as that which has been shown to him in his redemption? The question is abundantly justified. But there is a danger once again of falling into error. There is, even in human friendship, a communication of soul with soul that goes far beyond the bounds of ethical relations ; something far more spacious than even mutual service and a forgiving and understanding spirit. There is no ethical book-keeping between the soul and its Saviour. To be " in Christ " is something apart and beyond. When reconciliation is achieved and we know our sins to be forgiven, that is not the end: there is God's love still ; it is not something that is exhausted in the act of reconciliation ; and the response of the forgiven soul is not adequately described as reverence, or even as gratitude, though these are inevitably present and often dominant ; but it is rather something that might best be described as *resting* in His infinite grace. We are called not servants but friends. And we are to think of *Agape* as revelation not of God's essential being (that phrase has little meaning) but of His redeeming activity in relation to us men. And, since our sins prevent it growing as it should, it would be better to speak of the love which He is seeking to inspire in us, rather than of the love which men show towards God. It is an ideal: we cannot point to its realisation. And though its coming is a miracle of divine grace it does not come without striving and tribulation.

> Oh, where the immortal to our mortal flows,
> Flushing our grey clay heart to its own rose,
> Spirit supreme
> Upon me gleam ;
> Make me Thine own ; I reckon not the throes . . .
>
> Oh, to the point where man and God unite,
> Raise me, Thou God ; transfuse me with Thy light ;
> Where I would go
> Thou, God, dost know ;
> For Thy sake I will face the starless night.[1]

With these considerations in mind, we can complete the picture—an ideal picture, but one which the soul has been permitted to catch sight of. This love, which through God's gift and grace is of the same quality as His love for men, is different from faith ; it has passed beyond wonder and reverence and gratitude. "The soul that loves, loves, and knows nought else. . . . Love is the only one of all the movements, feelings, and affections of the soul in which the creature is able to respond to its Creator, though not upon equal terms, and to repay like with like. For example, if God is wroth with me, may I be similarly wroth with Him? Certainly not, but I shall fear and tremble and implore pardon. But how different it is with love! . . . She can make a return to Him by a love which is reciprocal. . . . 'He that is joined to God is one spirit.'"[2]

The word "Love" can be employed *univoce*: it may be used of God's love towards men not by an analogy but in exact description. "Do you perceive that even His Majesty yields to His love? It is so, indeed, brethren ; love looks up to no one, but neither does it look down upon any. It regards with an equal eye all who are united among themselves by a perfect bond of love ; it combines together in its own self the loftiest

1 George Barlow, *The Immortal and the Mortal.*
2 St. Bernard, *In Cant.*, LXXXIII.

with the lowest; nor does it merely make them to be equals, but makes them to be one. You think perhaps that God is excepted from this rule of love; but do you not know that he that is joined unto the Lord is one spirit?"[1] We are humbly aware of the vast gulf between the Beloved and ourselves. This is not an attachment and union between two persons who are of equal condition. In this love appears "the supreme felicity of the one and the marvellous condescension of the other".[2] Yet the love, though so different in quantity, is of the same quality. "It is true that the honour of a king loves judgment (Ps. xcix. 4); but the love of the Bridegroom, or rather of the Bridegroom who is Himself Love, requires only love and faithfulness in return. Let it then be permitted to the Bride to love in return. How could she do otherwise who is the Bride, and the Bride of Love? How can Love fail to be loved? . . . Although, being a creature, she loves less than He by whom she is loved, because she is less; yet if she loves with her whole self, nothing can be wanting where the whole being is offered."[3] The love of God for the soul of man produces the love of the soul for God Faith finds its realisation in Love. πίστις δι' ἀγάπης ἐνεργουμένη (Gal. v. 6). This Love is the medium by which the soul of man is permitted to gain a momentary glimpse of the light of God's eternal love. In it God is calling us and enabling us to love Him with that same love wherewith He loves us, and whereof He has shown us the pattern in the earthly life of our Lord Jesus Christ.

---

[1] *In Cant.*, Sermon LIX, para. 2.   [2] Sermon LXVII, para. 8.
[3] Sermon LXXXIII, paras. 5-6. Cf. Sermon LXIX, para. 7. St. Bernard, it is true, acknowledged that it is not any individual who is the Bride of Christ, but the Church. It was Origen who gave the impetus to the individual interpretation, which has generally prevailed in mystical literature. Cf. Dalby, *Christian Mysticism and the Natural World*, ch. vi.

CHAPTER IV

OBEDIENCE, GRACE, AND VICTORY

A THIRD condition affecting man's response to revelation is found in *Obedience*. We must examine it in the light of divine grace and the victory promised to man. The theme is a timely one. It is significant that the delegates to the same conference of Christian youth in Oslo set themselves to answer this other question, " Does the Bible help us to know how to act? " They raised the right problems. The spiritual dynamic of the Christian life is not respect for a sacred book, just as it is not respect for law, or for morality. It is, in fact, found in personal communion with the Risen Christ. That does not mean acceptance, necessarily, of every word of the Resurrection accounts. There is room here for disagreement ; since we can clearly discern faults of memory. (Our own friendships with others do not imply that we remember accurately every detail of our first meeting nor even every detail of their present life and occupation.) Nor are the Scriptures immune from error in scientific fact or in historical record. Indeed many a devout reader of the Bible rejoices in this lack of infallibility, since it prevents him from falling into the idolatry to which we are all inclined, the worship of a book ; and saves him from the temptation of taking the line of least resistance and, instead of working out strenuously and prayerfully the right decision in any perplexity, trying to have the decision made for him by the words of the Bible. The recognition of inaccuracies in Scripture delivers us from Bibliolatry. So Calvinists and Lutherans alike, though firmly anchored in Scripture, avoid claiming external infallibility for the written word and insist on the *spiritual* principle of interpretation. The Westminster Confession, after speaking of the incomparable excellencies of Scripture, goes on, " yet, notwithstanding, our full persuasion and assurance of the infallible truth, and divine authority thereof, is from the inward work of the Holy Spirit, bearing witness by and with the Word in our hearts ". In the Thirty-nine Articles of the Church of England there is no claim of infallibility for the Bible but rather for " the sufficiency of the Holy Scriptures for Salvation ".

THE BIBLE AS GUIDE TO CONDUCT

What is our position, then, when we ask, Does the Bible help us to know how to act? Take a single instance from many. In Matthew v. 39 we read " But I say unto you, That ye resist not evil : but whosoever shall smite thee on thy right cheek, turn to him the other also ". Professor L. A. Reid says in his *Preface to Faith* (p. 193) that " the chief difficulty about the gospel of non-resistance is not that it is extremely difficult to turn the other cheek, but that most of us cannot believe that it would be a good rule to act upon. The bully would thrive . . . I honestly believe that if somebody pushes himself or (much worse) herself in front of me into the wrong place in a queue I am encouraging bad manners and worse if I merely submit to be browbeaten." We all sympathise with this. While we desire to be Christian, we do not feel called upon to be Christian door-mats. Professor Reid's conclusion is that this word of Jesus cannot be made into a general rule ; and was never meant to be a general rule. Moreover, obedience to the strict letter of the verse would cease to be the highest form of Christian conduct, since it would imply doing something not because it is right but because it is according to rule. " A world which is based on the use of force is certainly a world which is going from bad to worse : there is value in the assertion of a value which is infinitely higher than force, and there are certainly occasions when this principle should be expressed at all costs. But the occasions are individual occasions, to be judged by the individual who has seen the vision and knows all the circumstances. To make a general rule would be to nullify the value of the principle which, becoming a rule, would cease to be a principle of absolute value."

To express this more positively, there are four points which ought, I think, to be made :

1. *Bible study brings a man to the right frame of mind,* the mood in which he is prepared to say, " Not my will, but Thine "; the state of mind in which alone he can be sure that his decisions

are free from personal prejudice and the thought of his own ease, advancement, or comfort; the state of mind in which he is humble, obedient, teachable, reverent, dedicated.

2. Others have passed this way before us. Their problems have shown some similarity to ours. *The Bible sets before men the example of the saints* of the Old Testament and of the New Testament, patriarchs, prophets, apostles.

3. *In the New Testament we have the example of Jesus.* A famous book which swept the world with a curious fervour forty years ago was called *In His Steps*. The author, Charles Sheldon, suggested that the simple rule of conduct was that of the *Imitatio Christi*. We have only to ask, when in perplexity, What would Jesus do? and our way becomes clear. It is easily recognised that there are one or two fundamental difficulties in the way of applying this rule, apart from our doubtful ability to visualise His way. One is that many of the perplexities in which we are involved arise out of our own foolishness and error and sin. When we ask, What would Jesus do in this position? we know at once that He would never have been in it. The other difficulty lies in the fact that His vocation is not ours. The Father's will for Him was unique : it is not simply applicable to human situations. We should, therefore, rather ask, What would Jesus have *me* to do?

4. *The Bible is not a legal or a moral code.* If that had been all, then Jesus would have failed in His purpose. We should be back at the old level of " doing our duty ", perhaps with a grudge; "keeping within the law", perhaps with the success of the Pharisees but also with their unattractiveness and their censoriousness. Nor was the Bible meant to give the opposite, a charter of libertinism. In Alice Meynell's *The Newer Vainglory*, it is the publican who boasts

> For I am tolerant, generous, keep no rules,
> And the age honours me.
> Thank God, I am not as these rigid fools,
> Even as this Pharisee.

There are two caricatures of the evangelical doctrine of the Bible. The first holds, in effect, that the Bible contains magic, and therefore that it is verbally inerrant ; there can be no mistakes in it. This view is to be rejected, but it has the merit of being the caricature of a *truth*—namely, that the Word is sacramental: it is not a word *about* God, but one in which God *acts*. The second misconception regards faith, because of its being bound to the Word, as chiefly an affair of the intellect. (This may in part account for the Scottish emphasis on doctrinal sermons.) This also contains an element of truth; for, when the revelation does come, it gives timeless truth. There *is* a sphere in which reason ought to act.

Thus we conclude that the Bible is the record of crucial and classical instances of God speaking to man; that God speaks in some *event*, inner or outer; that the event may become the occasion for God speaking to new audiences all down the ages; for the Word is the eternal contemporary. We read the Bible today therefore in order to worship God aright; to be in touch with Him ; and to hear His Word for us today.

THE INTERPLAY OF THOUGHT AND ACTION

Having looked at the bearing of revelation on conduct, we must now reverse the picture and inquire what is the effect of obedience on our response to revelation. Very quickly we become aware of the marked influence exerted by action on our thought and on our belief. The most outstanding Scriptural passage is that in John vii. 17, where Jesus says: "If any man will do His will, he shall know of the doctrine, whether it be of God, or whether I speak of Myself." In identifying true revelation a large part is played by obedience. The disobedient spirit cannot hope for conviction, but will be constantly the prey to uncertainty. Our own time has seen recovered emphasis on the interplay of thought and action, and the word "existential" gathers up much of the thought of the day on this subject.[1] Action may test the reliability of thought. Theory should continually be subjected to practical verification. It is told of Lord Mersey that he was once defending before a jury a company which was charged with responsibility for the explosion on a ship by which much damage had been done. His line of argument was that the oil on which blame was laid was in fact noninflammable. He would prove it by a simple experiment. Pouring some of the oil into a pan, he asked the members of the jury to notice that nothing happened. He applied a match

[1] Cf. *supra*, p. 22.

—and caused an explosion that rocked the court-room and singed the eyebrows of most of the spectators. Lord Mersey, it is said, retired from the case. The wise theorist submits his hypothesis to verification in the practical sphere; and part of the contribution made by action to knowledge is just that added security which a successful experiment confers on a conclusion arrived at by Reason which we know to be fallible and in need of all available and legitimate tests. For the quest of absolute certainty by cognitive means Dewey would substitute the search for security by practical means.[1] His view, he claims (p. 38) "renounces the traditional notion that action is inherently inferior to knowledge and preference for the fixed over the changing; it involves the conviction that security attained by active control is to be more prized than certainty in theory." But the view also provokes the counter-questions, "More prized by whom?" and "More prized for what?" raising the familiar difficulty of pragmatism to determine, having decided that truth is that which works, what precisely is meant by "works". I sometimes think that Dewey is really tracking down another *kind* of knowledge, perhaps symbolised in an odd capacity which I discover, to my surprise, to be resident in the fingers but apparently not in the ordinary memory, to find the appropriate keys on my typewriter. (A few I could probably write down in order from memory: the strange thing is that the fingers can go to all of them accurately.) Dewey is aware of the difficulty suggested above, and hastens to add that his view does not imply "that action is higher and better than knowledge, and practice inherently superior to thought. Constant and effective interaction of knowledge and practice is something quite different from an exaltation of activity for its own sake."

There is one special application of the theory of the interplay of knowledge and action which demands attention today. The Marxist philosopher despises the pure theorist and the *bios theoretikos,* and maintains that reliable thought can emerge only from action. Lenin puts it in practical form in his *Left Communism; an Infantile Disorder* (pp. 76-77), where he is arguing that revolution is necessary, not merely to overthrow a bad régime which refuses to abolish itself willingly, but also because theory is never enough. It will not be sound theory

[1] *The Quest for Certainty.*

if it is not allied with practice. It is Revolution which creates the situation propitious to right thinking. "History in general, the history of revolutions in particular, has always been richer, more varied, and variform, more vital and 'cunning' than is conceived of by the best parties, by the most conscious vanguards of the most advanced classes."[1]

This serves to remind us that we must take note of a danger in existential thinking. We cannot lightly assume that action of any kind is certain to clarify thought and to direct it along right ways. Doing *wrong* things may, it is unhappily true, sometimes sharpen the insight, as we know from the clarity of hatred and of vested interests, but it cannot enlarge insight nor guide it save into ultimate blindness and disaster. Existential thinking may be deceptive. It is very important that action should be brought to bear on thought; but it is still more important that action should be of the right kind. Not energy is the important thing, but the direction in which it moves. The early forms of War Office Selection Boards, set up to choose potential candidates for army commissions, seem frequently to have fallen into error in this respect, and to have laid stress on the formal qualities of leadership rather than on the ability to identify the proper goal. "Leadership!" was the cry; and the still, small voice that whispered "Whither?" was stifled. We all know men who will lead others gallantly and confidently into spiritual bogs and over metaphorical precipices.

It is only an assumption, says Dewey, that the object of knowledge is that which existed prior to the act of knowing, and existed as something unchanging. In the sphere of religious knowledge, however, we can claim that the assumption is warranted. Both the things which Dewey deprecates we affirm, and with good reason and full justification—because *God is so.* But there is attached to the attitude of the knower, a fundamental condition which approaches Dewey's view of knowledge, namely the faith of the believer which has for one of its constituent elements readiness to commit everything to God, to meet the challenge of God by a decision for Him.

Study of the relation of theory and practice, the interaction of the rôles of spectator and of participator, and the

[1] Cf. *supra*, p. 21.

influence of action on thought suggests that the distinction here observed is not quite so simple as is at first imagined, but requires clarification. There are the contrasted types of mankind, symbolised, for instance, by the architect who is busied most of the time with blue-prints and, on the other hand, the master-mason of the medieval cathedral who worked out his plans in daily contact with the stone. Either of these fails if he wholly ignores the functions of the other. Only a wise combination is successful. The architect whose plans are airy and impracticable will not necessarily derive professional benefit through engaging in just any kind of practical activity— winter sports, or gardening, or bird-watching, let us say, however healthful and commendable these pursuits may be. State planners ought to be men of wide and varied interests, but as a first priority they should know the raw details of the national activities which they are engaged to assist. An officer of the agricultural services once told me on a country-walk that he was grateful for my reference to the ragwort grow-ing in the fields, for he had signed thousands of letters to farmers encouraging them to eradicate this pest, and now at last, after twenty years, could congratulate himself on having it identified. He felt, I am sure, that this would add interest to his daily work. We arranged to take another walk together in the following week, when I hoped to be able to point out a thistle to him. Unfortunately he was transferred to the depart-ment of Fisheries, and my trouble was wasted.

Neither action nor theory, however, are simple concepts. Hard thinking can be an intense form of activity. Gabriel Marcel puts in a word for the contemplation of the artist[1] as a very real form of participation. The distinction, when clarified, has rather to do with the presence or absence of chal-lenge and the response in decision; and in the ultimate analysis reduces itself to a difference in character. The man whose whole life is given to study, or theory, or contemplation, may be of the type that will spring into action when the need arises, and will do so with surprising commonsense and practical ability. His study has been dominated by character of that kind which is constantly accepting challenges and responding to them with sincerity and determination.

[1] *Mystery of Being*, vol. 1, pp. 121 ff.

TYPES OF RELIGIOUS ACTIVITY

For the acquisition of truth in religion, it would seem to follow, it is not necessary to be immersed in public affairs of ethical or political flavour. Admittedly, the spectator attitude is not conducive to progress in real religion: active commitment is essential; but the first qualification is to be found in the practice—not of politics, nor of social service—but the practice of *religion*. To place that qualification first is not to fall into the errors of the Ivory Tower, of other-worldliness. There will be a wise intermixture of practice with theory, of participation with speculation, of works with faith. Suppose then that the approach is made from the other side (the side of duty well done), as must often be the case and increasingly so in an age when it cannot be assumed that most people are grounded in religious truth. God has many ways of knocking at the human heart. Sometimes it is by the hand of one of His messengers that He chooses to call us. The summons of conscience is such a messenger. The man who knows his duty and turns from it moves farther away from the Light: he who sees the right way and sets his feet in it, however falteringly, is on the road towards the Truth. Where there is, as yet, no faith, but only the conscientious performance of duty, we must not dismiss it as "mere moralism". With some contemporary writers, "moralism" has become a kind of theological swearword. In any case we ought to suspect the use of "mere" after the pleasant instance of the small boy, chaffed by his father over the school-report for being "beaten by a mere girl" and replying, "But, Daddy, girls are not so mere as they were in your time". Assuredly, the response to duty will not be joyous and sustained in the absence of faith and worship. It will be faulty, precarious and, probably, ephemeral; it may easily decline into "mere moralism". It was significant to notice, in a recent radio discussion on the question, How do we know what is right and what is wrong? that the answers varied widely, some declaring that the knowledge came from the example of parents, others pointing to the training given by teachers. None of the group raised the further question, Where did the parents, and where did the teachers get *their* knowledge? and no one seemed to remember the Ten Commandments or the Sermon on the Mount.

We have already seen that, if duty is simply the right response to the total environment, we must still raise the question whether God is not indicated by the total environment; and we have seen[1] that to argue for a non-theistic moral world is to make reality more opaque than it need be; but there remains the question whether the attempt to be "good without God" can hope to succeed. It is the testimony of very many trained observers that it does not often endure beyond the third generation. Goodness without God may last a long time; but its roots are severed. It is only awaiting its end. It has no continuance. The second trouble about it is suggested if we raise the other question, If we fail, what then? The grim answer is that non-religious goodness can never speak the word "Pardon". If we fail, we are for ever a failure: we carry the stigma eternally. And we know that we *shall* fail. If we are setting our standards even moderately high, in our own strength we can never hope to achieve what we ought. As men say when they have ruined their own life or someone else's, "I can never forgive myself!" They are right. But that which we cannot do for ourselves, God has done in Jesus Christ.

DUTY AND GRACE

Elsewhere[2] I have argued against the idea that the ethical system is autonomous and against the view that man is independent in making his moral decisions. Neither in the form of the claim made by Fichte nor in that put forward by Nicolai Hartmann has a strong case been made. We must raise here the special issue of grace. Dutifulness and love are different things. All agree that love is superior and most are convinced that we should feel shame in showing only dutifulness where we ought to offer love. The ethics of duty are incomplete without the impulse of love; and love is not to be commanded. It is from God. Grace comes as more than a reinforcement of the human personality in the ethical struggle. It is a kind of possession by the Spirit of God over against the danger of possession from below. It will not do to take our stand in either of the extreme positions. If we insist that saving grace is irresistible, we shall be forced to the logical consequence that God

[1] *Supra*, p. 75.   [2] *Revelation and Response.*

must save all men. Condemning everything human, we finish
up in universalism. If we adopt the other extreme, and exalt
the human possibilities and the responsibility which goes with
them, then we easily lose all hope as to man's final destiny.
Clearly we are in paradox here, and must suspect any neat
solution from either extreme.

The word "grace" is not used by Jesus, nor is there any
indication in the Gospels that the thing itself, which is everywhere implied, can never be found acting on the non-religious,
or mediated by them. Tillich quotes[1] the case of continental
religious socialism as recognising that God may speak for a
time more powerfully through a non-religious and even anti-
Christian movement such as the earlier social democracies than
through the Christian churches. The good pagan ought to be
a perpetual, wholesome rebuke to the sincere Christian. S. L.
Frank makes this point[2] when he says: "A man who is intellectually an unbeliever, but whose heart is aglow with love for
his fellow-creatures, who is forgetful of self and thirsting for
goodness and righteousness, *really* believes—without being aware
of it—that God is love and that one must lose one's soul in order
to save it, i.e. in fact confesses the fundamental dogma of the
Christian life. And if a so-called 'believer' repeats the words
of the creed with conviction, but is a harsh and heartless egoist,
he is really an unbeliever, for *in fact* he rejects the Christian
dogma." And again (p. 120) "The fullness of the divine truth
manifested in Christ and His revelation may actually live and
act in men's hearts quite apart from the fact whether they
recognise the source of that truth". Where there is love, there
is the holy Catholic Church. No doubt Professor Frank's
splendid book is weakened by the meagreness of his discussion
of human sinfulness, and we must realise once again that the
"good pagan" may often see his duty but fail to find the power
to perform it. Only faith and the grace of redemption can give
that power. His goodness is precarious, possibly doomed. Social
workers suggest that they can even draw up a time-table of decay.
One generation is both dutiful and pious, and all is well. The
next begins to sit loose to the claim of worship. For many
reasons, not all of them wholly blameworthy, they become
irregular in attendance at church—they are on night-shift, or

[1] *The Protestant Era*, p. 213.   [2] *God With Us*, p. 98.

they have had illness in the home, or they have moved from one district to another and are shy about making new church contacts, or they have taken offence at something said or imagined. But they have a deep reservoir of spiritual power on which to draw, and all is still well. They remain decent citizens, good neighbours. It is in the third generation that trouble often breaks out. The spiritual reservoir is exhausted, the capital is spent, this generation has been living parasitically in the matter of goodness, and the parent-plant has no more sustenance to give. It is this third generation which, in the experience of youth workers, has been observed to supply many of the boys who gather into gangs that steal and stab and shoot. But the other side of the picture must never be obscured. The religious man ought to be ready to learn from the decent pagan, and to learn with shame. Conceivably, our arrogance, our *hybris*, may lie not in acknowledging general revelation, but in despising it. The thesis most familiar to our ears is that special revelation is needed because of man's sin. The time has come to propound the other as also true, that general revelation is needed for the same reason, because man's sinfulness may take the form of pride and exclusiveness—in his Christianity. It is unfortunate that philosophers and theologians are not "speaking the same language". The former very frequently convey the impression through some of their most copious writers that they are engaged almost wholly on the analysis of words and matters of grammar: the latter may easily appear to be employing words in an unusual sense of their own which makes it impossible to launch discussion on profitable lines. The result is that the philosopher appears in the theologian's eyes as naive and superficial, and the theologian is regarded by the philosopher as obscurantist and irrational.

Nevertheless, in thinking of this theme of obedience, with special reference to its consequence in religious illumination, we must always bear in mind that there is in mankind a hard core of rebellion. If he is not aware of it, a man is living on too superficial a level. Allowance must be made for the sincere conviction that an honest decision for the right is a man's own decision and an occasion, if not for pride, since that word is tainted, at least for rejoicing that the decision fell that way and not another; but it is only on the lower planes of thought that we can be content with this description. We acknowledge that in some fashion, inexplicable yet undeniable, all our good is of God. We cannot claim merit, when we are on our knees before Him. The paradoxical formulation of the theologian cannot offer any clear-cut picture of the case, but it touches a depth of experience which has eluded the moralist. James Moffatt employed a useful simile in *Grace in the New Testament* (p. 397). "By insisting that 'grace and faith' are the primary factor in the religious life, Christianity is not ignoring the moral consciousness but urging that unless the moral consciousness is to become feverish and futile, it must include a transcendent order, or rather, it must be included in such an order. The moralistic emphasis upon the central importance of man's strivings and standards really corresponds to the old Ptolemaic astronomy, which made earth the axle of the universe, all heavenly bodies revolving around it in their courses. So Comte assumed, for example; humanity is our source and centre. When Christianity sounds the note of grace, it is upholding the new and true astronomy of religion: the world of human conduct moves within the sphere of the Sun, deriving from the Centre its light and impetus, and in that relationship is the final clue to what we know and what we do. At the core of the gospel this conviction lies, that to be thus humble, conscious of indebtedness to God, is to be strong."

GRACE AND HISTORY

It has often been said that the age in which we are living gives us an unrivalled opportunity, if we would take it, of understanding something of the impact of divine grace on the spirit of man and consequently of the manner in which grace has moulded human history. The very fact that a vast proportion of men and women today have not been deeply influenced by traditional religious education means that there are innumerable instances in which we can observe the *direct* impact of revelation on the soul. Again, the tragic wanderings of whole populations, driven out of their homes as political victims or as refugees from bombardment and the devastation of battle, have brought vividly before our own eyes the intricate pattern of the world's good and evil and have pressed home the lesson of the unity of all mankind in the complicated web of history. Moreover, by the intimate knowledge which all of us inevitably acquired of the upsurging of evil forces, we have learned that the neat, rational categories into which we tend to divide human reactions are not adequate for the task. Reason fails to account, at the very beginning, for the differentiation among people and nations; for to the human observer it seems that the fantastic disproportion of endowment and circumstance and vicissitude observable among individuals and communities can be described only as irrational; and, looking still deeper than the differences of condition and opportunity, we discover that human decisions in response to these cannot be rationalised, for the past is always rising up to invade the present, brooding over it in the form of guilt and powerlessness. The working out of evil is the ultimate irrationality; we cannot explain how it has invaded the world; why it persists; and, most perplexing of all, why it appears at times and for long ages together even to be victorious. Reinhold Niebuhr's conclusion of a study of such factors as these is to the effect that history witnesses the execution of moral judgments, but never with precision, and that therefore the Christian philosophy can be regarded as a rational one only in the sense that the alternatives to it are partial and misleading and inadequate.[1] Emil Brunner goes farther and holds that there is no Christian philosophy of history, for that would mean interpreting history by preconceived principles, but only a Christian understanding of history which takes note of events, and relates them all to the one Fact of the Divine Word made flesh.[2]

When Calvin pressed to a logical conclusion his doctrine of the divine majesty, he was attempting to combine the transcendence of God with an intelligible system of eternal decrees, but the two are incompatible. To insist that the eternal decree is hidden shuts us off even from guessing its nature. There is much that is revealed, and there is much that is hidden; but the hidden *is* hidden. We must not presume to draw conclusions from it. In doing so, Calvin was going beyond the testimony of the Bible.

In the same chapter[3] of the *Institutes*, Calvin has himself given a wholesome warning that it is "not right that man

---

[1] *Faith and History*, ch. viii.   [2] *Man in Revolt*, p. 439.
[3] Bk. III, ch. xxi.

should with impunity pry into things which the Lord has been pleased to conceal within Himself, and scan that sublime eternal wisdom which it is His pleasure that we should not apprehend but adore, that therein also His perfections may appear. Those secrets of His will, which He has seen it meet to manifest, are revealed in His word—revealed in so far as He knew it to be conducive to our interest and welfare." Later (section 3) he develops the last thought. "For Scripture is the school of the Holy Spirit, in which as nothing useful and necessary to be known has been omitted, so nothing is taught but what it is of importance to know." Then, propounding the double doctrine of predestination in section 5: "All are not created on equal terms, but some are preordained to eternal life, others to eternal damnation", it is significant to notice, he draws all his proof-texts from passages which support only the fact of preordination to eternal life; which, indeed, is unconditional, for it is from God's love alone. Calvin would have been on less treacherous ground if he had continued in the vein of the first section in the chapter, where he speaks of "the unsearchable depth of the divine judgment". Unfortunately he ends the chapter by maintaining that "this counsel, as regards the elect, is founded on His free mercy, without any respect to human worth, while those whom He dooms to destruction are excluded from access to life by a just and blameless, but at the same time incomprehensible judgment". No man is in possession of the evidence which will justify him in saying *both* of these things at once—that the divine judgment is incomprehensible *and* that it is "just and blameless"; for this characterisation must be made in the light of human standards of what is just and what is blameless. We know no others. Often we wish that Calvin had taken the more becoming line of honestly admitting the paradoxes instead of denouncing as "petulant dogs" and "impious folk with an infatuated inquisitiveness" those who could not follow him. This is the one notable occasion on which he seems to have extracted divine qualities from the world of nature, with its irrationality, caprice, ruthlessness. His rancour in these passages reveals an unconscious lack of conviction.

It is pride on the part of man if he claims that he has deduced something of the nature of God from a decree that is

8

hidden from men. There is less danger of pride in drawing
conclusions from the manifest signs of divine grace in the history
of man. The Reformers were right to reject the crude idolatry
which exalted the Church ; but wrong in rejecting all thought
of divine victories here and now brought about by God's grace
acting through the Church. These victories were foretold by
Jesus when he addressed His final words of comfort and promise
to the disciples (John xvi). (The theme of victory is taken
up again in the Johannine epistles and in the Apocalypse. See,
in particular, 1 John v. 4-5, "Whatsoever is born of God overcometh the world: and this is the victory that overcometh the
world, even our faith. Who is he that overcometh the world,
but he that believeth that Jesus is the Son of God? ") All the
terrors which the world can launch against mankind have been
overcome by Christ through the Cross which He is soon to
endure ; and His followers are being given His own power to
enable them also to overcome. "In the world ye shall have
tribulation: but be of good cheer, I have overcome the world "
(John xvi. 33). "The world" is not the same as "nature",
though it includes the whole spectacle and menace and awesomeness of nature. Nature is not inherently evil, though it
may offer easy possibilities of sin. "The world" is rather to
be described as "humanity organising itself apart from God".
The overcoming of the world is not to be regarded as taking
place through purely human activities ; for they are involved
in the same condemnation. Dr. Niebuhr speaks of history as
the false Messiah of today; for, although we do rejoice in
every triumph of righteousness in the field of history, we cannot
be secure without something far greater than that. We cannot
think of the Kingdom of Heaven as being identified with even
the noblest cause championed by sinful men—though we are
not by that theological conclusion absolved from playing the
most strenuous part possible to us in all such cases.

THE CHURCH AND POLITICS

In similar fashion we must meet and answer the vexed question of whether the Church should have a political programme ;
whether it should take a leading part in this form of history-
making. It is not, I think, the part of the Church to make

political changes, though it belongs to her to train and to influence the men who will bring about the necessary changes. The minister of religion must give priority to the proclamation of the Word. If he refrain from drawing political conclusions from it, there are many others who are capable of doing that: at the worst it is a relative failure; but if he fail in preaching the Gospel, he fails absolutely.

Aristotle's sense of the word [1] is irretrievably lost for the modern world, and "politics" for most people means "party politics", and this fact is symptomatic of another. It is becoming increasingly difficult to draw the boundary-line between moral issues and a party line. The prophets of the Old Testament drew inferences—with a vengeance!—but these are more adequately described as ethical rather than as political. The Christian minister can say, and often is in duty bound to say, that the body politic is ailing here and here, but he is not bound to say, nor trained to say with competence, "The only cure is—Free Trade, or Controls; Closed Shops or Sit Down Strikes". The inferences which can legitimately be drawn by the preacher in his privileged position are those only which can be prefaced by "Thus saith the Lord". Other inferences and other issues should be discussed by Christian people seriously and constantly, but not in the act of worship when the minister is declaring the Word of God. No doubt many ministers will desire to take part in "politics" in their capacity as private citizens, perhaps even as "influential citizens". The adjective will be employed with greater justification if in the pulpit a seemly restraint is exercised concerning these same matters. My personal view would therefore be that he should abstain from political inferences, because, in the first place, they may become a barrier between him and his congregation, many of whom may quite sincerely and with equal passionateness draw different conclusions; because, in the second place, he has not the technical training to make him competent in this field; he may appear just as an incompetent amateur among experts and, by seeking to pronounce with authority on matters beyond his province, he may discredit himself in those spheres in which he is admittedly an expert. Ministers of religion are trained and set

[1] See *Nic. Eth.* I, 2, 1094 b8—Politics as the completion or even the verification of Ethics in a true philosophy of man.

apart to look after what concerns us as creatures who are made
to live for ever, and we are not to ask them to perform a function
for which they have never been adequately trained.   Thirdly,
members of the preacher's audience are all too apt to find in the
political aspects a pleasant field of discussion in which they can
loiter without exposing themselves to the challenge of Christ;
and, fourthly, if the man in the pulpit (elevated, as the saying
is, six feet above criticism) takes sides, as he is almost bound to
do, his own party will expect political slogans from him and
will be disappointed if they hear "only the Gospel": his oppon-
ents will probably stay away so that they may not be exasperated
by the exposition of theories which they abhor, without the
opportunity of hitting back.   Dr. C. S. Lewis in *Christian
Behaviour* (p. 17) says: "The job is really on us, on the laymen.
The application of Christian principles, say, to Trades Unionism
or education, must come from Christian Trades Unionists and
Christian school-masters; just as Christian literature comes from
Christian novelists and dramatists—not from the Bench of
Bishops getting together and trying to write plays and novels in
their spare time."

On the general question of the overcoming of evil there is
the old philosophical dilemma: If evil is illusory, the moral
struggle is a piece of play-acting: if evil is real, we cannot be
sure of the final victory of good. Christianity meets the dilemma
by affirming that evil is real; and it is already overcome by
Christ.

VICTORY OVER FEAR

To know that God is Light is to be made victorious over fear,
one of the most substantial forms of darkness. As love increases,
fear diminishes. "There is no fear in love; but perfect love
casteth out fear" (1 John iv. 18). A remarkable document was
published in the United States with the title *A Gentleman in
Prison* (George H. Doran, New York). It was written in the
condemned cell of an Eastern prison in the closing months of
the First World War. The writer, Tokichi Ishii, had lived a life
of notorious crime, but a new light was thrown on his character
when, like Victor Hugo's Jean Valjean, he voluntarily confessed
to a charge for which another man was condemned to death.

The sentence fell on him, and in his last days of imprisonment he wrote down briefly the story of his life. The end was touched with triumph, for the visits of two women missionaries brought to him the Gospel of the love of God, and we have the first-hand record of one of the most note-worthy instances of Christian conversion. His last words were in the form of a poem

> My name is defiled,
> My body dies in prison,
> But my soul purified
> Today returns to the City of God.

At the age of seventeen he had witnessed an earthquake. A village lay between two mountains, both of which caved in. Only the roof of the temple remained above ground; everything else, houses and people alike, were completely buried. That terrible spectacle, seen from a neighbouring hill, left him with an uncontrollable fear that haunted him day and night; and the fear never once left him until he learned to love God. Then there was no room for it. "It continued", he writes in his simple narrative, "until I learned to know God. Through His power I am not in the least afraid of earthquakes any more. Christians fear only God, and nothing else can make them afraid.... This is true not only of me but of all Christians, that they do not fear, even if they are ill or endure distress or suffer greatly. They quietly leave everything in the hands of God, and even while they suffer, they rejoice and wait patiently until they recover."

SOME FEARS LEGITIMATE, OTHERS NOT

There is a right fear as well as wrong fears. There is the fear of the Lord of which the Bible speaks so often as an essential part of true religion. "The Lord reigneth: let the people tremble." This attitude is a mingling of awe and love to make reverence; and it is the basis of faith. The fear of the Lord is the beginning of wisdom.

From physical fear only the very exceptional are completely free. The bravest men often confess to one fear, the fear of being found afraid. Our age has gladly admitted that there is nothing odd or shameful in being terrified of devastation raining from the skies, of injury, death, disaster, bereavement. Physical shrinking from pain and wounding is instinctive in men: it safeguards them against callousness towards danger. There is nothing strange in it; and there is nothing shameful in it when the determination is to face these things, if they come, with all the courage and coolness and self-forgetfulness which we can command. A natural emotion need not become an obsession. Miss Dorothy Canfield has given a vivid picture of a scene in Paris during the First World War on that day when mysterious explosions occurred in the city. There were no enemy aeroplanes overhead. The citizens were bewildered, for it was only later that they learned that the Germans had brought up their long-range gun and were shelling Paris. Down in the basement of a convent-school the headmistress is addressing her tiny charges, " Eh bien, mes enfants, your chance has come at last. This is a great day for you! Everyone else, your fathers and mothers, the soldiers, the hospitals, the nurses, all the grown-ups, have been able, ever so many times, to show how brave-hearted men and women can be. But who ever thought that little children would have a chance too? " . . . Bang! came a loud nearby explosion, followed by the crash of breaking glass upstairs. The stout, elderly woman's head went up. " Do you hear that, mes enfants? That noise calls out to everyone of you, 'This is *your* day of glory!' . . . If you meet danger bravely everybody who ever hears about it even years from now, perhaps when you are old people, will be braver when his turn comes to meet danger, because he'll think —what children did, I can do." [1]

A third type of fear is altogether wholesome and essential. We *ought* to be afraid of failures, of indolence, of disloyalty. Aeschylus called fear " the guardian of the soul ". It is good, he said, that men should carry a threatening shadow in their hearts under the full sunshine. They should for ever be afraid of wrong-doing, never making terms with evil. And He who was fearless of all other things has said, " Be not afraid of them that kill the body, and after that have no more that they can do. But I will forewarn you whom ye shall fear: Fear him which after he hath killed hath power to cast into hell; yea, I say unto you, Fear him." (Luke xii. 4-5). Mr. Middleton Murry

[1] *The Deepening Stream,* p. 368.

has said that the picture of Jesus in the boat on the lake, sleeping throughout the storm, is a picture of a supremely lonely man. His fearlessness set Him altogether apart from others. He could not understand why men should think that God was any farther off because a storm was sweeping over the water. His love towards men and God was all-embracing: His heart had no room for fear.

Other fears fall into two classes. First are those which arise from the sin of Adam; second, those which come from the sin of Cain; the one from a breach in man's communion with God, the other from the rupture of man's fellowship with other men. Adam disobeyed and hid from God in fear. We see the counterpart of this fear in the numberless superstitions, which are forgivable in barbarous nations who have never heard of God, but not in civilised people. Yet they persist—superstitions about the wearing of green, the spilling of salt, walking under a ladder. These fears arise from scepticism about the character of God and the meaning of the universe. Fear is the antithesis of faith. All the vague, superstitious fears which break out with renewed violence in time of war or pestilence, drawing after them a whole retinue of charms and amulets and mascots—all these are a sign that men have broken down the bond of fellowship between themselves and God the Father. They are fears which arise from the sin of Adam. Those others, which arise from the sin of Cain, out of the breakdown of brotherhood, lead to distrust, the collapse of credit and confidence between nations and finally to war. And the cure of both kinds is love. As man's love of God increases, so superstitious fear diminishes. As man grows in love for his fellowmen, so fear and distrust will vanish. But there are other fears, the special study of our own age, morbid fears, undefined but threatening, the material of the nerve-specialist and the psychiatrist. It is symptomatic that so many nervous disorders in our tired epoch are described by the name of 'phobias'. These are the dark psychological bogies which have led in our time to a more thorough study of the dark geography of the human mind. If we could banish fear from our modern life, it has been conjectured, we should liberate men from half their mental ills. They are not always precisely defined. Among historic cases are those of Erasmus who was filled with a nameless apprehension at the sight of—

a fish; Newton and Paganini when confronted by a basin filled
with water; Schumann, Chopin and Edgar Allan Poe terrified
by fog; and de Maupassant by an open door, through which,
as he believed, at any moment the nameless thing might enter
and say " I have come ". (The guest whom he expected was
madness: he came at the last.)   And there is the fear which
has been recognised from immemorial antiquity.   It also is
an indefinable dread of something which is summed up in the
Biblical words " the powers of darkness ".   These were very
real to men and women of New Testament times.   St. Paul
wrestled with principalities and powers; and that is not only
mythology.   They may come in different fashion from those
which threatened Paul or Luther, to both of whom the fight
with evil was anything but a sham-fight; but we cannot abandon
all thought of them.   They represent what we might call
" capitalised evil ".   The bad influence of bad men and bad
actions has no limit which we can set to it.   The evil that men
do lives after them.   There is a kingdom of sin striving against
the Kingdom of God.   Into this situation comes the message
of the Risen Christ.   It brings salvation, deliverance.   It does
not say that these fears are unreal: it says that they are con-
quered; there is no power of darkness which can resist the
power of God.

We may learn how this works out in practice.   In Central
Africa a young chief and his native doctor have committed a
horrible crime ; have been discovered, arrested, and condemned.
The story is told.   A short time before, the chief came to believe
that some demonic influence had robbed him of his power over
the tribe; he summoned his medicine-man to restore it.   The
prescription had been that the chief must be treated with human
blood.   Fear and horror seized upon the village, for the decree
meant the murder of someone, so that the fresh blood might
be obtained.   The plot is hatched at midnight.   There is a little
boy, three years old, in the village, the son of the native evangelist.   The chief's son is his playmate, and it is arranged that
he shall decoy the child from home.   That is easily done.   He
is hidden in a hut and there the two men repair when darkness
has fallen, to return with the unholy medicine, the life of a
small, lovable boy.   It is not that the African has no love for
children.   It is that his great fears are bigger than his little

love. Only the love of Christ can cast out these fears, so that chaos and darkness shall take flight. "I am persuaded", said St. Paul " that neither death nor life, nor angels nor principalities nor powers . . . shall be able to separate us from the love of God which is in Christ Jesus our Lord."

The victory is offered to man: he need only accept it.

Christ is overcoming the world by *confirming the faith of Christian people;* revealing Himself ever anew as the Saviour and the Risen Lord.

Christ is overcoming the world by *strengthening the dutifulness of Christian people;* in particular sending them out as witnesses to the Saviour and Risen Lord.

Christ is overcoming the world by *illuminating the world's* darkness of suffering and distress.

Christ is overcoming the world by *pointing beyond* the end of this earthly life, saying " Be of good cheer: I have overcome the world."

It is not possible to propound a Christian philosophy of history; but we know history as the sphere in which grace can operate. We recognise therefore the double nature of the world, as that which is dominated by sin and death but also that realm in which God chooses to work His marvels. And thus we believe, not indeed in the nobility of man, for he forfeited that by disobedience, but in the nobility of God's plans for him in spite of that forfeiture.

CHAPTER V

MAN'S KNOWLEDGE OF GOD

WE are now to examine the *epistemological* implications of the symbol of light and of all that it stands for. The familiar postulate of mysticism holds that we can know a thing only by becoming like it. "We could not see the sun, if there were not something sunlike in ourselves, nor could a soul which has not become beautiful have any knowledge of beauty" (Plotinus). To know God who is Light, must the soul acquire the properties of light? The distinction between likeness and identification is not always maintained. The *Theologia Germanica* utters a warning: "The false light dreameth itself to be God, and taketh to itself what belongeth to God as God is in eternity without the creature." Out of his own mystical experience and out of his faithful and strenuous pondering on its meaning, St. Paul wrote the sound sense of it in *First Corinthians*. The Spirit is the organ of revelation and also of response, working through human faculties but transcending them (1 Cor. ii. 10). Even as the deep things of a man's own heart are known only to himself, unless he take the deliberate step of conveying them to another, (and even that is not always possible) so the thoughts of God can be known only if God choose to communicate them by Word and Spirit. The unspiritual man cannot therefore be a judge of religious matters, even as a deaf man cannot adjudicate on music. But the man who has the Spirit of God is the one who can safely search, examine, investigate (ἀνακρίνω). God's infinite wisdom inspires man's organs of revelation and response ; and it is therefore the mind of Christ that men *have*, when they are in His presence. Union with Him is the heart of our Christian experience. "He that is spiritual judgeth all things, yet he himself is judged of no man. For who hath known the mind of the Lord, that he may instruct him? But we have the mind of Christ" (1 Cor. ii. 15).

THE HORIZONS OF KNOWLEDGE

It is customary to notice that the scientific disciplines and the researches of the laboratories can take into account only what I have called the "metric" aspect of the universe. By controlled observation and repeatable experiment, the scientist can give a very accurate account of a very restricted portion of reality. Breadth of view is deliberately sacrificed for the sake of precision. Science proceeds by abstracting and no harm is done so long as the process of abstraction is recognised and remembered.

Let us notice that philosophy also is subject to what we may still call a "metric" limitation. Philosophy wishes to put its findings in communicable form and therefore in propositional embodiment; but there is much in human experience that will not fall into such a pattern. Once more, for the sake of precision in statement, breadth must be sacrificed; and again the procedure is harmless so long as the limitation is acknowledged. Philosophical idealism did at least endeavour to keep the disadvantages within bounds by holding to a criterion of truth which was not described as coherence alone, but as coherence *and* comprehensiveness.

Is there a corresponding limitation in the sphere of religion? Surely there is. Religion has its "metric" aspect, represented in the main by dogma. Faith is not the subscription of propositional statements concerning God and the world; and yet for the sake of precision in communication, faith constantly tends towards this. Again, the process is harmless so long as it is acknowledged, and its limitation accepted, but this cannot always be taken for granted. It is perhaps significant that when Professor Brand Blanshard, of Yale University, delivered his Gifford Lectures at St. Andrews in 1952, a trenchant analysis of Protestant theology left Protestant hearers deeply interested and stimulated, while a similar examination of the philosophy of Thomas Aquinas seemed to provoke alarm and even anger among Thomists in the audience. The second reaction was no doubt a sign of uncertainty and insecurity, but it is also something more, namely a failure to realise that the scholastic system offers an abstraction, at the best only one aspect of truth.

The same "metric" limitation may hold in certain aspects of the study of Scripture. There is a province of the Bible legitimately open to textual criticism, to historical inquiry, and to doctrinal speculation; but, if there is to be precision of statement, the boundaries of that province must be drawn far short of the true horizons of Biblical revelation. The essence of Scripture is nearer to the realm of poetry and music and art than to that of logic. Real communication is possible only when the reader occupies the place of the writer; and the means by which that identification of reader and writer is brought about is the working in each of the same Holy Spirit.

Of the Bible, God appears to say, By this medium I choose to give you everything. It does not seem necessary to believe that He adds, Elsewhere I give nothing.

We naturally inquire what place may be allotted to human reason. Without seeking accurately to define that puzzling word, we might indicate that reason is at least the faculty by which we apprehend necessary truth and try to build it up into a stable and self-harmonious system. Reason is an activity of the whole man functioning in a sound way. Admittedly both of these phrases demand further definition. How are we to tell what is to be included in "the whole man"? And how do we indicate what is meant by "in a sound way"? The criterion of the former is comprehensiveness and of the latter coherence, and as always, the two may be in conflict. There are, for example, instincts which are undoubtedly *human* instincts, and yet are *unsound*. Is there a circle here? Who decides which impulses are to be ascribed to the functioning of human nature in a sound way? Is reason the arbiter? and are we therefore begging the question? I think not, for reason at its highest level is in effect a manifestation of the witness of the Spirit. And there are many levels. Rationalism may connote no more than reliance on the senses. Or it may mean implicit trust in the discoveries of natural science. Again it may indicate acceptance of the logical reasoning of the schoolmen. A fourth possibility is that it stands for religion without mystery, as in the writings of the Deists in Britain, especially John Toland's *Christianity not Mysterious showing that there is Nothing in the Gospel contrary to Reason nor above it, and that no Christian Doctrine can properly be called a Mystery* (1696), or Julian Huxley's

Religion Without Revelation (1927). There is also a fifth possible connotation of the term rationalism. It may stand for the acceptance of all that the sincere, obedient, illuminated reason can penetrate and for the suspension of judgment concerning all that lies beyond. This attitude may not please the earnest believer, but it is an honest frame of mind and one that must be respected. Indeed it is worthy of much more than respect. Its very sincerity may well place it higher than the conventional belief of multitudes of Christian people ; and it offers the ideal soil in which the enthusiastic faith of another can sow the seed of a rich harvest. There are therefore, it would appear [1] several types of non-believer. There is the sincere humanist, believing in the values discovered by human nature in its highest endowment. There is the advocate of a philosophy opposed to the Christian faith, as for instance the Marxist or the follower of Islam. There is the person who is selfishly indifferent to all questions of truth and value. And there is the cynical self-seeker who is so extreme in his cynicism and self-seeking, that he must be classed as a pervert. Over against the third and fourth nothing will serve any good purpose save the direct and continuous proclamation of Christian truth ; but it is always a mistake to confuse the first and the second with the third and the fourth. The Christian Gospel has a point of contact already in every humble and sincere thinker.

FROM BELIEF TO ENLIGHTENMENT

Revelation is not created by human understanding and is not amenable to judgment by it ; nevertheless it is to the human understanding that revelation is given ; only reason can apprehend and elucidate it. Thus we have Anselm's watchword *Credo ut intelligam (Proslogion* 1). "Belief leads to enlightenment." In general there are four common attitudes on the matter. (1) We may have a creed which is unintelligible ; belief which is unenlightened—not because it is dealing with that which is transcendent, but because it is prematurely satisfied ; it is guilty of a kind of philosophical suicide, and thus easily falls into prejudice,

[1] Canon Richardson has developed the thought in his *Christian Apologetics*, p. 26.

obstinate dogmatism, superstition. (2) We may have an intelligence which is incredulous; enlightenment which is unbelieving —not because it is free from prejudice and superstition; though it may be all that; but because it is determined only to know, never to believe. It fails therefore, because it does not admit nor understand that there is *given* to it material which it did not create and without which it cannot make a beginning nor proceed. (3) There is such a thing as intellect which leads to a creed; enlightenment producing belief. We may not rule out this possibility at the start on the grounds that human reason goes far wrong because of man's fallibility, that intellect is therefore unreliable, and faith alone to be trusted; for we cannot help remembering how far faith, belief and theology have erred in painful and tragic episodes of ecclesiastical history such as the persecutions and the Inquisition. But certainly the result will be a philosopher's creed, appropriate to the *savants* and the *philosophes;* a creed like that of Karl Jaspers, reminiscent of the eighteenth century Deists, with its five principles: God is; There is an unconditional imperative; Man is finite and imperfectible; Man can live in God's guidance; The reality of the world subsists ephemerally between God and existence.[1] (4) We may have a creed leading to a satisfaction of the intellect. Here also we must be careful not to imagine that the intellect is a static force, waiting passively to be convinced. It is present in the first *credo* and throughout all its development: it is a vital factor in the elucidation of belief and need not be an alien factor anywhere in the course of its unfolding.

It was the intensive study of Anselm's works that led to a radical change in Karl Barth's thought concerning the relation of faith and reason.[2] His interpretation of Anselm led him to say that the *credo ut intelligam* involved no transition from faith to another genus, no μετάβασις εἰς ἄλλο γένος but rather the bringing into captivity of every thought to the obedience of Christ. In this, Anselm differs from Aquinas and endeavours, not to establish faith on rational grounds but to arrive at the understanding of faith on faith's own implications. The *intellectus,* the *gnosis,* the knowledge, is the knowledge of faith and in Anselm's presentation is always regarded as being within the

1 *Vide, Way to Wisdom.*
2 See Barth's *Fides quaerens intellectum: Anselms Beweis der Existenz Gottes,* 1931.

fellowship of the faith. Knowledge of God is therefore, according to Barth, to be conceived rather as *acknowledgment*.[1] In this section of Barth's Church Dogmatics the word "acknowledgment" is made to include a great deal—the experience of a personal relationship ; self-adaptation to a necessity in bowing before the purposes of God ; discovery of the contemporaneousness of revelation ; a decision for faith or unbelief ; the recognition that the Word of God is " always at the same time veiled and unveiled or unveiled and veiled", and so forth. It is a heavy burden for one word to carry, but the main point is clear, that man's reason is determined by its object and that in faith we have reason directed to its object in God. Man's critical reflection on the Church's proclamation must always be determined by its divine object and not by its human origin and essence. Dogmatics, for example, can be open and obedient without restrictions only on one side, namely the side of the Church's proclamation : it has no side in common with any kind of philosophy.[2]

There is the obvious danger here of so separating the reason of man's secular life from that of his religious experience as to make them two different things. If we are driven to postulate a different reason we are opening the door wide to irrationalism and chaos. Discontinuity cannot be the final word.[3] A better way of expressing the truth would be that reason, in being brought face to face with God, recognises that it cannot *reasonably rest there*. In loyalty to itself it must go on to obedience and decision. Where it has been true to itself, reason is not deposed by faith, but transformed ; not discredited, but transfigured. Thus in Romans xii. 2, we have the exhortation, " Be not conformed to this world : but be ye transformed by the renewing (ἀνακαινώσει) of your mind, that ye may prove (δοκιμάζειν) what is that good, and acceptable, and perfect, will of God ".

The implication of the phrase *credo ut intelligam* before which the scientifically minded appear to shudder as if it were something shameful, is not that the believer accepts a hypothesis,

---

[1] *Doctrine of the Word of God*, E.T., pp. 233 ff.
[2] *Ibid.*, p. 94.
[3] The fact is that Anselm was not required to move out of the sphere of faith, for he was never challenged, as Aquinas facing Moslem thought was to be challenged, by a system other than that of Christian philosophy.

for the scientist does that constantly ; could not advance without it : but that the believer accepts the hypothesis as final, unquestionable, authoritative. In fact, the gulf is not so vast as might appear. If the believer has now closed his mind, he is not on the road which is described by the phrase ; he will never "understand"; for God cannot reveal His truth to a closed mind. No ; what the believer possesses is a conviction which nothing can shake or alter except the revelation of a wider truth. And on the other hand the greatest scientists have often held grimly and obstinately to their hypothesis, when everything seemed against it ; they have believed in it for very much the same reasons as those which influence the man of faith, abstract from their religious world everything except that may rest content at that stage. They must impart the truth. Therefore, as the scientist abstracts from his world everything except that which is subject to his metric approach, in order that it may be expressed in generalised terms, so the philosopher of religion, and the individual believer when he reflects on his faith, abstract from their religious world everything except that which is amenable to rational treatment. Nor is it temerity to maintain that God speaks by luminous thought as much as by the ineffable vision. More valuable than a vague feeling of oneness with the Alone is a thought which can be shared with others. The incommunicable might as well be the speaking with tongues. Religion is not merely an atmosphere of wellbeing, an aura of security and comfort, but a mental clarification. God is accessible, it is true, not through thinking but through faith and obedience. Nevertheless it is also true that to faith and obedience God gives something more than a vague sense of His presence. He gives *thoughts* of Himself ; of His goodness, His love, His holiness, His mercy. Hence the power exercised by the theistic "proofs" long after it has been demonstrated that they are not philosophically valid, and that in any case they establish the existence of a God who is not the living God of believing experience. A God who can be proved is no God, but a thing in the world ; yet the "proofs" are the felt coincidence of the thoughts which God has put in man's mind with the sense of His transcendent presence. Thoughts, too, are symbols, in that they are pictures, counters, metaphors, which enable us so to convey our meaning to others not that they may directly understand everything, but that they may stand in the place where we have stood and so experience what we have experienced. "There are roads of thought" says Karl Jaspers, "by which we come to limits at which the consciousness of God suddenly becomes a natural presence".[1] Through the communication of speech, thought dissolves into radiance.

HUMAN WISDOM AND DIVINE SALVATION

St. Paul commended prophecy above the gift of tongues, saying that he would rather speak five words with the understanding than ten thousand words in ecstatic utterance. It is true that we must set over against this chapter (1 Cor. xiv) the passage with which the same epistle opens, where St. Paul is insisting that the Gospel is not a philosophy to be discussed in the school and the debating-society, but a message of God to be believed. The wisdom of speech (σοφία λόγου) is not needed to convey good news. It may indeed distort the good news by giving the impression that we have to do with a philosophical system and not with a divine *act* of mercy. Godet writes in his commentary on this passage (1 Cor. i. 17) *L'évangile n'est pas une sagesse, c'est un salut.* I think the danger lies not in a *sagesse* that is dedicated, but in one which believes that it has its own *salut.* Consecrated wisdom is not alien to the realm of redemption, but only wisdom which has lost its head and grown presumptuous. It is common enough to find ourselves saying, " God has revealed the truth by His Word : no human analogy is required ". But then we are simply thrown back on the problem of Divine speech. Every word and phrase in which the Divine message is conveyed is a human word, a human phrase, which works by analogy. Even the " word of the Cross " (ὁ λόγος ὁ τοῦ σταυροῦ) does not raise us out of this difficulty, for the terms in which the Divine act is interpreted by us demand the human word as well as the Divine Word. " Ransom ", " reconciliation ", " sacrifice ", " atonement ", " justification "—all are human words and our understanding of them depends on the rightful application of analogy. On the other hand, the parables usually emphasise the difference between human conditions and those existing between man and God.

[1] *Op. cit.* p. 42.

9

The parable of the labourers in the vineyard, for example, and
the payment of the same wage "unto this last" as to those who
had borne the burden and heat of the day—all this would certainly appear absurd conduct in the realm of man's economic
life ; and we can imagine the complications that would arise in
the labour market through the adoption of such a system. The
parable is concerned to say that the terms on which man faces
God are infinitely unlike those on which negotiations may be
conducted between one man and another. Yet this parable
and many others indicate at the same time that there is indeed
an analogy between things human and things divine. We can
learn from the inadequacies, conflicts, and yearnings of human
life something of the fullness of the divine. A theology of crisis
is one-sided and incomplete without a theology of encounter,
of challenge, of decision, of responsibility ; and who can presume to determine the precise limits of the part which God has
allocated to man ; how far, in other words, a true theology is
also an anthropology in grace? A purely transcendent theology
with its accompanying irrationalism is probably a less serious
danger than one which is too humanistic or too deistic ; but that
is no excuse for remaining in error. Delusion and distortion will
inevitably enter, if reason is not put to its rightful function of
distinguishing between sense and nonsense. Truth is truth
whether it is revealed to faith or to reason or to conscience ; but
the human faculties are not left unchanged when revelation
takes place. "Reason is turned into light and will into love."[1]
The static conception of reason and of conscience as human
faculties brought to bear on reality like observers and assessors
has led thought astray. They are not to be envisaged as unchanging instruments or constant yard-sticks, but as pliable
media moulding themselves to the material on which they are
at work, or endowments growing in capacity as they are rightly
employed. In this development there is a point at which the
acceleration may be particularly rapid and there is an illumination of knowledge so extraordinary that it is like the union
of three sounds to make, not a fourth sound but a star ; and the
maturing of conscience may go forward with such energy that,
not only the power of discernment of right and wrong is transformed but the man himself who exercises it.

[1] Walter Hylton, *The Scale of Perfection.*

Since the beginnings of Christianity there have been good Christians who were suspicious of human thought. God has spoken, they declared: there is no need for men to think. Only believe! "What has Athens to do with Jerusalem?" asks Tertullian.[1] But there must be some place for reason, if only to determine whether the statements of faith make sense or not, or to assess the evidence for believing that revelation has been given, for instance, in the accepted text of Scripture. There is, however, no call to go to the other extreme and to say with Anselm in the preface to *Cur Deus Homo* "setting Christ aside (as though He had never been)" let us seek to prove "by logical arguments that it is impossible for any man to be saved without Him". It is just not true that God has everywhere given such light as to enable mankind even dimly to guess what he needs for salvation. It cannot, however, be argued simply that the most earnest and conscientious philosopher is in total darkness. If he has indeed come nearer the truth, he has been drawn thither by God. To confront him with a Christian philosophy, alienated from all contact with "merely human" wisdom, is to embarrass him unnecessarily. From this sense of frustration comes the savagery of Karl Jaspers' comment on John Calvin.[2] "Calvin's greatness lies in disciplined, methodic form, iron logic, unswerving and dauntless adherence to principles. But his loveless intolerance makes him, in his theoretical as in his practical activities, the repellent antithesis of philosophy. It is good to have looked him in the face in order to recognise this wherever, in veiled or fragmentary form, it is manifested in the world. He is the supreme incarnation of that Christian intolerance against which there is no weapon but intolerance." It will not serve simply to say to the philosopher, Believe and you will come to understand: *Nisi credideritis, non intelligetis;* for he has perhaps as yet no firm belief, and faith cannot be compelled. The method of the Thomist is to handle philosophical problems as a philosopher and theological problems as a theologian; but this is no solution. It may end some of the strife; but it leaves a gulf which is a denial of the unity of truth. God has spoken in the Word; in the Church; in the soul of man. Suppose the testimony is conflicting. What then? Aquinas had little

---

[1] *On Prescription Against Heretics*, ch. vii.
[2] *Way to Wisdom*, p. 183.

place for religious experience as evidential. He emphasised history and miracle (especially the miracle of the Church); but we know that the interpretations, made by the Church, of Bible history can be as fallible as those made by reason working on religious experience. The danger attaching to reason is not that it is always a faulty tool, but that it is liable to mislead. It may degenerate into wishful thinking; or (quite unconsciously) it may seek so to wrest the evidence as to minister to power and prejudice. From time to time, indeed, it may fail to realise that an abstraction has been made and that conclusions which are reliable enough in a restricted field cease to be trustworthy when applied in unsuitable circumstances.

REASON ADDRESSED—AND JUDGED—BY REVELATION

The late Dr. J. K. Mozley indicates that there is a danger in using phraseology to suggest that Reason can in any way be employed as a *test* of revelation.[1] I entirely agree. The word " test " might be taken to infer that Reason is a kind of litmus paper to be applied mechanically to the content of faith ; and such a simile would give too passive a connotation; or that Reason operates like a process in the laboratory initiated and controlled by a master-mind who, himself quite disinterested, knows what reaction should follow if the element under investigation is genuine ; and such a comparison would make Reason too dominant. Nor can it be compared to the mirror which reflects everything as it is, but remains unchanged by what it reflects. Reason is more like the mirror that distorts, yet is precious because it is our only one. To save the metaphor of reflection we should have to think of a mirror that was sympathetic, changing with the scene it registers, chameleon-like taking colour from its object.

To seek for a description without metaphor, we are bound to say that Reason does several things. It identifies revelation. (That is a better word than " tests ".) It receives revelation, apprehends it, elucidates it, responds to it, *and bows before it.* An important fact that must not be overlooked is that Reason is not static: it is constantly learning from the Revelation and

---

[1] See *Some Tendencies in British Theology*, pp. 156-157, where he is discussing my Kerr Lectures *Revelation and Response*.

altering because of it. Nor is the alteration necessarily for the better. It is a fact that true Revelation has been rejected in the process of human reasoning; and we must hold that the rejection came about because Reason failed to develop aright as Revelation played upon it; was stubborn, defiant, allowing prejudice, probably unconscious prejudice, to have its way. Condemned if it try to stand in place of Revelation, Reason is commended when it is content to mediate Revelation. We are dealing therefore, not with a changeless Reason which, like the analyst in the laboratory, has all the answers and waits only to see if they are correctly given by the material under investigation, so that he may proclaim it genuine or spurious; but with Reason which is profoundly modified by the Revelation with which it deals. Reason, which identifies Revelation, then becomes *identified with* Revelation: the two processes are co-relative and commingled. As Reason identifies itself with Revelation in decision and obedience, it acclaims the Revelation as true. Reason does not *explain* Revelation: it provides a *sympathetic understanding* of Revelation.

The function of Reason and its capabilities may be illustrated by a pleasant encounter in a famous Border parish. On the highroad, or on the moors, or in a country lane you may meet the parish minister almost any afternoon, trotting around his flock on horseback. It seems the sensible way; but it was all very new when he first came to the charge and, on inquiring the price of a horse, he discovered that it was far beyond the reach of his modest stipend. However, the minister realised that an *unbroken* horse was much less expensive. He therefore purchased, first an unbroken horse; second a book entitled *How to Break in a Horse*. Together they cost much less than had originally been asked.

In the case of our Reason there is one difference. We have to write the text-book as we go along (it is like playing the violin in public and mastering the instrument as you play); and yet we cannot wait to make use of Reason till we have completed the final chapter and read the proofs. Indeed the truth is apprehended only as we make use of it, as Napoleon said of many of his most vital decisions, that they had to await the moment of action. *On s'engage, puis on voit.*

Those who decry Reason and Nature and the ethnic faiths

as media of revelation are doubtless indulging in a more or less conscious exaggeration in order to assist the ordinary man to avoid the dangers of over-estimating Reason, Nature, and the ethnic faiths; erecting, as it were, fences higher than need be and enlarging DANGER notices in case the weak, the foolish and the ignorant are injured. It is the natural tendency to over-value Nature; it seems reasonable to trust Reason; and to reverence the ethnic faiths has an air of tolerance. Here, more than in many other spheres, natural man is disposed to be led astray; therefore it is necessary to take special precautions. The emphasis laid by the Theology of Crisis on the other side has not yet reached the great majority of non-theological Christians and the preacher may therefore feel justified in conveying the truth contained in that school of theology by overstressing one part of the truth. Nevertheless there is an equal and opposite danger in the very exaggeration, even when its aim is to avoid humanistic views of the "Blue Domers" (who claim to worship God under the vault of heaven); or to warn against a weak toleration of the idolatries of the ethnic faiths; or to proclaim the uniqueness of Christianity and stand by the scandal of its particularity. We must constantly remind ourselves that it was the exaggerated expression of a truth by the later Reformers which gave to us the tyranny of a Bible supposed to be verbally inspired, and delayed for many generations the coming of the full liberty of the Gospel with its enriched understanding of the Christian faith. Over-emphasis on the Biblical text had the laudable aim of protecting believers against the constant temptation to reduce divine revelation to human discovery. There were, indeed, many scholars of the Bible who were more scholarly than Biblical, whose studies were so narrowly technical that they missed the spiritual quality of the texts they examined; and these brought scientific Biblical study into some disrepute. It is time to say that this school of criticism was never dominated by enemies of the faith, still less confined to such enemies, as timid Christians were too ready to suppose. Today we need most of all the kind of scholar who combines a strong faith in criticism with a strong faith in God, who will mix his keenest argument with his most fervent prayers. Professor H. H. Rowley is confident (in his book *The Relevance of the Bible* (1942), pp. 15-17) that we have reached the proper view-point:

In recent years a new change is coming over Biblical study, whose significance is far too little perceived. The newer attitude does not reject the work of the earlier study but seeks to conserve all that is of worth in the fruits of every approach. Yet it desires to transcend them. It accepts substantially the work of Biblical criticism, but beyond the desire to know the date and authorship of the books of the Bible and the meaning they had for their first readers, it seeks the abiding significance of the Bible, and in particular its significance for this generation. It recognises all the human processes that went into the making of the Bible, without reducing it to the level of a merely human document, and it acknowledges that its scientific study, which is still valued and continued, is not enough. For the Bible is first and foremost a religious Book. . . . The newer attitude still recognises the clear marks of progress in the Biblical revelation, yet it does not reduce revelation to discovery. It does not cease to be interested in the development of religion, but its centre of interest is not in man, but in God. It does not find the story of man's growth in the understanding of God of such absorbing interest that it becomes an end in itself, but rather seeks to perceive in every stage of the process that which is enduringly true of God.

IS ALL KNOWLEDGE *REVEALED* KNOWLEDGE ?

The next conclusion might seem to be that all knowledge is revelation; and there is a very real sense in which that is true. No aspect of truth can be apprehended unless God Himself shall make it manifest. God is the light of all our seeing. But we must distinguish. Even as it is unsatisfactory to say with Schleiermacher that everything is miracle, that " miracle " is just the religious word for event; so here. Where everyone is someone, no one is anyone. While aware that no human thought is independent of divine illumination, we must still find it convenient and necessary to distinguish revelation and discovery. In some spheres of the activity of mind and heart discovery is at a minimum, in others at a maximum. Religious experience falls into that category where the human contribution is least apparent. Nevertheless it would be a mistake to suppose that here we have something quite unrelated to authority, to Scripture, to home, to upbringing. All these have had their influence in bringing the man to that place in which God has chosen to reveal Himself to him in " religious experience ". In particular, religious experience is not divorced from the religious fellowship. Its form may be individual, but its content, if it is genuine, intimates the fellowship of Christian brotherhood. "Faith is false, the Word of God is not heard aright, when I am not claimed in all my being for the service of my brother, in the very fact of being claimed for the service of God."[1]

GENERAL REVELATION

As revelation is associated with an event in the world—an act accomplished or a word spoken for a particular moment; indeed both of these together, for the act is not revelation without the word that interprets it—so it is in the individual soul. Illumination comes, not by ideas of reason, which lie within the province of discovery, but by divine actions, which lead some to speak of "The Lord's work with me". Does it follow the same pattern as the revelation given to a nation or a community? Normally, that appears to be true. General revelation has a striking appeal in childhood; it is followed by the history of an elect one, growingly aware of the divine call; and is at last fulfilled and transcended in the conviction of forgiveness and victory through Jesus and in the assurance of the abiding power of the Spirit.

How authentic is the first stage all preachers know who have found it so easy to talk to children on themes of natural theology; who ask themselves how often their teaching of elementary Christianity to the very young has left them with only a beautiful story of Bethlehem and Galilee, and a shedding of tears over Calvary; while conscious of the vivid reality in the child mind of the starry heavens above and the moral law within. The profound attachment to general revelation is something that continues throughout the whole life of many Christian people. It is true that this is not always so; for, where there is mature faith combined with an ability to express it in Christian terms, there is a type of character which is unforgettable, whose influence is incalculable. But it can commonly be observed that the Christian layman, if he has escaped the impact of the theology of crisis, as many have, when invited to testify to his faith, will almost invariably speak in terms of

[1] Emil Brunner, *God and Man*, E.T., by Professor David Cairns, p. 130.

natural theology. The theistic proofs may be very dear to him. Is it only shyness? Does he find it easier to speak in the more impersonal terms of the philosophy of religion than in the warm accents of spiritual experience? Or is this the reaction only of those who have undergone higher education? Have humanist studies so deeply modified the form of his witness? Certainly he finds it more natural to speak of the wonders of creation than of his sin and his Saviour. Others again, it is true, more readily turn to testify to the experience of redemption ; but here also too often the terminology is one taken over from evangelical circles, sometimes perhaps even a terminology without an experience. On the other hand, we have probably fostered too sedulously a horror of pantheism. Dr. Donald Fraser loved to tell how as a young man he sailed down the estuary of the River Clyde and exclaimed enthusiastically on the loveliness of the sunset, only to be rebuked by a stern Scottish elder at his side, "Young man, beware of pantheism!" We must respect the witness of those who are found of God in Nature, who experience the sense of exaltation from even the simplest miracles of His creation—

> The blue of a kingfisher haunting a bridge
> And the sun on an ancient tower

—who are led by this path easily and inevitably into the divine Presence

> And follow with childlike faith the way
> To the luminous fields of eternal day.[1]

The Word of God is God's self-communication, and we cannot believe that in Nature He is withholding Himself from us : for, if that were so, we should be left with Nature as a surd, an irrational realm. It is not that. With all its inscrutableness, it is not that. Admittedly it is often opaque ; but in spite of all its rawness and cruelty, it is God's : it is good. And in looking on it we must take all the facts into the reckoning. "To select the earthquake or the parasites is as mistaken, and almost as irritating, as to select the sunsets and the lilies. Nature is not an arena or a picture-house where we can indulge our sadism

---

[1] Ishbel Dickie, from the poem entitled, *The Field of the Gossamer Threads.*

or tickle our taste for prettiness." It is a symbol and instrument
of reality and, in the words of John Ray, to enquire of it is
"part of the business of a Sabbath-day".[1] The interpretation
of it is indeed fraught with difficulty; but so also is the interpretation of the Bible. Both need the aid of the Holy Spirit.
We shall not go far wrong if we find in Christ the fulfilment of
the joy that is in Nature; the answer to the challenge which
Nature brings, when our littleness is contrasted with Nature's
majesty; and the source of power for the endurance which
Nature demands. Victor Hugo has a poem called *A Villequier.*
That is the name of the place where his young daughter and
her husband were drowned when sailing on the river. At last he
has been able to re-visit it and has found solace in his desolation
by looking on the wonders and the immensity of Nature:

> Voyant ma petitesse et voyant vos miracles.

It may be that Nature can bring a man to personal encounter
with God. It is probably unusual; but we dare not deny the
work of the Holy Spirit; nor try to explain it away as pantheism
or as superstition when the busy scientist turns aside for a
moment to praise God, or the countryman doffs his hat before
the bright glory of the evening sky. The point to be raised
lies in the question, Can nature, can conscience, can the ethnic
faiths or profane history offer a preparatory background for
the coming of Christ to the soul, which is at all comparable
with the background and preparation of the Old Testament?
We are seeking, not the evidence of syllogistic reasoning, but the
evidence of personal encounter (the only evidence that is
relevant to knowledge of God) and we are asking, Does that
evidence exist at any other level than that of Biblical revelation?
If we are not be involved in irrationalism, we must acknowledge that these have real worth. If we are not to be involved
in obscurantism, we must admit that there are instances where
these have been sufficient and adequate preparation; where
these have brought men to the place of challenge and decision.
Assuredly we do not go on to say that these, together with the
Scriptures—as if they could be brought together in one category!
—are the Old Testament of the religion of the future. Certainly
we insist that the way which God in fact chose is that by which

1 C. E. Raven, *Science, Religion, and the Future*, p. 104.

He led his people of the Old Testament. Yet we acknowledge that His ways are not all open to our scrutiny. He has His own secret workings. If we close our eyes to God in Nature and in the ethnic faiths, we shall not see all that God desires to reveal in Jesus Christ. And by this is meant, not simply that we, from the Christian viewpoint, can see God therein; but that He has been pleased therein to reveal Himself to others of His children.

Calvin[1] reiterates that the natural knowledge is enough to show God as Creator and Governor. "To this first knowledge was afterwards added the more intimate knowledge which alone quickens dead souls, and by which God is known, not only as the Creator of the world and sole author and disposer of all events, but also as a Redeemer, in the person of the Mediator." "Therefore, while it becomes man seriously to employ his eyes in considering the works of God, since a place has been assigned him in this most glorious theatre that he may be a spectator of them, his special duty is to give ear to the Word, that he may the better profit."[2] This is clear, but not yet conclusive, for while it is true that faith alone makes possible a right knowledge of God in His *works*, it is also faith alone which makes possible a right knowledge of God in His *Word*. Calvin is obviously embarrassed when he comes to deal with the incidents concerning Naaman and Cornelius and the Ethiopian eunuch. "I admit that in some respect, their faith was not explicit either as to the person of Christ, or the power and office assigned Him by the Father. Still it is certain that they were imbued with principles which might give some, though a slender, foretaste of Christ. This should not be thought strange; for the eunuch would not have hastened from a distant country to Jerusalem to an unknown God; nor could Cornelius, after having once embraced the Jewish religion, have lived so long in Judea without becoming acquainted with the rudiments of sound doctrine. In regard to Naaman, it is absurd to suppose that Elisha, while he gave him many minute precepts, said nothing of the principal matter. Therefore, although their knowledge of Christ may have been obscure, we cannot suppose that they had no such knowledge at all. They used the sacrifices of the Law, and must

[1] *Institutes*, bk. I, ch. vi, § I.
[2] E.T. by Beveridge, vol. I, pp. 65 and 66.

have distinguished them from the spurious sacrifices of the Gentiles, by the end to which they referred, viz. Christ." [1]

The weakness of this reply indicates that we have not yet arrived at an absolute distinction, but are left asking whether Revelation anywhere tells us that Revelation is to be found in such and such a place and there only; or in such and such a form and thus only? Where does Revelation tell us this? and, if it does, is there not a circular argument somewhere? We need constantly to pray for deliverance from the temptation to elevate our own " religion " instead of adoring and honouring our Lord. There is one eloquence which springs from conviction, and of that we can never have too much; and there is another eloquence which is the fruit of insecurity: against this eloquence the Christian as well as the agnostic should be on his guard. When Paul and Barnabas were rejected by the Jews they exclaimed " It was necessary that the word of God should first have been spoken to you: but seeing ye put it from you, and judge yourselves unworthy of everlasting life, lo, we turn to the Gentiles " (Acts xiii. 46). It is true that this refers to the *promise* (the Gospel is for all the world, and prior to the covenant with Abraham was the covenant with Noah, the symbol of the mercy of God extending over all mankind) and does not refer to Gentile religion as a preparation for the Gospel; but it is also true that the apostles were sure that the Gentiles were ready to hear; they had not been without witness. Christ, the Saviour of all men, could not have left them in utter darkness. We may affirm that the true Gentile believer is on the way, though he has not arrived at the goal, and even that he is on the way which God chose for him.

If Christian people were all one in thought and worship and polity, there would be more justification for intransigence; but the actual situation in the matter of Christian unity suggests that our Christian response has been so faulty that we must have missed much of the truth that God sought to impart. From the ethnic faiths there may be something to learn that He has not been able to communicate because of the dullness of our blinded sight. Thus many of our most experienced missionaries are insistent that we must go to work among other peoples as learners and not only as teachers; for the mere

[1] *Institutes*, bk. iii, ch. ii, § 32.

iconoclast will not achieve the success that ought to be his. The whole field of growth indicates that the formula, of pattern *plus* novelty, underlies all life. There is nothing wrong with the concept of spiritual development, and of progressive revelation with its consummation in Christ, except where we imagine that there is nothing specifically new in the coming of Christ. In human love, we are not depreciating other people's friendship, but stating the plain fact when we declare that there is now "only one in all the world", as in *The Song of the Camp* where

> Each heart recalled a different name,
> But all sang " Annie Laurie "

In the realm of faith, the conviction dominates the heart that nowhere else is there salvation. "There is none other name under heaven given among men, whereby we must be saved" (Acts iv. 12). Peter, when he used these words, was not making any pronouncement on the value of the non-Christian religions, but was simply stating his own experience. There is none to be placed alongside Christ. To meet Him is to know all others insufficient. In human experience it is one for each ; in religion, one for all. Dr. John A. Mackay has pointed out that Christian saints and thinkers so far apart as Irenaeus and the Sadhu Sundhar Singh have expressed in almost identical terms their view of the uniqueness of Christ. To the followers of Marcion, inquiring, " What new thing did Jesus bring ? " Irenaeus replied, "He brought all that was new in bringing Himself ". When a Hindu professor of philosophy asked the Christian Sadhu "What have you found in Christianity which you did not find in the religions of India ? " the simple response was, " I have found Jesus Christ ".[1]

THE CHOSEN PEOPLE

Manifestly, God has been at work in the history of all nations, not only in that of the Hebrews ; but it so happened that among the Hebrews were found certain people who were able to interpret the working of His hands. The phrase "it so happened" conceals the mystery. We do not know *why* God raised up the

[1] Report of the Jerusalem Meeting of the International Missionary Council, vol I, p. 441.

succession of prophets in Israel and not in Babylon or Greece, in Persia or Rome. It is certainly not that the Hebrews were a race of saints. On the contrary, they were often conspicuous for rejecting the divine approach and for defying the commands laid on them by the Lord God (*vide* Deut. vii. 7 ; ix. 6). "The scandal of particularity" cannot be avoided by finding in the Chosen People a natural aptitude for faith and obedience. God chose them in the mystery of election.[1]

It can even be said that Israel did not become gradually better, purer, more religious and more capable of being used ; that on the contrary its existence is a unique confirmation of human unfaithfulness. There is always, it is true, a Remnant, a root which survives when the branches are cut off, even when the trunk is felled ; yet even these faithful and obedient ones are bound up in the solidarity of Israel's guilt.[2] We should not allow the fact, that the Remnant in Israel identified itself with the people's sin and confessed its own guiltiness, to cancel out our sense of proportion, as has happened surely when Karl Barth goes out of his way to say that in the end even the faithful disciples of Jesus were in the same position as Judas and Caiaphas. "In the same position" begs the question. If it means that they too were sinners, needing the grace of God, it says little that is not obvious ; if it means that God could as easily have used Judas and Caiaphas as apostles and missionaries, it says something dangerously like nonsense. Hosea made it plain to Israel that all man's reliance is on God's mercy ; that even when man has broken all his promises to God, the faithfulness of God still endures. The Remnant may do nothing more, it may be, than hold fast to that truth ; but the holding fast is something, when all others have despaired or rebelled. Part of the mystery of election is that God should choose those who have nothing to justify the choice ; but there is the other part of the mystery, that God chooses His people for that which He sees in them, when none other, least of all they themselves, could see it or suspect it. To His chosen people God gave the qualities neces- sary to carry out the purpose for which He had chosen them ; and, since we are in any case involved in mystery, it does not greatly matter how we express the fact. whether by saying that

[1] See Alan Richardson, *Christian Apologetics*, pp. 139 ff.
[2] See Barth, *The Knowledge of God and the Service of God*, pp. 61 ff.

He chose them because He saw certain qualities potentially in them, or by saying that He endowed them with those qualities after He had chosen them. A time-schedule is particularly absurd here. The central truth is all that matters, namely that God is behind all worthy human character and achievement. When He said to Israel (Isa. xlix. 16) "I have graven thee on the palms of My hands", it was indicated that He saw all His people's weakness and disobedience but nevertheless He saw Israel as it could be, the ideal people of God. Thus it has recently been said:[1] "The main concern of Israel was not with culture, civilisation, world-conquest, political power or commercial success; these factors played their part in her life and often she was tempted to follow them and reject her divine destiny, but finally one element predominated over all the rest, the obedience to Yahweh's declared will, as that will and its obligations were made clearer through the historical crises in which she was involved. It was the relationship of the nation to Yahweh which determined the form of its social life, the nature of its economic order and the development of its literature, as well as the constitution of its religious cultus and its priestly orders. The relationship of Israel to other nations, depended not upon nationalistic ambitions but upon her obedience to Yahweh and her fulfilment of His will." Nor can we penetrate the mystery of election at the other point by trying to assess how much is of grace and how much of human responsibility and self-determination in the obedience and receptiveness of the prophets which made possible the fuller revelation. All we know is that they, like the nation, perhaps representing the nation as it was ideally meant to be, were called to special service of God by God's love and mercy and faithfulness. It is not of the will of man, but of God. (John i. 13.)

It is possible, however, for this dogma of the aloneness of the Old Testament, as preparation for the Gospel, to lend itself to a misconception, like that of Bibliolatry. As the richness of Christ has sometimes been reduced to little more than the literal interpretation of the words He spoke, so the universality of God's self-communication has been narrowed to the history of the elect nation. The truth in each inadequate theory is that God has chosen a particular way of coming to mankind

---

[1] E. C. Rust, *The Christian Understanding of History*, p. 99.

which man neglects at his peril. The error in each is the making of a book, in the one case, and a human history in the other the authoritative centre of faith, in place of Christ Himself and His challenge to the human soul. It is not given to us to construct a system into which all religious truth will fit; but we have the light of Christ.

THE DISTORTION OF REASON

Whenever we try to return to even a modified assertion of general revelation, we are bound to inquire as to the bearing of it on our view of human thinking. It is no part of Protestant theology to minimise the importance of human reason, though it may be a duty to rebuke ourselves if we find reason becoming self-sufficient. It is not reason that is objectionable, but rationalism. Assuredly, we must affirm that reason is deeply affected by man's fallen state, and has suffered corruption; but this must not blind us to the truth. Saying that it is all corrupt may be part of the taint. Our fallen nature may have fostered in us a pathological fear of Reason. A mathematician is not any better at mathematics because he is a Christian. Emil Brunner directs attention once again[1] to a distinction which is not always clearly maintained, between knowledge that comes *from* God and knowledge *of* God. Like all scientific knowledge, mathematics comes from God, but it is different from theology as it is different from faith in God, the Source of all knowledge. The disturbance caused in human reason by man's fallen state is seen at its maximum when reason seeks to apply itself unaided to the spiritual nature of man and his relations with God, and at its minimum when it is engaged in the sciences and in the sphere of the formal. "The more impersonal the sphere, the less disturbance there is; the more personal, the greater is the disturbance. Mathematical thought and technical dexterity are far less affected than marriage and the life of the family. The disturbance is great wherever personal human relations are involved. . . . Through Christ we do not receive a different mathematics, physics, or chemistry, but we do find a different kind of marriage, family life, a different relation to our

[1] *Revelation and Reason*, pp. 318, 383, 429 of the English Translation.

fellow men, and hence, influenced by that, a different kind of public justice."

Observing the distortion of man's faculties which has been brought about by his sinfulness, we affirm, not that the divine image in him has been annihilated, but that it has been perverted. And that is a terrifying situation to contemplate. It means that if we break away from the guiding hand of God and follow our own bent, we may come to accept as true what is a travesty of the truth, and that, as we have seen, in those spheres of our life which matter most for our attitude to God and to our fellows. There is, however, no need to take the next step, as if it were an inevitable conclusion. It is not to be deduced as a corollary that the sincere, humble use of the reasoning faculty must be regarded as a breaking away from the guiding hand of God. When we quote the words of Zophar and inquire "Canst thou by searching find out God?" (Job xi. 7), a question which "expects the answer, No", and agree that it is good Hebrew but bad Greek, we may then go on to suggest that the Greeks were able to achieve something whose worth was hidden from the intensity of the Hebrews, the truth, namely, that God is revealing Himself through every quest of sincere philosophising.[1] It is, of course, true that there may not be time, in this or that man's brief existence, for both the full life of faith and the full life of philosophy, and then philosophy may be characterised as leisured self-indulgence (as, it is said, the Basques gave up the pursuit of art because there was no time to cultivate it in addition to the life of religion); but to the average man the discipline of ordered thinking is one of the modes in which God is seeking to restore the clarity of thought which sin has perverted.

In thus referring to reason, it is essential to particularise by using some such term as "disciplined", since one symptom of the disturbance introduced by man's sin into his rational activity is precisely the tendency to wishful thinking. The rigorous employment of reason will imply a right attitude to authority, where authority is conceived as the legitimate influence exercised by the thoughts of others and by the insights embodied in history and tradition. Both in thought and in belief, much has to be accepted on the testimony of others, where we cannot

[1] See *supra*, p. 9.

ourselves experience, but can only judge that the testimony is reliable. Ultimately it is true, of course, that the testimony of others, however reliable or exalted those others may be, however great may be our confidence in them and our reverence for them, is capable only of presenting the case to us for our own decision. The responsibility is ours. We decide on the reliability of the witness and on the reasonableness of the claim to truth of that which is presented to us. A man may be "an heretic in the truth" if he believes things "only because his pastor says so". "The very truth he holds becomes his heresy."[1] The final authority lies with the light of Truth itself.

AUTHORITY IN RELIGION

Transposing this conclusion into the more appropriate terms of religion, we affirm that God in Christ is the sole authority in belief. Inadequate expressions of this sole authority are found in our doctrines of Scripture, of the Church, of the Inner Light; and the important matter is to discover which of these is the least misleading and wherein each of them is inadequate. Each of these subordinate expressions of divine authority, if isolated, may lend itself to perversions of thought, to spiritual blindness and refusal to repent. There are those who bow to the authority of power, but, as Whichcote wrote, "The longest sword, the strongest lungs, the most voices are false measures of truth". There are others who, while not sufficiently naive to accept those cruder forms of assertiveness, nevertheless long for authority of some sort. In their flight from freedom and in their fear of private initiative they would gladly consent to be led blindfold if only they could be sure of being led aright. They will even, says Dean Inge, put on manacles to keep their hands from trembling.[2] In giving due emphasis to the Bible and the Church, it may seem that we have a logical circle, the Bible supplying the credentials of the Church, and the Church determining the boundaries of canonical Scripture and the rightful interpretation of it. It would be truer to say that in Bible and Church we have correlatives; and they must correct and enrich each other. The Roman Catholic comes to the Bible

[1] *Areopagitica*, ii, 431. [2] W. R. Inge, *Mysticism in Religion*, p. 14.

with his presupposition of the inerrancy of the Church, and the fundamentalist comes with his presupposition of the inerrancy of Scripture. For neither party can there be genuine interpretation—not for the Roman Catholic, because the Church has done it all for him; not for the fundamentalist since interpretation is replaced by repetition.

THE INTEGRITY OF REASON

Thus we should not be too ready to forget the pioneer work heroically accomplished over two centuries of controversy, when for the sake of true religion scientific criticism fought against prejudice and superstition and entrenched ecclesiastical interest; and therefore we must acknowledge the abiding values of a theology which is apt to be dismissed today, lightly and even condescendingly, as "liberal". When this school of theological thought stumbled, it was generally through a tendency to show unwarranted deference to the scientific structure which it had erected, and then to attempt to fit Christianity into it; and to neglect the supremely novel and supernatural aspect of Christianity, which, as divine revelation, showed to man that which could never otherwise be available to him. Liberal theology at least made possible two outstanding achievements which must never be surrendered. It gave Christian people the courage to examine the Scriptures with unprejudiced minds and so to shed from their faith a whole series of burdensome accretions and to recover the Bible in its true splendour. It also gave Christian people the courage required to place a greater value on truth than on security and so enabled them to rise above magical assurances, in fidelity to the principle expressed by Pascal, that "there is no consolation save in the truth". While convinced that none can lie open to the coming of revelation unless "existentially" disposed, we must realise that personal involvement requires always to be balanced by scientific objectivity. Unless it is thus combined, personal involvement may distort the vision, since we are all prone, as sinful and selfish creatures, to seek security when we imagine that we are still seeking truth.

KNOWLEDGE BY ENCOUNTER

The immediacy of man's knowledge of God has lately been challenged again from two sides, and it is always of first importance that faith should be defended against misinterpretations in the direction of a mysticism which is less than Christian. Emil Brunner has called this immediacy in question so far as it ignores the divine event through which revelation comes. This will be referred to later.[1] The other recent challenge comes from Dr. Austin Farrer.[2] Instead of holding that there is knowledge *about* God and also knowledge *of* God, he would say that there is truth about God and *revealed* truth about God[3] and this revealed truth comes by supernatural means. God Himself has given it. He would deny the authenticity of what we have called knowledge by encounter, in the sense of direct knowledge coming from God unmediated. He recalls his own early experience. Having been reared in personalism which might satisfy the most ardent disciple of Martin Buber, and thinking of himself as set over against God as one man faces another across a table, he looked for a sign of the divine presence in the form of some sort of address, speech, colloquy; but, he continues, "no 'other' stood beside me, no shadow of presence fell upon me" (p. 7). Our natural knowledge of God, he thinks, is at its highest in the divine moving of man's best thought, the divine causality illuminating man's mind. But there is also a supernatural action of God by which God works through second causes certain effects which do not arise from the natural powers of those causes (p. 11). This may possibly be a matter of words only, but more probably there is a profound difference and one which finds expression in the choice of metaphor. Since theological thinking must depend on metaphors, it is important to choose the best. Dr. Farrer's is almost a mechanical one, for he envisages the current of man's thinking being reinforced by an inrush of power from another source; and it is significant that he proceeds to derive the supernatural from beginnings in primitive magic. Where this metaphor is most apt to halt is at the point where we must acknowledge that man's thinking is in need of more than reinforcement: it stands in need of

[1] See ch. vii, p. 208.   [2] *The Glass of Vision.*
[3] See especially Lecture 1.

judgment. When Dr. Farrer questions the reality of personal communication of God with men he is, I believe, seeking to avoid a real danger, that of introducing at this level another kind of irrationalism akin to that introduced by Kierkegaard at the level of obedience, and so far as there is here a caution against this real error, the position is sound and healthy. But in saying that "For us, the typical case of the supernatural is not seen in physical miracles, but in the empowering of the spirit of man by the Spirit of his Creator, to know and to love the supreme and causeless Act, the pure and endless Being, the saving Charity" (p. 15), there is a more insidious danger. It looks out in the word "empowering". When Dr. Farrer takes this line and passes from the thought of a personal encounter of God with man, he parts company with the prophets and psalmists, the saints and mystics, who by the grace of God have heard God speaking to them as a man speaks to his friend. The absence of any sense of an Other, of the shadow of a Presence, which characterised Dr. Farrer's early experience can, of course, be countered by innumerable examples of the opposite. One which is familiar in Scottish tradition is that of Master Robert Bruce. When he preached at Larbert Kirk, there was near by a room where he used to go between sermons. "One day" says Wodrow's *Life*, "some noblemen and gentlemen, who had been hearing him, wearied between sermons, when he stayed longer than he used. They having a good way to ride after sermon, they called for the bellman, and desired him to go to him in the little room, where he was retired, and knock softly at the door, and, if he opened, to acquaint him, they desired he might begin as soon as conveniently he could, because some of them had far to ride. The bellman did as he was commanded; but Mr. Bruce was taken up so in wrestling that he did not hear him. However, the bellman, while at the door, heard some of Mr. Bruce's words, which, poor man, he did not understand; and so he came back to those that sent him, and told them that he did not know when the minister would come out. He believed there was somebody with him, for he heard him many times say, with the greatest seriousness, 'That he would not—he could not go—unless He came with him; and that he would not go alone'; adding, that he never heard the other answer him a word."

The metaphor of speech, and particularly of the speech of friend to friend, is startlingly anthropomorphic; but it has the advantage of being Scriptural and it is less inadequate than one drawn from non-personal realms. When, in these stimulating and charming Bampton Lectures, Dr. Farrer declares, concerning the claim of "personal communication" and the suggestion that God must speak to us somewhat as we speak to one another, that "this obviously does not happen, nor is it going to happen", he is quite right in the sense that the voice of God is not in the order of sounds that could be, let us say, electrically recorded. The divine speech is for the inward ear. But of course the metaphor of the voice of God is familiar (and appropriate, surely) in prophet and psalmist and elsewhere throughout the Bible. In prayer, as in human friendship, there is something much more than the statement of needs or the search for help. There is the intimate companionship, the warmth and joy of the other's presence. The term "personal communication", which Dr. Farrer questions, must at least be interpreted widely enough to include these experiences. Moreover, we ought to take into account the story of the baptism of Jesus. No doubt He was Himself the sole source of the information concerning the divine voice which then spoke to Him. It was for His inward ear. When Dr. Brunner (as we shall see in ch. vii) challenges the immediacy of religious knowledge, he is on strong ground, for he is emphasising the essential nature of the divine *event*, and the fact that Jesus is the sole Mediator and that He alone can have unmediated knowledge of God. But Dr. Farrer is not so strongly placed, since it is clear, surely, that the knowledge which Jesus had of God during His earthly Incarnation, was dependent on the same kind of mediation as is our knowledge. The difference between His and ours lies not in the fact that His was exempt from all mediation, but that it was uncorrupted by sin and therefore, as ours can never be, pure and untrammelled. Thus it is not the illumination nor the reinforcement of man's thinking about God which is the important theme, but the judgment of it.

When Dr. Farrer discusses the relation of Scripture to man's knowledge of God [1] he argues that the divine supernatural action on man's mind "bestows an apprehension of divine mysteries,

1 See especially Lecture III.

inaccessible to natural reason, reflection, intuition, or wit. Christians suppose such mysteries to be communicated to them through the Scriptures. In particular, we believe that in the New Testament we can as it were overhear men doing super-natural thinking of a privileged order, with pens in their hands." He is equally insistent [1] that the primary revelation was Christ, His life, words, passion, resurrection. "This at least in modern thought upon the subject is true: the primary revelation is Jesus Christ Himself." The consequence would appear to be that, where there is consciousness of "personal communication", this is to be regarded as response rather than as revelation. We need not worry about terminology, and it is impossible to draw the precise boundaries between the activity of man and the revela-tion of God in the inner process of faith and the apprehension of religious truth, but I should myself prefer to hold that the right response is here not to be sharply differentiated from revelation. It would not be the *right* response if the divine revelation were not prolonged through it, so making it possible. Dr. Farrer has more than a suggestion of this in a different con-nection (p. 42)—"Development is development, and neither addition nor alteration. The first and decisive development is the work of the Apostolic age. The interpretative work of the Apostles must be understood as participation in the mind of Christ, through the Holy Ghost: they are the members, upon whom inflows the life of the Head."

Dr. Farrer's early disappointment arose from the fact that, child-like, he was looking for an encounter with a divine being who was an object in the world like other objects in the world. Even in adult life this expectation is difficult to eradicate. It is part of the problem referred to by Dr. Laurence Bendit in *Paranormal Cognition* (p. 53), the translation into terms of space and matter of things which, to the scientist, "are not there". "All description and expression is symbolic and can only be understood by the mind in terms of the time-space world."

We have to recognise, then, that our knowledge of universals comes only through the particulars, yet is not exhausted in the particulars, nor is to be described as an inference from the par-ticulars; that our knowledge of others comes only through their actions, yet is not exhausted in their actions nor to be described

[1] Pp. 37, 39 ff.

as only inference from their actions ; that knowledge of God comes only through events, or through the words of inspired men, or by way of our inmost thoughts and resolves, yet is not exhausted in the events, is not circumscribed by the human words, transcends our thoughts and resolves, and is not to be conceived as only an inference from any one of them or from all of them together.   The encounter of which we are speaking is something quite unique ; it is encounter with a person who is not there to be manipulated for our own purposes, who is not passive under our scrutiny ; who lays commands on us ; and who in the last resort lays claim legitimately to all we are and all we have.   Thus we are bound to say of all attempts to " prove " the existence of God, and in particular of the attempt which reaches its zenith in Aquinas, that a God who is arrived at by argument is no God ; conviction concerning God's exist- ence is not a result of philosophical inquiry, but one of the pre- suppositions of it.   We could not even begin to seek God unless He had already found us.

It is told of Thomas Aquinas that he startled his teacher at school by suddenly bursting out with the question, " What is God? "   Long afterwards he gave his own answer.   The most proper name for God is *He Who Is*.   From the master, Aristotle, he acquired the most Grecian conception of God, as the spectator of all time and all existence ; and this had to be reconciled with the revelation given from Christian sources.   Here were *two* authorities, each final ; and here therefore lay the certainty of hopeless tension.   The worst feature of the Thomist philo- sophy is no doubt that it is not prepared to follow the argument where it leads.   The conclusion is already determined.   (Ber- trand Russell reports in his *History of Western Philosophy* (p. 474) the storm which broke over him when he dared to criticise Aristotle.   His teachings were sacrosanct to the Roman Catholic believer.)   And this refusal to follow the argument where it leads is, in effect, a failure of *faith*.   It is pessimism— the fear that the ultimate will not be what we think it should be.   And the pessimism comes, in this instance, through the stressing of correct doctrine instead of faith in God.   It might appear that the other " final " authority for the Thomist is the Bible ; but it is, of course, the Bible as interpreted by the Church, and to the decisions of the Church Councils is given complete and unquestioning trust. Growing up though it did in the atmosphere of reverence and worship, this philosophy was nevertheless a denial of the Spirit, both in the Spirit's work in the development of Reason (for the Aristotelian philosophy is definitive) and in the Spirit's guidance of believers (for beyond the Church, represented by her Councils, there is no appeal). It is the claim of this philosophy that the existence of God and His fundamental attributes can be demonstrated by Reason alone, that Revelation is not required for the knowledge of God, but only to complete it and to give knowledge of salvation. God, as Aristotle's *Actus Purus,* contains within Himself all perfections. Since His existence and His essence are one the proposition that God exists must be self-evident in itself (since the predicate is the same as the subject); but it is not self-evident to us, for man's intellect cannot conceive what God is. His existence must be demonstrated " by means of those things which are more evident to us though less so in themselves, that is by its effects ".[1] The difficulty, of course, lies in attaching any meaning to " a proposition which is self-evident in itself " though not to us, since propositions do not go about knowing themselves. And there is a corresponding difficulty involved in this treatment of the attributes of God. Those " perfections " in God to which primary consideration is given are those of the " metaphysical " attributes such as unity, infinity, simplicity, and these perfections are considered in Himself independent of all relations with the world. " Sublime audacity ", says Dr. W. R. Matthews " which elevates the created mind to assume a knowledge of God 'in Himself'! " and he goes on to indicate how this sublime audacity has its nemesis.[2]

It is at this point that the carefully built system begins to break down. The " metaphysical " attributes take control. There is no room left in the divine nature for God's personal communication of Himself in love to mankind. God is utterly self-sufficient in His own being, needing nothing; finding no enrichment and no joy in the life, the faith, the repentance, the adoration of His creatures. Creation, indeed, can find a place in the system only by what is plainly an intrusion: it can make no difference to God, can add nothing to His perfection. And

1 *Summa Theol.* I. a. q. 2: I.c.
2 W. R. Matthews, *God in Christian Thought and Experience,* p. 102.

Redemption loses most of its meaning. The God of the scholastic philosophy is not wounded by the sins of men, nor can He rejoice at the prodigal's return from the far country. We have a Creator who cannot take pleasure in the works of His hands and a Redeemer who can experience only a "metaphorical" satisfaction in the sinner who repents.

"When Aristotle was enlisted in the service of Christian theology, the recruit became the general and the philosopher prevailed over the evangelist."[1]

It is true that all this is combined with reverence and worship; but worship and thought fall apart. A valiant attempt is made by Dr. Mascall in his book with the title *He Who Is* to deal sympathetically with this conundrum. The Thomist tradition holds that there is something more fundamental than Love; something out of which love itself and all the other divine attributes must spring—and that is *Being;* and we therefore are confronted by a dilemma, since worship is in fact directed *not* to pure Being but to a personal and loving God. Dr. Mascall's reply is[2] that what is primary for devotion need not be primary for theology. The reply is not quite convincing for, if what is primary for worship is not necessarily primary for theology, we are exposed to the alarming deduction that either devotion is worshipping an unreal God and is merely sentimental, or that theology is constructing an abstract and unreal fiction. To depart from the New Testament teaching that God is Love is to run the risk of the most disturbing consequences. It is not an accident that the same Thomas Aquinas, as Dr. Inge reminds us,[3] can coolly state his dreadful conviction, "In order that nothing may be wanting to the felicity of blessed spirits, a perfect view is granted them of the torments of the damned".

Professor Ferré's book *The Christian Understanding of God* is a useful corrective to the tendency to return to the scholastic type of reasoning. He emphasises the truth that there is no *abstract* love: love is always the behaviour of persons (p. 29).[4]

1 W. R. Matthews, *God in Christian Thought and Experience*, p. 227.
2 *Op. cit.* p. 11.
3 *Mysticism in Religion*, p. 68. *Vide Summa Theol.* III. Suppl. Q. 94. 1.
4 Cf. Emil Brunner, *The Church in the New Social Order*, S.C.M. Press 1952, p. 11: "The essence of the Kingdom is love ; God's love given to man, man's love towards man. Love, however, cannot be institutionalised. The *Ekklesia* is in no way an institution, an order, but a personal life flowing from beyond the temporal world ; it is God's own life sharing itself with men through the Mediator, Christ."

And he affirms once again that love is never sufficient unto itself (p. 32). The divine urge to create the world is not a deficiency in God's nature, for God would not be diminished if the world were to pass away, but is the inevitable outcome of the divine love, which needs the world, or at least needs men to be His children. "If God is absolute love, what follows? The very nature of the ultimate, the absolute, God as love, a self-existing and self-directing being, is to have relations. As a matter of fact, love freely creates relations. Such is its nature. Since, moreover, love does not manufacture puppets, because it is basically not causative but purposive, love not only has and creates relations, but also redeems these relations to whatever extent there is need of it. Love as the absolute by nature reclaims the mistakes and reconciles the over-againstness of finite freedom" (p. 19).

RELIGIOUS EXPERIENCE

What part, then, is played by religious experience in our coming to a knowledge of God? In particular, is there any organ or innate sense which gives direct knowledge of God? Aquinas answers these questions by condemning what is called "ontologism". The Thomist contribution falls naturally into two parts.

(1) If there *is* any specific sense which apprehends God directly, it is maintained, it is different from all the other senses in this at least that, whereas the bodily senses can report on the presence of a physical object simply by being turned to it, there is clearly no religious sense which can at any time and at will produce a similar apprehension of God.

This is not at all convincing, because it sets off on the wrong track. Might not the difference, we are constrained at once to ask, lie not in the percipient organ but in the object perceived? Some objects—in particular those physical ones of which the argument speaks—are static; they "stay put"; they show no initiative; they take no part in the proceedings. But there are other objects which show signs of independence—in particular, human beings, many of whom are not easy to understand because they are far above the rest of us; they pass through the world, but the world, as we say, does not *appreciate* them. In the apprehension of God, the initiative lies all with Him. And if this seems to suggest favouritism—that God reveals Himself to some more often, more readily, more fully, than to others, the reply is that it is not favouritism ; the truth, rather, is found in such a metaphor as that of Dr. C. S. Lewis. The light is inevitably reflected better from a bright mirror than from a dusty one.

(2) The second part of the Thomist contribution argues that religious experience may indeed be convincing, but it is ineffable. Those who have had the most intimate religious experience are all agreed on this matter and we may therefore be compelled to ask of such experiences as Gilson asked after reading accounts of them given by William James, "I still want to know if my religious experience is an experience of God, or an experience of myself".[1] The experience may be absolutely convincing to the man who has it, and quite unconvincing to everyone else. Hence in Roman Catholic mystical theology, "revelations" are discouraged, rather than sought after. (There may, of course, be a quite obvious reason for this in the desire to avoid every form of Montanism : the authoritative church cannot give free rein to the individual's spiritual idiosyncrasies and private revelations.) It is supernatural charity, rather than revelations, that unites the soul with God. In the spiritual marriage, spectacular mystical phenomena almost invariably cease.

It scarcely needs to be said that this view of religious experience is an extremely narrow one. Reluctant to admit direct apprehension or immediate knowledge of God, and condemning it as "ontologism", Roman Catholic theology admits as the sole exception the mystic union, and there it is God who seizes upon the soul. (Again, of course, there may be a quite obvious ulterior motive at work, consciously or not ; since it is essential for a church that lives by ordering the lives of its adherents to retain the necessity of the traditional apparatus of worship.) The narrow interpretation of "religious experience" leads the Thomist to think that he has elsewhere the key to belief in a God who is personal. This is given, he thinks, in reason : it does not necessarily come by religious experience.

In his chapter on "The Urgent Presence", Principal Baillie

[1] *Reason and Revelation in the Middle Ages*, p. 67.

says of the Roman condemnation of ontologism "it is really intending to condemn the view that the knowledge of God is *innate*, part of a fixed and given constitution with which the human species was initially endowed ; and that indeed is a view to be rejected. But what ought to be affirmed in opposition to it is not the inferential nature of our knowledge of God, but rather the *continual* invasion of our life by His holy Presence." [1]

When all has been done that must be done through Word and Church and Sacrament to reveal to sinful man the depth and wonder of God's redeeming love, there comes at last the luminous moment in which a man stands in immediate encounter with God. The question is thus partly a matter of words—Can we use the term *immediate* of this encounter, by whatever means it may have been brought about? I believe that we can. It is of the unmediated presence of the divine that a man is made aware, and this awareness does not detract from his conviction that the Son is the sole mediator in creation and in revelation as in the redemption of mankind, nor from the surety that the love of Christ lies at the heart of that divine paradox whereby in redeeming mankind for Himself God is ever seeking that which His perfection does not need.

DIVINE LAW AND DIVINE MYSTERY

The right conclusion lies, therefore, in a properly conceived ontologism, which takes into account man's fallen nature and God's election (which sometimes may look to our eyes very like favouritism) and remembers always that the medium of revelation is the Word of God. Then one more problem arises. Where response to revelation is a right response and faith is pure, it will always be impossible to indicate the march-fence between divine action and human reaction. Thus the boundaries are apt to be obscured also between illumination of man's thought and judgment of it, since illumination may come through judgment, and judgment may happen by way of illumination. One matter is clear, however. The vital consideration and the one that must be considered in this connection even to over-emphasis is that man's knowledge of God is under judgment. It is always

[1] *Our Knowledge of God*, p. 174.

in danger of slipping down into complacence or pride. Yet judgment need not be finally for condemnation. Its aim is man's salvation, and the judgment is a call to man to submit himself to God. Not slavishly, but in the loyalty and gratitude and devotion of a son. Man's knowledge of God and man's salvation are thus brought into close connection. The concept of "saving knowledge" will be examined later.[1] Here we look more particularly at the familiar contradiction. It is given in the words of St. Paul (Phil. ii. 12-13): "Work out your own salvation with fear and trembling. For it is God which worketh in you both to will and to do of His good pleasure." The apparent contradiction is not confined to religion. A notable scientist of last century, James Clerk Maxwell, once said that "it is a universal condition of the enjoyable that the mind must believe in the existence of a law yet have a mystery to move about in." The *law* is plain enough—a man must fight his own battles, or perish. And there have been men of strong character, self-reliant and self-sufficient, who were prepared to live on the assumption that this law was all, that there is no mystery, that man simply stands alone in his struggles. On the bitter day of March, when Beethoven was dying, his biographer tells, storms of snow and hail raged outside, a blinding flash of lightning lit up the room, and a peal of thunder seemed to rock the whole house. The dying musician raised himself in bed, looked with gallant eyes into the tempest and shook his clenched fist. Then he fell back exhausted. It was his last gesture of defiance to that fate against which he had struggled valiantly all his life through. We know, as Beethoven himself knew in his mystical piety, that such defiances are tragically pathetic when we consider our frailty in the scheme of things. We are the creatures of time and circumstance. The battle is not always to the strong. But there is more—and worse. In that dramatic glimpse of the end of Beethoven's life, we might, for most people, put temptations in the place of the elements. The helplessness of man becomes then all the more evident and all the more dangerous in its consequences. It will not do to paint an idealistic picture of life, leaving out its temptations. When de Florian was writing his lovely pastoral descriptions, a French critic said of them, "They are very charming, but a

[1] Ch. viii, p. 225.

wolf would improve them". We cannot ignore the existence
of the demonic. If we have never trembled before the dark
possibilities of the human heart, we have not really taken life
seriously. St. Paul had no illusions on this point. He had
watched the athletes training for the Greek games and pre-
paring themselves by mock-engagements; but, he says, when
you come to do battle with the temptations of the world, then
it is no sham-fight. "I maul and master my body, to bring it
into control." To that extent, man *has* to work out his own
salvation. The choice is his, freely and deliberately made.
"Myself I willed it" says St. Augustine "myself I nilled it".
And that is an essential truth in the life of the soul—our
individual responsibility for our conduct, our character, our
eternal destiny. But the same St. Augustine is found expressing
the complementary truth—and the greater half of the truth.
He recognises that there was some power which took matters
out of his hands when as a young man he was going to make
certain shipwreck. Looking back on it, he said, "Thou O God
wert at the helm, though very secretly". "Tossed about with
every wind, yet was I secretly piloted by Thee."

There *is* help. We do not stand alone. At least, we need
not. Professor Henry Drummond once heard of an acquaintance, a coachman, who was ruining his life by drunkenness,
and intemperance of all kinds. He went to him, in the friendly
way which no one could resent and few could resist, and asked,
"What would you do if your two horses ran away, turned down
a steep hill, and were in danger of disaster?" "Nothing",
replied the coachman. "By that time they would be beyond my
strength. I could only wait for the end." (He knew quite well
what was the reference.) "But if, in your exhaustion you found
a strong man on the box beside you, what would you do?"
"Give *him* the reins." That was the way of salvation which
St. Paul had in mind, even when he wrote, "Work out your
own salvation". We see it from what goes before—he has been
speaking of the work of Jesus which has made deliverance sure:
there *is* that strong one to take the reins. And we see it from
what follows. "It is God which worketh in you."

Over this well-known contradiction good people have been
sharply divided; and theologians have spilled much ink and not
a little blood. Nor has the debate been confined to Christian

theologians. In the Hindu philosophies of the great flowering
in the thirteenth century, the discussion went on briskly between
the same two schools of thought, one proclaiming the *kitten-
hold* theory, because of its belief that man had as little part to
play in his salvation as has the kitten which is carried off to
safety by the mother-cat; the other propounding the *baby-
monkey* view, believing that man makes his partial contribution,
as the monkey holds on with all the tenacity of its tiny paws.
It would be a pity if such controversy ceased, for that would
mean that we were content to believe that there was no mystery
left worth speculating upon in these grave matters; but it would
be still more unfortunate if discussion were to obscure the real
truth which the author is setting forth, that *we* cannot work
out anything except as *God works in us.* We realise now,
perhaps, that all efforts to mark out the ground meticulously
between divine grace and human faith may go far astray. In
the inward process of salvation God does all, and also man does
all. For receiving in faith, man is responsible, but it is God who
takes precedence! We can work *out* our deliverance only as
God works *in* us.

We saw that it is not only the religious man who is conscious
of the seeming contradiction. Perhaps General Omar Bradley
had something of this in mind when he wrote his *Soldier's Story.*
He describes the secret staff conferences for OVERLORD, the
invasion of Europe in June 1944. To the private soldier these
must always be mystery—and he dedicates his book: "To
those Soldiers who must often have wondered WHY they were
going where they did." Then comes the dramatic moment when
the decision was taken. He puts it in five vivid words: "The
Plan had taken over." A little later, he sees it in terms of
human struggle and human hazard. "Though we could see
it dimly through the haze and hear the echo of its guns, the
battle belonged that morning to the thin, wet line of khaki that
dragged itself ashore on the Channel coast of France." That is
the humanist way of putting the apparent contradiction. The
mysterious Plan does it all—and the fighting soldier does it all.
Finally, he allows the conviction shyly to escape that there was
a more profound mystery than that of the Plan. In the assault
on Utah beach, the navy missed its guide-point and landed the
regiment 2000 yards south of its mark. " Apparently Providence

had put its hand to the helm. Not only were the underwater obstacles planted less thickly on these beaches, but the shore defences proved less formidable than they were found to be farther north." [1] He uses (unwittingly, I expect) the metaphor of Augustine—" Apparently Providence had put its hand to the helm."

God is active on man's behalf, eager and anxious that man should come through nobly and worthily. That is part of the profound hopefulness which Christianity brought to the world. God sees, cares, helps. He is at the helm, though very secretly. At one stage, the only safety may be to give up the reins to One who can avert disaster; but at a later stage, we are no longer meant to lean altogether. God gives men something to do. During the period between the wars, one of the inherent tragedies of an industrial age was realised in the phenomenon of wide-spread unemployment, and with that phenomenon came the miniature tragedy seen in the emergence of the grim, ill-omened word "unemployable". There were men who had been so long out of work that their skill had vanished, as there are always some whose skill is not suitable even for a mechanical age. They may lose the dignity of life that comes from the self-respect of craftsmanship. So, looking on the poor capacities of mankind in the spiritual world, we might imagine that in the eyes of God His children must appear as simply unemployable; yet God thinks out ways in which they may turn a hand to His work, even at the risk—and it is a solemnising thought—of damaging delicate machinery; for men are entrusted with their own lives and with the lives of countless others whom they inevitably influence; with human souls, and with the divine plan for the world. Our knowledge of God comes pre-eminently from the consciousness of the salvation which He has wrought in us, but it comes partly also from acting in obedience to God's call. We are fellow-labourers with God. There are, apparently, some things which God does not choose to do, unless we help Him. If the sick child is not skilfully attended, it will die: God cannot save it without the aid of a trained surgeon's knife; a nurse's care; a hygienic ward; a suitable bed; appropriate nourishment. Service is "the rent we pay for our room on earth". Thus there are two threads

[1] Pp. 264, 271, 275.

interwoven in the texture of this passage from St. Paul's letter—not only working the work of God, but willing the will of God. To obey the divine will is not simply submission. It means consecration of the entire life; definite things to be done, high adventures, heroic obedience. The Book of Common Prayer sums it up excellently: It is to love the things which God commands and to desire that which He doth promise.

CHAPTER VI

THE TESTIMONY OF THE HOLY SPIRIT

OVER against wrong ideas of Authority we set the *Testimony of the Holy Spirit*. The Word of God, said Calvin, is like the old man's spectacles, which make clear to his eyes much that had been dim and confused before, dissipating the darkness and showing the true God clearly: but in the following chapter [1] he has to meet the specious suggestion that the Church's judgment is needed to give authority to the Scriptures. The truth, he says, is very different. God does not give daily responses from heaven: therefore the Scriptures are the only records to which He has been pleased to consign His truth for perpetual remembrance. How foolish then to imagine that the eternal and inviolable truth of God should depend on the suffrage of the Church, as if the good-will of men were required to determine where reverence is due. That would indeed be a precarious authority. All that the Church can do is to acknowledge Scripture as divine truth. Nothing can be more absurd than "the fiction, that the power of judging Scripture is in the Church, and that on her nod its certainty depends. When the Church receives it, and gives it the stamp of her authority, she does not make that authentic which was otherwise doubtful or controverted, but, acknowledging it as the truth of God, she, as in duty bound, shows her reverence by an unhesitating assent." And if we ask, How shall we know that it is in fact the divine Word which confronts us? it is just the same as if we asked, How shall we distinguish light from darkness, white from black, sweet from bitter? "Scripture bears upon the face of it as clear evidence of its truth, as white and black do of their colour, sweet and bitter of their taste." Scripture is its own evidence. Our conviction of its truth is derived from a higher source than human guesses and judgments and reasons. It comes from "the secret testimony of the Spirit" (*ab arcano testimonio Spiritus*). The Spirit which spoke to the

[1] *Institutes*, bk. I, ch. vii.

163

writers must speak to the readers. Scripture can give a saving knowledge of God only when its certainty is founded on the inward persuasion of the Holy Spirit. The confirmation of human testimony is useful, if kept in subordination to that chief and highest proof, but it is foolish to attempt to prove to infidels that the Scripture is the Word of God. That knowledge can come only by faith.[1]

There are two points in Calvin's exposition here which call for comment. (1) *The Church simply acknowledges the Word of God.* As in its rite of ordination to the ministry, the Church is just publicly acknowledging what God has done. As God calls a man to the ministry and the Church proclaims the fact of the call, so the Church does not make the Bible authentic, but proclaims the truth which it finds there. It pleased God to appoint the Scriptures as His special mode of utterance, and this lies beyond our speculation: it must simply be accepted. So the argument runs. The trouble is that a similar argument can easily be constructed to give the first place to the inner light or to the Church. There is always a danger in taking refuge in a mystery: the same right may be claimed by other schools of thought. (2) The second point is therefore the crucial one. *Scripture is self-authenticating.* The Church is not needed to identify the Word: the Word announces itself and silences doubt. Calvin deals with the passage which is frequently quoted from Augustine against such a position as his.[2] When Augustine said that he would not believe the Gospel were he not moved by the authority of the Church, he was speaking, we must remember (cf. *supra*, p. 27) in the heat of controversy with the Manicheans. And, secondly, we must note that the suggestion which some have read into the words is nowhere else discernible in his writings. Professor Burleigh points out, in particular, that you will search in vain for such a thought in the *Confessions*.[3] The truth is grasped, Augustine believed, because the mind has its own interior teacher who is Christ Himself, the very **Truth.**

---

[1] *Institutes*, bk. 1, ch. viii, § 13.
[2] The sentence is in Augustine's *Contra Epistolam Manichaei quam vocant Fundamenti*, c. 6.
[3] J. H. S. Burleigh, *The City of God*, p. 96.

THE CHURCH IS JUDGED BY THE WORD

The difficulty lies, surely, in this further fact that the Spirit, the Inward Master, employs some medium through which to testify. That medium may not be simply identified with the inner light of a flash of private interpretation. The Church enters again as the fellowship of Christian people to whom, rather than to the private Christian, revelation comes. Unhappily, there may be a Church that acts without the Spirit, and then it is not the Christian Church and not the medium of revelation. The Church's witness can be unworthy and inadequate; and the Church can far more readily go wrong and lead men astray than can the Scriptures. The Church has a duty to cherish the Word and to elucidate the Word; but the Church is always *under the judgment of the Word*.

Here once more we see the familiar process unfolding in the meeting of the soul with Christ. Men learn *about* Him in *Scripture;* then there appears a point at which nothing is added, no further information is conveyed, but a light shines, a page is illumined, a challenge is made clear, the flame appears. The inner witness of the Spirit is at work. It is in the Bible that we meet with Christ, but it is this meeting with Christ that makes the Bible the Word of God. We believe in the Bible because we believe in Christ, not *vice versa*. Without the Spirit everything is seen through the mists of sinful error. It is the light of the Spirit which enables us to see the self-revelation of God in Jesus Christ. The true preacher of the Gospel is he who points men through the Word to the Lord of the Word.

THE CONTENT OF THE WORD

At this stage we ought to notice that one of the most severe of the difficulties encountered by the contemporary Theology of Crisis is that of giving definite content to the Word of God. It is its inevitable, almost unconscious aim to give it the familiar content which religion has traditionally had; but there is a hindrance: for words like justice, grace, Father, and many other Scriptural terms, because they appear in the Bible, do not cease to mean what they signify in ordinary human speech. Most

readers would acknowledge that the Scriptural use transmutes
and enriches a word ; but this theology advocates a case, not
of enrichment only but of radical and complete alteration, so
that not even analogy remains as a guide. It is this, perhaps,
more than any other feature of such a theology, which makes
it extremely hard for the philosopher to enter the discussion ;
and much is lost by both sides. This unfortunate schism between
sincere seekers after truth must remain unless the conception
of the *Testimonium Spiritus Sancti Internum* is broadened in
several ways. It must be realised that the Spirit is at work in
man's acquisition of knowledge of the created world ; for without that, there would be nothing but perversion and pagan
idolatry ; and that the Spirit is at work in the interpretation
of history, for without that, history would be ambiguous and
opaque ; that the Spirit is active in the mandates of conscience,
for without that, conscience would be at the mercy of man's
measureless capacity for self-delusion, and it must be realised
that the Spirit is at work in the individual's decisions and in the
individual's vocation.

It is equally true, however, that in another sense the conception of the Spirit's witness must be narrowed. No light can be
given to those who are proud, or spiritually myopic, nor to
those who are narrowly dogmatic, unaware of their liability to
error. Before the *testimonium Spiritus sancti* can operate, there
must be an attitude of sincerity towards truth already offered.
That truth may have come through the medium of the Bible,
or of the Church ; through the impact of human history or
through loyalty to conscience. Loss of the inward witness may
arise through the neglect of any of these ; but it is also important
to realise that the loss may arise from excessively timid attachment to them. A Bible transformed into a fetish, a Church
turned dictator, an interpretation of history on predetermined
lines, such as those of the Marxist, or conscience become
tyrannical through some pathological condition or simply
through forgetfulness of the fact that it is the conscience of
a man and thus the subordinate, not the master, of divine
revelation—these may all become barriers to the entrance of new
truth. In a witty passage, with malice towards none but Barth,
Professor Etienne Gilson shows how the hindrance may be
located in a rigid orthodoxy. "God speaks, says Karl Barth,

and man listens and repeats what God has said. But unfortunately, as is inevitable as soon as a man makes himself God's interpreter, God speaks and the Barthian listens and repeats what Barth has said."[1] How easily the tables can be turned is seen by re-writing the passage with a simple change: "God speaks, says the neo-Thomist, and man listens and repeats what God has said. But unfortunately as is inevitable as soon as a fallible Church makes itself God's interpreter, God speaks and the devout Roman Catholic listens and repeats what the Pope has said." Distortion of truth and the avoidance of the challenge of truth must inevitably lead, and have often led, to spiritual blindness.[2]

THE CONTRIBUTION OF S. L. FRANK

A wiser antidote to authoritarianism than that suggested by Professor Gilson is given in a notable book written in notable circumstances by Semyon Ludwigovitch Frank. He was born in Moscow in 1877, became a convinced Marxist in his academic years, then a penetrating critic of Marxism; and finally, like Berdyaev and Bulgakov, became a Christian. He was first a lecturer in philosophy in St. Petersburg, then professor in Moscow, and in 1922 was arrested by the Soviet government on a charge similar to that which was laid against Socrates of "exerting harmful influences on youth". Exile took him to Germany but in 1936 he was uprooted once again with the rise to power of the National Socialists under Hitler; and he found refuge in the south of France. When disaster fell upon France in 1940 it was possible for him to communicate only with extreme caution with his son Victor in Britain. His manuscript was sent, a few pages at a time, and in such minute handwriting because of postal restrictions that no typist could decipher it and his son had to copy it out for the translator. The last pages were safely dispatched only a short time before

---

[1] *Christianisme et Philosophie*, p. 151.
[2] Cf. Professor Nels Ferré, *The Christian Understanding of God*, p. 180. "On the one hand, it is dangerous not to put emphatic stress on God's work in the Church, the Bible, the creed or the sacraments; while on the other, perhaps our easiest way to hide ourselves from God is behind these. The Word of God is always a living Word, and though the letter is needed by the Spirit, the letter as letter always kills."

the interruption of communications in October 1942. The
manuscript was published as *God With Us.*[1]

It is the First Meditation of this book which is of special
interest to us at this stage. In examining the nature of faith,
Frank inquires whether it is to be described as confidence or
as certainty. Much of our daily life depends on confidence,
our trust in buyers and sellers ; our reliance on friends who will
not, we firmly believe, prove unfaithful. The activity of every
day is based on a confidence which cannot be justified by
demonstration ; it cannot be proved, and we do not ask for
proofs. Sometimes, it is true, actuality disappoints us, showing
that our confidence is not logical at all, but moral ; a matter,
therefore, of probability, not of binding necessity. When New-
man built his *Grammar of Assent* on this type of confidence
he was confusing the calculus of probability on which our
practical life is founded with a very different thing, religious
faith. The object of faith is not the more probable, but the
very opposite, the less probable. It is foolishness to the Greeks.
The existence of God is not the most likely hypothesis. There
are no scientific proofs of the existence of a God of love. Pious
efforts to explain the tragedies of personal life are derided by
the sceptics and are denounced in the book of Job by God Himself as blasphemous. If, then, reason cannot be quoted in
justification of our trust, may we fall back on authority? Should
we take refuge in Scriptures, or in the tradition of the Church ;
in the supposed infallibility of a Pope ; or in the actual words
of the founder of Christianity? The answer must be negative ;
for, although we may have in the fact of authority a satisfactory
description of the manner in which the religion arose in the first
instance, we must not press what is only a psychological account
of origins till it takes on the dignity of an exposition of the
nature and essence of faith. In appealing to authority, there is
always an involvement in a circular argument. Who is to
choose the authority to which man is invited to bow? And what
substantiates the claim of the authority to sole reverence? We
must return, sooner or later, to *direct insight,* immediate certainty, or self-evidence. In the last resort, faith is an encounter
of the human heart with God ; God's manifestation of Himself
to a man. Frank believes that there are people alive today who

[1] Jonathan Cape, 1946.

are cut off from all human channels of approach to God among whom nevertheless conversions take place. This can only be by the direct action of God on the soul of man. "We find that some Gospel saying suddenly melts their hearts with the unutterable beauty of God's truth" (p. 21). Every believer has at some time experienced this *faith as certainty;* and those who have never felt it should not be called believers, even if they recognise the authority of all that the Church holds sacred. Faith is knowledge—a direct knowledge of God, which may be clearer in babes than in scribes versed in the Scriptures, the law and tradition.

This attitude to revelation appears to bring us to complete subjectivism; to dispense with the given revealed faith; even, may it not be said, to make Christ unnecessary, since trust in Christ and obedience to Him seem not to be of the essence of faith. But in the meantime, Frank is concerned to show what a monstrosity we have in the religious "wager" proposed by Pascal (*Pensées*, 233). The stakes, says Pascal, are altogether different when we are betting on faith and when we choose unbelief. If we stake on faith and lose, we lose only the paltry things of a brief earthly life; but if we stake on unbelief and lose, we lose the prospect of eternal bliss and run the risk of eternal damnation. Thus, however small are the chances that our faith is true, consideration of the risk involved and of possible gain makes us wager on faith. It is true that Frank overlooks one consideration. Pascal intended the argument to express something quite profound and quite true, namely that, if we start on the path of faith "at random", we discover by experience as we go on that it is the true path. Faith is an experiment that ends in an experience. But the *wager* gives a very bad expression of this truth. The unbeliever can say, "I do not believe that God exists; and, even if He did exist, I should prefer to appear before Him and say, 'I have sought conscientiously and, finding no convincing evidence for faith, have chosen to be sincere and remain in unbelief'." Or he may say to us, "If your God exists, He is a God Who respects truth and sincerity: He would prefer honest scepticism to belief that is motivated by the possible gains of eternity. I do not for a moment imagine that He will condemn me for a sincere error."

Faith cannot be forced: it is by its very nature, says Frank, free, involuntary, irrepressible, easy, joyful, spontaneous. Somewhere, therefore, this faith as confidence is based on faith as certainty and certainty must mean the actual presence of the object of thought *in our consciousness*. Certainty thus means religious experience, a phrase which was apparently coined by William James, but undoubtedly misunderstood by him, as shown by the fact that he wanted corroboration of his own experience and was, we are told, impatient to die so that he might at last attain access to the mysteries of divine reality.

Is there, then, such a thing as supersensuous experience? Outside religion, Frank believes, music gives the clearest example. It is true that musical sounds must reach us through the ear, by way of the sense of hearing; but it is also true that the thing of which they speak, which cannot be put into words, is directly apprehended by the mind. Another instance may be found in architecture—"music frozen in space"; but best of all is the case of goodness. When we experience this quality of human life, it is by way of what can only be called *encounter*; and our encounter with goodness is closely analogous to our perception of beauty. It is not merely by chance that we speak of "moral beauty". Frank quotes the interesting history of a Russian writer of the nineteenth century, Gleb Uspensky. He had no religious beliefs and little perception of beauty; but one day in Paris he wandered into the Louvre, and was confronted by the Vénus de Milo. At that moment he experienced a change of heart, which he described in the phrase "she put me straight". His dejection vanished. He was convinced that there *is* truth and justice in the world. Frank holds that this man without knowing it had, by contemplating a Greek statue, passed through a genuine religious experience which brought him spiritual regeneration; and he quotes, in this connection, Turgenev, who, writing about the futility and tragic senselessness of human life and destiny, makes one significant reservation: "Of course Vénus de Milo is *more certain* than the principles of 1789."

Thus the argument is that both inspiration (which lies behind artistic creativeness) and moral decision mean encounter with the superhuman; mean the influx into the mind of forces which are not of earthly origin. Real faith, according to this argument, is knowledge by experience; and it renders doubt, negation, search, deliberation, and choice between two alternatives, quite meaningless.

It has been customary, says Frank, to divide reality into two categories, the material and the mental. There is a third. Call it the ideal. It includes Time; beauty; goodness; and all that is suggested by the Platonic "forms" or "ideas". But we remember the ancient dictum that "like is known by like"; as it was expressed by Plotinus. "If an eye were not similar to the sun we would not see the sun; if our spirit were not akin to the deity we could not apprehend God." We recall that St. John has said something not vastly different "Hereby know we that we dwell in Him and He in us, because He hath given us of His Spirit" (1 John iv. 13). The very important conclusion can be drawn that man, in the depths of his personality, is godlike. The soul is not a sealed vessel: there is fathomless depth in it, and in that depth it is open to God and in contact with Him. The ultimate state of the human soul is not loneliness, not solitude, but twinness (not *Einsamkeit* but *Zweisamkeit*). Thus, Frank concludes, faith is not an arbitrary, unverifiable assertion about something inaccessible to us, but a simple and self-evident recognition of a reality given in experience.

How, then, we are apt to inquire, can there be unbelievers at all? If there are, do they not appear to be simply the victims of divine neglect? God has not revealed Himself to them.

Frank's way of meeting this objection is not very satisfactory. He asserts, in effect, that belief is just a bit of extra knowledge over and above unbelief. "It is not a case of one person seeing white where another sees black; a believer differs from an unbeliever as a man with good eyesight differs from a short-sighted one, or a musical man from an unmusical one. In addition to what they perceive in common, a believer also perceives that which the unbeliever fails to notice and therefore denies. . . . The essence of unbelief lies in the consciousness that the world as a 'brute fact' is meaningless, blind and incomplete and the human self in it is doomed to loneliness and frustration; man's hopes and strivings can avail nothing against the indifferent and therefore cruel forces of nature, including the natural elementary passions of man. All this can and indeed must be recognised by the believer. In the last resort his only difference from the unbeliever is that he *supplements* the latter's experience by another—by the experience of a super-cosmic dimension of reality giving rise to the consciousness that the human soul is safe, secure, and at peace in those depths of being which are its home and resting-place."[1] Faith, as experience, cannot doubt its object: it can only doubt the relation of it to other facts. However grave and painful our religious doubts may be, they do not refer to the real object of faith but to something utterly different, namely, to reconciling that reality with other facts; to reconciling religious experience with our other, "earthly" experience.[2]

Some criticisms should be made at this point.

Frank's onslaught on authority is the flogging of a fairly dead horse, but a later chapter in this same book is worth reading; since he deals there with more urgent aspects of this question.

More important for us now is his description of faith as knowledge. We need not quarrel with the word, but we should require to add that faith is knowledge of a very special kind and *not* simply an additional quota or ration of the same kind of knowledge which is shared by the unbeliever. The knowledge of faith comes to judge, not only to supplement, that knowledge which is otherwise obtained. This very special type of knowledge is indeed that *confidence* in a Person which Frank has already passed by. It will not serve to say that the knowledge comes from an experience which renders doubt, negation, search quite meaningless; for so many have claimed to have such experience whose claims none would care to acknowledge. When Emanuel Swedenborg, at the age of fifty-five, was admitted to intercourse with angels and spirits through direct speech with them, while remaining conscious in the normal way of what was happening around him on this earth, he was naturally met with considerable scepticism concerning his claim. Anticipating objections of this kind, he wrote in his first theological work,[3] "I am well aware that many will insist that it is impossible to converse with spirits and angels during our life-time in this body; many will say that such intercourse must be mere fancy; some, that I have invented such relations in order to gain credit;

---

[1] Pp. 51-52.   [2] Cf. p. 53.   [3] *Arcana Coelestia*, § 68.

whilst others will make other objections. For all these, however, I care not, since I have seen, heard, and felt." But the plain truth is that there are illusory voices and there are deceptive visions. To prove their authenticity, voices and visions must convince the reason to which God speaks. When Frank speaks of self-evidence, he has adduced no argument to show that this self-evidence cannot lie in the sphere of personal trust. Surely it is true that confidence in God (transcendent as well as immanent) does not mean abandonment of reason. It is, on the contrary, a fulfilment and illumination of reason.

Certainty, says Frank, must be based on experience, and we may well agree; but "experience" is a very vague term; one of the most nebulous. It provides only the actuality of "a something". Yet he is surely on the right road when he lays stress on faith as encounter (*Begegnung*).

The most damaging criticism of Frank's immanent philosophy of religion arises at the stage where he says that we men are conscious, not merely of having been created by God as a fragile vessel is created by a potter, but also of being born from above, of the spirit, of God (John iii. 3, 5; 1 John iii. 9). For we have to ask him, Who is it who knows all this? Is it the natural man or the redeemed man? Frank makes the fatal mistake: he fails to deal at all adequately with man's sin. In a later meditation ("The Way of the Cross": ch. vii of his book) he takes up the question, but the treatment is slight; and, in any case, it ought to have consideration here, since the corruption of man's soul by his sin cannot fail to have its repercussions on his encounter with the divine.

It is inevitable that Frank should be compelled to face the question, What account can we give, on these terms, of the natural drift and tendency to unbelief? It cannot be solely an oversight on the part of God that He has failed to make Himself convincingly known. First, therefore, he notices that the act of faith involves experience of a transcendental reality. What we have is knowledge of something that is hidden: nevertheless, it *is* knowledge, and may even be certainty. This is a very remarkable phenomenon; it can at the moment only be registered as a fact—that we do know with immediate certainty something about the hidden content of reality. Examples are easily found outside the scope of faith—we know that the parts of space which lie beyond our sensuous experience have the same qualities and geometrical laws as those within the reach of our senses ; we know that the past and the future, which transcend our sense experience, have the same character and temporal flow as the present and the past which we have sensuously experienced. More important still, we know that the feelings and impulses of other minds are essentially the same as the feelings and impulses which are our own. Sometimes, indeed, we apprehend the hidden depths of other minds with absolute certainty. Religion, then, like every other experience thus analysed, has the dimension of depth or of distance. In philosophical terms, we have an immanent experience of a transcendental reality. We are aware of a living intimate contact with that which comes from afar. St. Augustine expresses it by saying: "Thou didst cry to me from afar . . . and I heard as the heart heareth." A message comes to us from beyond and " we feel the contact of other worlds " (Dostoevsky).

We can pause here to ask why Frank claims the possibility of certainty being obtainable in our knowledge of other minds, though he formerly denied the possibility in relations of trust and confidence. For these, he argued, only probability can be claimed. It seems more likely that the certainty is present just in those relations of trust and not in our knowledge of another's mental states. Suppose, for example, we have a friend to whom we have to appeal for counsel and help in a complicated situation. He acts on our behalf—wisely, as we knew he would. (We were quite *certain* about that; quite sure about his generous attitude to us ; quite certain that he would act in our best interest.) But he may in fact do something far wiser than anything we had ourselves contemplated—perhaps because he *is* wiser, or simply because he brings a fresh mind to the problem, and sees it unembarrassed by our personal implications. The point is that we cannot be certain about the precise workings of his mind. Certainty lies, if anywhere, in our trust in his good disposition towards us.

Frank misses this point, but he makes another, which is important for the psychology of religion. How is it, he asks, that unbelief is so easy and so widespread? His answer is this: Man is overwhelmingly a sensuous creature. He has to be: it is biologically essential that he should react swiftly to the immediate environment of his body. If his reactions fail, or are delayed or faulty, he may perish. Supersensuous experience, on the other hand, does not as a rule reach this intensity and this convincing power. In spite of all our high-sounding talk, what matters most to us earthly, carnal creatures is food, warmth, sunshine, the tangible presence of those we love. How hard it is to comfort a bereaved mother by the faith that her child lives now " in another world ". She wants the touch of a vanished hand, the sound of a voice that is still. All this is relevant to the study of belief. That which we call the voice of God comes to us not as a deafening shout which we cannot help attending to ; but as a " still small voice ". The easiest thing in the world is not to attend to it ; not to respond ; not to admit its existence.

Thus faith implies an act of will ; the control of attention ; the will to attend. " The will to believe is nothing other than the will to attend, to see, to observe, to perceive that which, once perceived, is unquestionable truth." Truth is offered with a clarity that admits of no doubt : all we have to do is to turn our eyes towards it. If we seek it keenly and whole-heartedly, it does " strike the eye " and is " given freely ". The only thing that is difficult and demands strenuous effort of moral will is to be ready to receive the gift, to go to meet the giver.

Frank anticipates a criticism.—This inner religious experience gives no clear and reliable knowledge of the nature of God. Can we, relying on it, know even that God is personal? Frank's answer is to admit the charge implied in the question. For him, God cannot be subsumed under the conception of personality. His nature is beyond all thought, inexpressible. (He quotes Goethe's ironical formula : *"Der Professor ist eine Person, Gott ist keine."*) To say " A personal God exists " is not an adequate expression of faith. Both words, " exists " and " personal " narrow down and impoverish the true idea of God. What we should say is not "God is a person" but "I stand in a personal relation to God"—that is the real testimony of faith. Just as we know the sun in the heavens not by looking at it, but by experiencing its light and warmth, so we know God by the effects of His presence ; He penetrates and irradiates our heart. Since God is love, he who has no love for his brother does not know God or believe in Him. To say "God exists" is almost an expression of *un*belief: if we are profoundly conscious of His presence here and now, we could not presume to speak of Him in the third person—and almost as if He were absent. In common with the existential theologians, Frank affirms that in human communion, and still more clearly in communion of man with the divine, the "thou" precedes the "he". Communion with another human being takes place directly, in and through mutual contact. Only later and derivatively the "thou" is transformed into "he". "Only in so far as we remember the meeting and are intellectually conscious of it can we formulate the judgment 'he exists'." Even so, we learn of the existence of God because in the depths of our hearts we "hear His voice" and have the unutterable experience which we call communion with God.[1] Thus, for Frank, dogma is not the most important factor in belief. Liturgical expression is more important than dogma. Many dogmas are obsolete or at least obsolescent. The test of a living dogma is its significance as a practical guide in life. But this must not blind us to the fact that dogmas which at first sight may seem abstruse and theoretical may in fact belong to the very heart of living faith, and he quotes the notorious case of Thomas Carlyle saying of the Arian controversy on *homoousia* and *homoiousia* that Christendom was rent over a semi-vowel; but, as a blind old man, not long before his death, exclaiming as he listened to the reading of the Gospel, "Yes, if you are really God, it is all true; but if you are only a man, why should you know better than I do?" The quarrel about an iota was the controversy as to whether Jesus was a created human being, merely "like God" or whether the true essence of Godhead was actually present in Him—and that distinction is far from trifling.

Frank's final chapter in this first meditation is concerned with authority and revelation; but, when he formulates the equation: Revelation *equals* religious experience *equals* encounter with God, he still leaves unanswered the question, *How* does God bring about this encounter? Is it through Nature, History, Scripture, Church? Is it through the person and work of Jesus? This question remains open.

The Society of Friends faced a similar problem. At first they thought of the Inner Light as being divorced from man's

[1] *Vide* p. 78.

normal faculties, supernaturally placed in man like a candle in a lantern. The same attitude is no doubt persistent in their thought and practice even today, as it is still in the prejudice of many good Presbyterians against "read sermons"; but modern Quakers have in general a sounder philosophy and are prepared to think of the Spirit as speaking through our natural faculties.

If we share this view, we are, it would seem, committed to the conclusion that there is no infallible test by which revelation can be clearly and finally distinguished from the highest reaches of human discovery; yet we must aver that there is a timeless truth which cannot perish and there is also truth which has been reached through man's thinking and which, through the efforts of subsequent thought, will be superseded. In the first category may be placed the certainties of mathematics and of logic and the convictions of moral obligation. Of divine truth it must further be said that it comes by the act of God in history. (That is what the Fourth Gospel is constantly emphasising.) It is not an isolated gleam but a steady illumination of events. It might seem natural therefore to conclude that the remainder of the New Testament is given to interpretation of events which have already occurred and to the testimony of those who have read of or been told about the earthly life, the redemptive death, and the victorious rising again of Jesus Christ. That would be a mistaken conclusion. Events continued to take place. We think not only of the dramatic happenings of Pentecost and of the appearance of Christ to St. Paul on the road to Damascus, but of the true encounter of many souls with their Living Lord. These too are "events"; historic happenings in which the Risen Christ acted and spoke. The fellowship of the Spirit, which is the Church, is the realm in which such events take place.

THE BIBLE AND THE CHURCH

The witness of the Holy Spirit has not always received adequate treatment or been given sufficient prominence in the Christian Churches of the West. The Roman Church has neglected the doctrine of the Spirit because of a fear of the consequences of new truth on its own position in the world; and in those circles of Protestantism where the tendency was towards belief in the verbal inerrancy of the text of Scripture, less than justice has been done to the work of the Holy Spirit's testimony. Where Church and Bible appear to be in conflict it is to be remembered constantly that the Church to which authority belongs is not the Church of today or the Church of any past day ; not this or that branch, division, or denomination of the Church, however numerous and however confident, but the continuous fellowship of faithful Christian believers in every age. The witness from such a source is of the most vital significance ; but nevertheless the Church of every age, in every branch, division, and denomination, stands under the judgment of the written Word which comes from the foundation period of the Church.

THE SPIRIT AND THE WORD

It is too frequently assumed by powerful churches that the witness of the Spirit comes to confer the consciousness of rightful authority : it may be well to realise that it comes, quite as frequently, to convict of error. On the question of the Spirit and the Word, Calvinism sets three principles in the forefront. First is the conviction that these two cannot be separated ; and, where Robert Barclay and the Quakers in general would be content to maintain that the inner light will never be found to conflict with Scripture, the Calvinist is sure that nothing is worth consideration if it lie manifestly outside Scripture. But in the second place, Scripture is not to be considered in any narrow sense. Scholarship, therefore, the weapon of reason, is permitted full play, so that no ignorant interpretation may impede the operation of the Word. Thirdly, the Church occupies a place of vital importance in the activity of Word and Spirit, since the Spirit is given only to those who are within the fellowship of the Church.[1] The third principle here quoted must not however be misinterpreted to mean that the Spirit is conferred only on those who are prominent within the Church ; only on the scholars or the powerful people or the ecclesiastical statesmen. It may be that the *anicula Christiana*, the little old woman who keeps the faith, will prove, however strenuously she may disclaim the distinction, to be the real recipient.

[1] *Vide* Professor G. D. Henderson, *The Claims of the Church of Scotland,* p. 25.

Once it is received, the Word is no longer only transcendent. There is an individual decision even with regard to the Bible message. That message is clear enough, and comprehensive enough to give the material for a decision to be made; but it does not extract it or compel it. The Word comes from beyond, but it must be welcomed and hospitably entreated before it can become man's own possession. As the liberty to reject the Word remains with man, so the Lord of the Word says to man, "Behold I stand at the door and knock: if any man hear my voice and open the door, I will come in to him". To whom does the Spirit come? Must we say, "Solely to the privileged, chosen people of the Old Testament and of the Christian Church"? or can we find vestiges at least of the Spirit's witness among the ethnic faiths? It was suggested earlier that the religious growth of the child shows many features that closely resemble the corresponding stages in the experience of the race; and it may be that the normal course of development brings in the train of the child's natural theology a growing consciousness of being an elect one. We all have the early awareness of something which mysteriously interferes with our destiny. Mature consciousness of election comes frequently at adolescence; indeed it is likely that, occurring before this, it has been induced prematurely by adult influence or agency. Significantly, it is often combined in the adolescent with a real conversion experience, not necessarily of the violent or spectacular sort. Thus the impression formed in the religious mind is normally the right one, not that of a privileged status above all others, but that of undeserved grace, eliciting gratitude and the desire to give everything in return. In the challenge presented by life we are aware that we must choose for Christ or against Him; and later, on looking back, we are sure, if the choice was rightly made, that it was graciously *made for us*.

The destiny of which we suddenly or gradually become aware has from all eternity been a part of God's plan. He has chosen us in Christ before the creation of the world, that we should be holy and without blame before Him in love (Eph. i. 4). This is perfectly in accord with the course taken by divine revelation to mankind. All nations were called by God, but Israel was summoned to a particular destiny. (Cf. Isa. lxi.) The elect nation was not chosen for any virtue of obedience. It may have

seemed at one time as if it were, and the prophets were urgent
in calling for obedience to the Lord ; but the mature judgment
of the religious consciousness set the matter in its true light.
"The idea of a human choice ", says Dr. N. H. Snaith [1] " is the
language of the newly converted, but . . . the certainty of the
divine choice is the language of the sanctified."

The election of Israel brings into prominence for us the whole
problem of the ethnic faiths.   Men's attention has been increasingly directed to them by the circumstances of our times.
Sailors, soldiers, and airmen have encountered adherents of
many different faiths, and few are content to take up the brusque
attitude of the officer who is supposed to have said, " The League
of Nations was all right till they brought in those foreigners "
or " The dagoes begin at Calais ".

From a hint given by Professor Heinrich Frick [2] we might
state the problem in pictorial terms.

1. There is the naïve claim to finality which is made by
the Christian for his own faith, simply because he has never
been brought into contact with any others, and has a vague
conviction at the back of his mind that in any case they do
not merit consideration.   This position might be characterised
as *the village-well attitude*.

2. Secondly, there are those who are convinced that
Christians ought to acquire all the knowledge available to them
concerning other faiths, but with the express purpose of showing
how worthless they all are.   All other religions will appear, it
is believed, as idolatry, the worship not of God but of demons.
This was the view of the first Christians, and it is in effect revived
by Karl Barth.   We call it the *hammer attitude*.   The Christian
is a witness to the truth and, when he meets with an enemy
of the truth, an iconoclast.

3. The opposite view holds, in its extreme expression, that
all religions are equally true.   " Better " says the Hindu " to
worship an elephant than to worship nothing at all."   And the
elephant is as good a symbol as any other for that which is in
any case unknown.   The view has been phrased with cynicism
in place of agnosticism by Gibbon when he says in *The Decline
and Fall of the Roman Empire* : [3]   The various modes of wor-

[1] *A Theological Word Book of the Bible*, p. 44, b.
[2] *The Gospel, Christianity and Other Faiths.*
[3] Ch. ii, *sub. init.*

ship, which prevailed in the Roman world, were all considered by the people as equally true ; by the philosopher as equally false ; and by the magistrate, as equally useful. And thus toleration produced not only mutual indulgence, but even religious concord." This extreme view breaks down at one point. It is generally agreed that there are some religions which can help and some which cannot help in conquering hatred and fear and in putting an end to squalor and oppression ; and the claim for parity is often therefore limited to the great ethnic faiths such as Mohammedanism, Hinduism, Buddhism, Confucianism, Judaism. This view may be referred to as the *seismograph attitude* and it has been eloquently argued in the American laymen's report *Re-Thinking Missions*. Such religions as these, together with Christianity, are to be regarded as the Old Testament of the coming religion. The New Dispensation of the future will, presumably, gather up all that is of value in each and produce that which far transcends them all.

4. *The compass attitude.* On this fourth view of the matter, the Christian believer is never insensitive to any manifestations of the Divine Spirit ; but always, having surveyed their whole range, he will return to point steadily to his own one magnetic pole. He knows that there are limits to syncretism beyond which we run into danger, that there is a core of adamant in the Christian faith which it is not ours to sell or barter.

From that village-well of which the first metaphor speaks there has come in the history of Christian people much fine, pure water, though it is true to say that none will know how fine and how pure it is until they know something of other sources. Nevertheless, for many simple, saintly souls, this is truly not only the village-well but a source as sacred and as satisfying as the well at Bethlehem.

The testimony of many of our best missionaries tells against the hammer view. Having lived and worked with non-Christian leaders they cannot bring themselves to believe that the religion which has sustained these people can be altogether false.[1] Thus the missionary must not go to the adherents of the ethnic faiths merely to disrupt and destroy their religion, in order to build on a vacant lot. God has nowhere left Himself without witness.

By following the theory of the seismograph it is all too easy

[1] See Nicol Macnicol, *Is Christianity Unique?*

to lose completely the sense of values. Where one is as good as another, none is of very much consequence. But we are right to see, as the Jerusalem Report of 1928 has insisted, the excellent moral precepts of Buddhism, while observing that the cheerful note introduced into Buddhist pamphlets in this country is quite at variance with pure Buddhism, for which there can be no joy, since there is no God and no human soul; we are right in appreciating the fine ethic of Confucianism, learning from it how much can be achieved by good manners and by the loyalty which distinguishes Chinese family life; we might do well to borrow some of the fire and devotion of Islam; and we might learn from the desire which is prominent in Hinduism for contact with Ultimate Reality; but when it is suggested that we take as our standard the Greatest Common Measure of all the more outstanding religions, then we halt. A religion, in any case, is not built up by synthesis and mechanical mixture. It is an organic unity.

It is thus the claim of Christianity that all the values found in other religions which are worth conserving are found in greater purity and greater strength in Christianity. We see in Sakyamuni a child of God who did not know his Father, and in all sincere worshippers in non-Christian communities the sons of God who are yet lost and prodigal sons. All of them have a longing to return but none can find the way back till the Father comes to seek him, as He has done in Jesus.

We adhere to the compass view and, if asked whether this is not just a return to the naïve claim of finality whereby we are betrayed into believing without evidence that the direction in which the compass points is necessarily the true direction, the answer must be, as always, in spiritual matters, that all profound convictions are in the long run personal decisions. When Peter affirmed (Acts. iv. 12), "Neither is there salvation in any other: for there is none other name under heaven given among men, whereby we must be saved" he was giving his own personal testimony. There are, it is true, two convenient crucibles for the identification of true religion, the first Truth, the second Morality. But Christianity is far more than the first: it is not just a coherent and comprehensive philosophy; and it far transcends the second: it is not just a guide to right conduct. If it is said that finality rests, not in doctrine but in Christian character and character cannot be refuted, we must still realise that Christian character goes with Christian faith, for the Christian acts always in loyalty to his Lord. Thus we are led to speak not of the finality of the Christian religion, but of the finality of Jesus for faith. He is the Lord, from whom are pardon, peace, and power.

" NONE OTHER NAME "

It was to Simon Peter, who spoke the words: " Neither is there salvation in any other: for there is none other name under heaven given among men, whereby we must be saved ", that there came the vision of the sheet let down from heaven. True, the story of Cornelius is intended to deny the uncleanness of the Gentiles in respect of their right to the Gospel. The Gospel alone will save them. But there is another aspect ; a caution against dismissing all Gentile faiths as idolatry and foolishness. The truth is that from our place within a special and final revelation we can see that none other is adequate ; but we should see also that the Christian revelation cannot be put into the same equation with those others. This point is well put by the Theology of Crisis, but it proceeds to draw an illegitimate conclusion from it. It argues that therefore those others are wholly profane and wholly in error. This is one of three instances in which a logical scheme has been followed, conspicuously to the detriment of spiritual truth. (1) The truth of the wonder and mystery of the Godhead has been pressed to the point of affirming a *deus absconditus*. But we worship a God Who has revealed Himself. If too great a stress is laid on the idea of the hidden God, it becomes questionable whether even the divine self-revelation in Christ can bring light ; and it is not surprising that those who cherish this concept are frequently driven to describe God in terms that are predominantly negative. But God is not only the hidden abyss ; He is also the hidden home of His people.[1] (2) Whereas Augustine presents the doctrine of predestination to life, that of salvation ; Calvin continues the logical train of thought till it produces the doctrine of double predestination, one to salvation, another to destruction.[2] " The predestination by which God adopts some to the hope of life,

[1] *Vide* infra 212. [2] *Institutes*, bk. III, ch. xxi, § 5.

and adjudges others to eternal death, no man who would be thought pious ventures simply to deny." This view, he says, in the phrase that follows, involves us in much disputation. And no wonder! There is only the slenderest of New Testament evidence for promulgating the doctrine in this form and much that is incompatible with it: it represents the intrusion into the teaching of the Gospel of a logical system, which is quite alien. There are matters on which the New Testament gives no leading, and this appears to be one of them.[1] (3) The subject under review is the third instance of a seemingly logical deduction taking the place of spiritual insight. How God has spoken to His other children we dare not dogmatically claim to know. We must rest content in acknowledging that our own special place within the redeemed community affords us no privileged illumination of God's secret ways of confronting those of His human creatures whom our indifferent efforts in world-evangelism may have failed to reach.

The uniqueness of the revelation in the Old Testament and in the Gospel does not imply the worthlessness of all others. The teaching of Genesis (ix. 1-17) is that no race of men is inferior. In this passage "even the most exclusive Old Testament writer, the priestly recorder, recognises that the heathen peoples are also set in a direct relation with God and have a similar responsibility to him, which the writer expresses in the same word, 'covenant', which is decisive for Israel's relation with God".[2] We may be sure that God intended the earliest animists to move on to His next lesson, and where they failed to advance from more primitive beliefs and practices, the deficiency was not in the revelation but in the response. The earliest animists did not all move on; but God had fore-ordained a people to be His own, and to them He gave the next lesson. They too had their grievous faults, but they could not fall away altogether. They were chosen. Where many halted, and many even went back; these went on. We are their heirs. But going on does not mean leaving behind the first lessons as useless. So far as men learned them aright, they are permanent lessons.

Those who were chosen were summoned not to privilege, but to service. That lesson, too, was hard to learn: not all

[1] See Emil Brunner, *The Doctrine of God, passim.*
[2] Eichrodt, *Man in the Old Testament,* p. 36.

mastered it; and there was a still more difficult one, that the chosen ones were inevitably submitted to a more severe judgment. "Hear this word that the Lord hath spoken against *you*, O children of Israel, against the whole family which I brought up from the land of Egypt, saying, You only have I known of all the families of the earth: *therefore* I will punish you for all your iniquities."[1] All such themes imply a "shadow side".[2] Election draws in its train the spectre of rejection. Paul, in frustration and anguish, turned to the Gentiles. Jesus gave to the disciples the symbolism for a sacrament of failure, shaking off the dust of the unresponsive city. But always the love of others pleads for the defiant ones, as Abraham intreated God for Sodom, as Moses prayed "Yet now, if Thou wilt forgive their sin—; and if not, blot me, I pray Thee, out of Thy book which Thou hast written" (Exod. xxxii. 32), as Paul declared "For I could wish that myself were accursed from Christ for my brethren, my kinsmen according to the flesh" (Rom. ix. 3). Man must not dare to dispute with God (Rom. ix. 20). In modern terms we might express it, says Professor Reid, by saying that "though there appear *logically* to be two classes in a developed doctrine of predestination, that of the blessed and that of the reprobate, Paul is unwilling to assign *real* persons to these classes. They remain mere logical, and of course spiritual, possibilities, categories without assigned or assignable members."

VICTORY AND POWER THROUGH THE SPIRIT

We have suggested an analogy between the religious development of the child to adolescence and the religious experience of the race. The third stage in both processes is that where the discovery is made that victory and power are available through the Spirit. And a similar problem arises. Does the Christian experience the power and victory *of* Christ, or power and victory *from* Christ? Does the Spirit annul the soul and act for it? or illumine the soul and act through it? The first answer is often put forward by "transcendent" theologies, and it is very true that an extremist statement of the second can be

[1] Amos iii. 2.
[2] See the article by J. K. S. Reid in *A Theological Word Book of the Bible*, p. 68 a.

further from the truth and can be more dangerous than an extremist statement of the first; but this may well be because extremist statements of the first carry no profound conviction, but, like the denials of the freedom of the will, are admitted only as theoretical extravagances, have no practical effects, and are virtually discounted. In any case a truth is not to be rejected because it is capable of being wrongly set forth; and it *is* a fact that God has created men free, responsible recipients of grace; potential sons, not slaves, of God.

In this connection the late Oliver Quick has noted[1] that, just as a theophany would not meet the purposes of God in redeeming mankind (since only the pure in heart could see God when He appeared) and He must therefore be veiled, and come by Incarnation; so it is certain that even the purest moral teaching would not suffice to win man, since man's will is corrupt and he could not comprehend; therefore what is needed is a radical change in man. In answering the question, What is the nature of this change wrought by Atonement and involving both remission of sins and the renewal of life? one reply seems to be given by St. John and Calvin, namely that there is a new birth, and that no goodness is present in those who have not yet passed through that experience; and another reply by St. Paul and Luther, to the effect that there takes place a resurrection of the old personality plainly identical with the old. And in the eschatological setting it seems that the second answer holds the field. It is of a καινὴ κτίσις not a νέα κτίσις that the New Testament speaks; of regeneration, renovation, being born again, hence the emergence not of a new person, but of a changed personality.

Clearly the process of regeneration is beyond the comprehension of human analysis, but there is a point on which modern psychology has been able to shed a small ray of light. Dr. William Brown[2] records the interesting discovery, during an analysis made of himself for scientific purposes by a leading psycho-analyst, that his religious convictions were not weakened, as many contemporary psychologists were intimating ought to be the case, but made stronger than before. The analysis had a purifying effect, ridding his religious feelings from much that was childish and sentimental, and leaving him more than

[1] *The Gospel of the New World.*   [2] *Mind and Personality*, p. 268.

ever convinced that religion is the most important thing in life and the main source of mental health. In his own patients he made the same discovery. "Although mere emotionalism and religiosity is diminished, the essentially religious outlook on life remains unimpaired."[1] These passages prompt in me the following reflection: In faith we are dealing, not with *contention* alone (the word employed by Baudouin to indicate a state of concentration without effort) nor with *attention* alone (which is characteristic of the conscious mind as opposed to the sub-conscious) but with *encounter*, which presents to God that frame of mind in which He can use both "suggestion" and "persuasion". The religious consciousness is neither on the conscious level alone, with its counterpart in rational thought and the instrument of persuasion; nor on the sub-conscious level alone, with its counterpart of unconscious cerebration and its medium of suggestion; but embraces both in a realm where will is the most important element. Persuasion operates most successfully when the unconscious is in abeyance: suggestion when the conscious is dormant. Revelation comes into its own when the two are held in right equilibrium; when the mind is clear, the will is operative, and the unconscious is liberated from its dark entanglements.

"The light of the body is the eye: therefore when thine eye is single, thy whole body also is full of light; but when thine eye is evil, thy body also is full of darkness.

"Take heed therefore that the light which is in thee be not darkness.

"If thy whole body therefore be full of light, having no part dark, the whole shall be full of light, as when the bright shining of a candle doth give thee light." (Luke xi : 34-36.)

[1] See also his *Personality and Religion*, p. 134.

CHAPTER VII

"THE SPIRITUAL IS MOST RATIONAL"

CONVICTION is one of the inalienable features of religion; for faith cannot be neutral or tentative, and both theology and personal witness have found numerous and varied ways of directing attention to the fact. One is found in the doctrine of the Inner Light, traced by the followers of George Fox and Robert Barclay to the words of St. John's Gospel (i. 9), "the Quaker's text": "That was the true light, which lighteth every man that cometh into the world."[1] As the emphasis is chiefly on the Light, rather than on the bearer of the Light, Quaker doctrine might be thought to interpret it in terms less than personal, and therefore care is taken to guard against this danger by reminding us that the light comes from God in the way of His revelation. The soul has its sense, as well as the body: so that religious knowledge is like sensation (as David could say, "Taste and see that God is good "). ἔστι καὶ ψυχῆς αἴσθησίς τις; but the object of faith is always *Deus Loquens,* God speaking.[2] Another method by which the central place of conviction is indicated is the doctrine of the *testimonium Spiritus Sancti internum,* the inner witness of the Holy Spirit, considered in the previous chapter; and because the stress here is on the Spirit, there is no need to defend the expression against the suspicion of being impersonal. A third way is seen in the psychological consideration frequently given to the *coercive* element in belief, as for example by Professor H. H. Farmer[3] in contrast to the overstatements current elsewhere of the pragmatic and reflective elements.

TYPES OF CONVICTION

It is very true that the term "conviction" is ambiguous and the thing itself often deceptive. The "Emotion of Conviction" Bagehot said[4] is "strongest in those points in which men differ

---

[1] *Vide* Barclay, *Apology*, Prop. v, vi, sec. xxi.   [2] Prop. II, ii end and viii.
[3] *Towards Belief in God*, pt. I.   [4] *Literary Studies*, III, 193.

most from each other. John Knox felt it in his anti-Catholicism; Ignatius Loyola in his anti-Protestantism; and both, I suppose, felt it as much as it is possible to feel it." That is one type, supposed by Bagehot to be due to sheer perversity.

In the second place, conviction may be due to the coercion of circumstances, through which, by upbringing, by psychological endowment, by heredity, by economic pressure (the truth that Karl Marx perceived) one man is compellingly driven to one belief and another to another. Third, however, it may arise from the force of evidence, where observation, judgment, comparison, and unprejudiced reasoning come into full play. Fourthly— and on this we ought to place special stress—it may arise through something more, namely that flash of illumination to which no man is altogether a stranger and to which the genius owes his more profound inspirations; that flash of spiritual light to which all the mystics bear witness. In *The Cloud of Unknowing*, for instance, an anonymous English scholar of the fourteenth century admonishes us: "Take heed to the marvellous manner of grace in thy soul. It speedily springs unto God as a spark from the coal." But, as Dean Inge recalls, quoting from the Indian Sama Veda, there is also the delusion of the "false light". That is the paradox of divine truth—"He who believes he knows it, knows it not; he who believes it not, knows it." Those who know it best find it incomprehensible; those who are most ignorant of it, believe that they know it perfectly.[1]

There is a vast field of investigation here, and many lines of contemporary thought are converging on it. A whole school of thought has grown up around the importance of the I-Thou relation.[2] Karl Heim made a particularly noteworthy contribution to the discussion of the theological problem uncovered by this philosophy, namely the question to what extent our knowledge of God is analogous to our knowledge of the other person, and in his *God Transcendent* he underlines the fact that, when we pass from one "dimension" to another, it is not by the way of syllogistic reasoning but by a species of illumination. The structure of a dimension cannot be discovered by inductive observation, but experience of it presupposes a particular mode

[1] *Mysticism in Religion*, pp. 125 and 149.
[2] Its beginnings and its development have been traced by Cullberg in *Das Du und die Wirklichkeit*.

of cognition. "Our seeking after God is like our search for a star in the night-sky. Again and again it eludes our eyes. We not only lose sight of the star itself, but we lose even the place where once it shone. We are always asking anew, 'Where is God my Maker?' (Job xxxv. 10). What is meant by 'God'? Surely God is an unframable thought? The change which takes place ever again in passing from one standpoint to the other is like the waking of a man from an oppressive dream which held him fast, or like the experience of a man born blind who gains his sight, so that a possibility is revealed to him which before was utterly unthinkable. From one standpoint the thought of God is unframable; from the other it is the clearest and most indispensable ground-idea, that in which all other ideas are rooted, and from which they must all be radically re-fashioned." [1] Side by side with this movement of thought has gone an increasing interest in the work of Wilhelm Dilthey. Drawing a sharp distinction between the natural sciences on the one hand and the humanistic studies on the other, he sums up his wide and stimulating research in the principle, "We *explain* nature; but we *understand* the human spirit." [2] That is to say, the world of things we can seek to reduce to laws and rational explanations; for here we are dealing with the universe only in its metric aspect, where it can be weighed and measured, counted and analysed; but the spirit of man we cannot capture by these methods, for in that realm only like can know like, and the way is the way of understanding. When all is known that can be known about another person, there is still the flash of insight—note again the inevitability of the phrase—by which the other is illumined and comprehended. In the knowledge of men, explanation must give way to experience.

PARANORMAL COGNITION

Interesting experimental verification of Dilthey's belief, that there is direct experience of the emotions of another person, is provided by the psychiatric work of Dr. Laurence Bendit described in his book *Paranormal Cognition*. In the second

[1] *God Transcendent* p. 218.
[2] "Die Natur erklären wir: das Seelenleben verstehen wir."

chapter of that volume he quotes a case of a young woman in her early twenties who was the victim of attacks of panic and agora-claustrophobia. During treatment she was talking one day, apparently quite naturally and calmly, about a sermon she had listened to in church, in which there was a good deal of reference to Hell fire and many of the cruder ideas of a once popular evangelism. Dr. Bendit continues: "As far as my conscious perceptions went, she was talking normally and un-emotionally, when I began to feel myself grow anxious and afraid. As soon as I realised this, I cast round for the reason, I asked myself whether, by any chance, at the bottom of my heart I were afraid of Hell fire and the like, but decided against this explanation: nor could I find any other reason for my fear. The idea then came into my mind: 'This may not be *your* fear, but the patient's, which you have allowed to invade you.' Immediately the sense of fear left me. I realised that I might have rationalised it back into the unconscious; or alternatively, I might simply have become positive and expelled it from my personality. I had now to try and find out whether or not the patient was on the edge of panic. It was difficult to do this without suggesting anything to her, but I took the risk of asking as casually as possible, 'Why are you panicking?' At this she sat up with a jerk and said, 'Good heavens! So I am, but I did not know it till you spoke. But how did you know?'"[1] Dr. Bendit realised that he had perceived an emotion other than his own, and that not through the normal senses (for it so happened that he had not at that moment been in a position to see her facial expression) but by some other means. He had disclosed in himself a power of perception far more acute than anything of which conscious observation is capable.

I have little doubt that this power is possessed by all of us, by some in greater by others in less measure; and that it lies at the back of our irrational likes and dislikes of other people and in particular that it explains the apparently inexplicable gift of character-reading which some possess in their judgments of men.

[1] L. J. Bendit, *Paranormal Cognition*, Faber and Faber, 1944, pp. 23-24.

INSIGHTS OF HISTORY

A wide vista is also opened up through the study of history. By the reading of history, Dilthey insists, we open up to ourselves possibilities of our own nature of which we should otherwise remain unaware. His own experience confirmed this. Professor Hodges quotes one passage.[1] " The possibility of experiencing (*zu erleben*) religious states in my own existence is for me " says Dilthey " as for most men today, strictly limited. But when I run through the letters and writings of Luther, the reports of his contemporaries, the records of the religious conferences and councils and of his official activities, I experience a religious process of such eruptive power, of such energy, in which life and death are at stake, that it lies beyond all possibility of being actually lived by a man of our day. But I can re-live it. . . . And so this process opens to us a religious world in him and in his contemporaries of early Reformation times, which broadens our horizon to include possibilities of human life which only so become accessible to us. . . . Man, bound and determined by the reality of life, is set free not only through art—as has often been set forth—but also through the understanding of history. And this effect of history, which its most modern detractors have not seen, is broadened and deepened in the further stages of the historical consciousness."

OUR KNOWLEDGE OF THE INDIVIDUAL

Both in reference to historical study and in the examination of our knowledge of other people, these investigations of Dilthey and their confirmation from the side of such psychological researches as those of Dr. Bendit have a philosophical counterpart in the important contribution made by the late Professor William de Burgh in his Riddell Memorial Lectures in Durham in 1939.[2] His argument runs along the following lines: Too long philosophy has followed the lure of science into the shadow-land of the universal. It is true that the concept of individuality asserts itself again at the summit, as in the Form of Plato and in the

[1] Dilthey: G. S., vii, 215-216. See H. A. Hodges, *The Philosophy of Wilhelm Dilthey*, Routledge and Kegan Paul, 1952, pp. 276-277.
[2] *Knowledge of the Individual*: Oxford University Press.

First Mover of Aristotle; but in general for the Greeks knowledge is of the universal, by the universal, for the universal. The same is true of scholastic philosophy. In spite of the new emphasis on the individual secured through the doctrine of the Incarnation and in spite of the claim made by Augustinian Platonism to intuitive knowledge of the self and of God, Aquinas reaffirmed the centrality of knowledge of the universal. True, there is non-conceptual knowledge (vision) of God in Paradise; and even in this life there is an anticipation of that vision possible for the higher mystics, but this is to be classed, not as *scientia*, but as *sapientia*, not as knowledge but as wisdom of some sort. For science today, truths of contingent fact can be called "knowledge" only when interpreted as instances of general law. Poets were the first to rebel. Now it is becoming clear that rationalism must be widened to include also knowledge of the individual, of the contingent, of the historical. Reason is the power to grasp truth; and truth embraces the particular. Every "such" is individualised. It is not simply *redness* as a universal quality that we see, but the *redness of this rose* or the *redness of that sunset*. The aim of Reason is thus to restore the unity which it has itself broken (by abstracting from actuality to study universals alone) and so to cease following the lure of science into the shadow-land of universality.

When we inquire whether history is a form of knowledge, the answer must be that historians have as their sole business *what happened*, facts for their own sake, *not* as instances of general law.

The synthesis of science falls far short of rationality, since it leaves two things altogether unreconciled, the facts and the law. The individual is robbed of its uniqueness and becomes a bare instance. It may yet be realised that nature too, in order to be understood, demands more than a science of explanation which reduces her processes to terms of law, and requires to be studied by the approach of sympathy.

Professor de Burgh's conclusion is that *sapientia* also is knowledge, though on a higher plane. The mistake of Roman Catholic theology has been to confine it to the higher grades of believer. "The criticism, so often voiced by Protestant writers, that Catholic theologians restrict faith to assent to propositions, to the exclusion of religious experience, is misplaced; their

shafts should rather be directed against the limitation of ex-
periential knowledge to the highest grade of spiritual efficiency,
achieved in the contemplative vision of the mystics." [1]

OUR KNOWLEDGE OF GOD

Dilthey, as we know, when he comes to discuss the knowledge of God, is altogether negative. But his epistemology can
be followed also in this realm without any necessity for his
sceptical conclusions. If we take such a writer as Thomas
Halyburton—Professor of Divinity in St. Andrews, 1710 to 1712—
we find constant reference to the highest experience of religion
as one of illumination. He speaks, for instance, of "the dreadful
strait I was in, with my Outgate"; and of the Outgate coming
through the Word indeed, but not any one word. There is no
superstitious attachment to any verse; nor even any *tolle lege;*
but there is prolonged study of the Scriptures and light from
many. He is earnest to note two features of his debt to the
Bible. The first is that God does the interpreting. The significance comes to him as an illumination. And second, it is not
merely a new idea about the world or about the nature of God.
It is a new relation between the Divine and the human; not
something "notional" but what today we should probably
describe as a new I-Thou relationship. This is a notable passage
on the Light. [2] The beginning and the end of it should be
quoted: "It was not the Word alone that conveyed the Discovery: For most of the passages whereby I was relieved, I had
formerly in my Distress read, and thought upon, without finding
any Relief in them. But now the Lord shin'd into my mind
by them. Formerly I was only acquaint with the Letter which
profits not: But now the Lord's Words were spirit and life, and
in His light, I saw light, God opening mine eyes to see wonders
out of His law. There was Light in them, a burning Light by
them shone into my Mind, to give me not merely some notional
Knowledge, but the Light of the knowledge of the glory of God,
in the face of Jesus Christ . . . it was not a Spark kindled by
my own Endeavours, but it shone suddenly about me; it came
by the Word of God, a Heavenly Mean. . . . It was a powerful
Light. It dissipated that thick Darkness that overspread my

---

[1] *Op. cit.* pp. 46-47.　　　　　　　　[2] Pt. 3, ch. ii of the *Memoirs.*

Mind, and made all those frightful Temptations, that had formerly disturbed me, fly before it . . . and it was composing, it did not, like a Flash of Lightning, suddenly appear, and fill the Soul only with Amazement and Fear; but it composed and quieted my Soul, and put all my Faculties in a due Posture, as it were, and gave me the Exercise of them. It destroyed not, but improved, my former Knowledge."

THE FUEL AND THE FLAME

For convenience of reference in this chapter it may be helpful to employ a domestic simile with which even theologians are now familiar—the fuel, the match, and the flame. It is a good simile, because in modesty we must admit that the flame, when it does reward our amateur fire-lighting efforts, is all of grace. It cannot really be the result of our fumbling attempts; and indeed a specially appropriate simile, since the Inner Light is both illumination and warmth.

The *fuel* is that which is given, including home and education; conscience and the moral society; the ethnic faiths; the inborn love of nature and consequent nature-mysticism; above all Scripture and the Church. But the fuel is not the flame. It may remain unkindled. What is that which causes it to take fire? Robert Barclay has a memorable passage[1] in which he distinguishes between the certain knowledge of God and the uncertain; between the spiritual and the literal; between "the saving heart-knowledge, and the soaring, airy head-knowledge". The first can be obtained in no other way than the inward immediate manifestation and revelation of God's Spirit, shining in and upon the heart, enlightening and opening the understanding. Even conscience is not to be placed in the first category. It is, as it were, only the lamp, and that is useless until there is a candle placed within. Conscience is compared with the lanthorn, and the light of Christ to the candle. It is not to man's natural conscience that we direct men, but to the light of Christ in conscience.

This is the first major problem. It can be simply stated— Is there an absolute gulf here, between the revealed and the natural? It cannot, I think, be so simply answered. Kierkegaard

[1] *Apology*, Proposition II.

in many passages makes the gulf absolute.[1] Again and again he returns to the story of the Binding of Isaac, as if it contained the whole essence of faith and the only clue to the problems of conscience, and in particular to his own personal tragedy of conduct. Abraham was commanded to slay Isaac; and we are to assume that he knew this to be a morally wrong act; but he set about obeying, in virtue of nothing else save his personal relationship to God; and he was enabled to do this by what Kierkegaard calls a "teleological suspension of the ethical". Faith is presented to us as altogether irrational and opaque. Ethical categories cannot embrace its meaning.[2] The case of Abraham is considered to be quite different from apparently similar instances in secular history and literature. By his action, Abraham went beyond the ethical stage and possessed a higher τέλος outside it, in favour of which he was able to suspend ethics. There is, it is said, a private duty of the individual to God which takes priority over the duty which he owes to his fellowmen. This places "the knight of faith" in a position altogether different from that of "the tragic hero". In the case of Agamemnon, called to renounce Iphigenia, and of others like him faced with tragic demands for the wider good of mankind, duty and desire are opposed, and the aim of the hero is to hold fast to duty and by enthusiasm for it to change it into desire. For the knight of faith duty and desire are also identical, but, whereas the tragic hero begins by renouncing his desire in order to fulfil his duty, the knight of faith is called upon to renounce both desire and duty.[3]

Every allowance must be made for the fact that Kierkegaard was here writing under great stress. He had broken off his engagement to Regine Olsen in the most heartless fashion and was seeking to justify, perhaps most of all to himself, his behaviour towards her.[4] But in one sense this makes it worse,

---

1 *Vide supra*, p. 57.

2 See the long and elaborate treatment in *Fear and Trembling*, and *Unscientific Postscript*, p. 525.   3 *Fear and Trembling*, p. 114.

4 He later acknowledged that the four portraits of Abraham in *Fear and Trembling* describe his separation from Regine. "When I left her, I asked one thing of God—that I might succeed in writing and finishing *Either—Or* (that was also for her sake, for the *Seducer's Diary* was meant to repel her from me, or as it is expressed in *Fear and Trembling*: when it is time for the child to be weaned the mother blackens her breast)." See note on p. 190 of *Fear and Trembling*. This whole business is material more for the psychiatrist than for the moral philosopher or the theologian.

for the theory which is put forward in elucidation of the story of Abraham would in fact, if it were possible to accept it, not only justify Kierkegaard's own conduct but would cover any other repulsive behaviour which set out to claim the protection of an irrational heavenly command. Our own time has been nauseated by many such claims in the realm of colour prejudice, anti-Semitism, and master-races.

In his Journal, Kierkegaard speaks of a plan of exegesis which he had hoped to develop whereby he would offer the explanation that Abraham pretended to have gone mad, in order that Isaac might not lose faith in God when he realised what his father was prepared to do under the belief that he was acting in obedience to a divine command. It is not surprising that many feel that Kierkegaard, in these passages on the Binding of Isaac, has lapsed into paganism and unreason. There cannot be a "suspension of the ethical". *God* does not suspend it; and in suggesting an illustration from the discussion of euthanasia, present-day writers have gone far wrong. Acceptance of euthanasia is not an instance of suspension of the ethical but, where honestly made, is the cancelling of one duty by another considered to be higher. So in the matter of the Binding of Isaac and in other cases of the same type, what we see is not the suspension of the ethical but man's inadequate or ignorant or sinful response to the divine revelation being overborne by new revelation and a worthier response. The new insight does not disrupt that which was good in the old, but judges that which was evil. Historically and in the setting of the evolution of morals, what we are witnessing in the Binding of Isaac is the dawning recognition of the right of private judgment after prayer, over against that which operates with overwhelming power in all but the strongest minds—the pressure of tribal customs, traditions, and demands. The event may best be interpreted as a prevision of that daring emancipation from the urgency of tribal morality which is seen in the Greek tragedies and in the message of the prophet Ezekiel. God does not give all His will in one eternal, comprehensive pronouncement, but speaks again and again in the unfolding of history, so that His people are called ever anew to face the challenge of their own time and circumstance. At definite points in the here and now, God's will "assumes definite and unrecurring form, in which it demands obedience ".[1] Is there then no relation to that which has preceded both the divine demand and the human choice to which a man is summoned? The reply once again must indicate that there is here the familiar blend of traditional pattern and creative novelty. The process of revelation is not inaugurated afresh with every divine self-manifestation. It is given to men with such and such a background, training, religion, and previous revelation. There is indeed no possibility of erecting a system of casuistry to cover every contingency. The Law must not be set above the God who gave the Law. He is always making fresh demands and giving new light in new situations; but this does not make each command and each decision irrational and magical. God's revelation is a unity: every obedience brings clearer insight into His will. If it darkens insight, then we may be sure that the obedience has been given to a command wrongly interpreted.

So we pass from conscience (which is always the boundary-line) to the knowledge of God. In presenting his theory of the Inner Light, Barclay had constantly to combat the suspicion that the light was a natural one. "Such is the malice of our adversaries, that they cease not sometimes to calumniate us as if we preached up a natural light, or the light of man's natural conscience." The distinction must be pressed, for this divine light is "not only distinct, but of a different nature from the soul of man and its faculties." The relation between the two is given in a simile: "As God gave two great lights to rule the outward world, the sun and moon, the greater light to rule the day, and the lesser to rule the night; so hath He given man the light of His Son, a Spiritual light, to rule him in things spiritual, and the light of reason to rule him in things natural. And even as the moon borrows her light from the sun, so ought men, if they would be rightly and comfortably ordered in natural things, to have their reason enlightened by this divine and pure light." It is true, indeed, that by the rational principle man may apprehend in his brain a knowledge of God and of spiritual things, but this not being the proper organ the knowledge cannot profit him towards salvation.

[1] Walther Eichrodt, *Man in the Old Testament*, S.C.M. Press, 1951, p. 26.

KNOWLEDGE OF HEARSAY AND KNOWLEDGE OF THE HEART

The question here therefore is that of distinguishing and comparing the two types of knowledge—knowledge *about* God and knowledge *of* God. The nature of faith is seen with particular clarity when we realise that religious knowledge is essentially knowledge of a *person*, and the methods of religious instruction which forget this are certain to be quite deplorable. (Leslie Stephen, for example, describes [1] a school in which the teacher used to converse with his pupils in this kind of fashion: " James, what is the difference between justification and sanctification?—Stephen, prove the omnipotence of God.")   And because we are dealing with knowledge of a person, we know that the acquisition of such knowledge will demand something more than intellectual integrity: it will require a certain character. William James offered a trivial illustration: " Just as a man who in a company of gentlemen made no advances, asked a warrant for every concession, and believed no one's word without proof, would cut himself off by such churlishness from all the social rewards that a more trusting spirit would earn—so here, one who should shut himself up in snarling logicality and try to make the gods extort his recognition willy-nilly, or not get it at all, might cut himself off for ever from his only opportunity of making the gods' acquaintance." [2]   More profound is the illustration from the book of Job (xii. 5) where we have the pregnant words, "I have heard of Thee by the hearing of the ear: but now mine eye seeth Thee ".   There are two kinds of knowledge, the knowledge of hearsay and the knowledge of the heart. The one is second-hand: the other is immediate. The difference is sometimes brought sharply home in the case of some human friendship.   At first we have known some person only very distantly. We recognise his appearance, his step, his movements. We know his home, his business, his habits. This is the stage of acquaintance. But one day, by a look in his eyes, or a word spoken, or a shared experience we suddenly see into his soul. The barrier is down ; the mask is off; we see his very heart. Hitherto we knew only *about* him: now we know *him*.

---

1 See James, *Will to Believe, sub init.*   2 *Will to Believe*, p. 28.

NATURE, CONSCIENCE, THE BIBLE

We know *about* God. From Nature, it may be; and the knowledge is not to be despised. An attempt was once made to stamp out religion from the peasantry of Brittany. But it would not succeed. The guillotine could not overcome belief. One of the revolutionaries said to the mayor of a village, "I will have your church-tower knocked down that you may have no object to recall to you your old superstitions". The mayor's reply was: "Anyhow, you will have to leave us the stars, and those we can see farther off than our church-tower" (Souvestre). The heavens are always there to declare the glory of God. It is one of the ways of knowing *about* Him. And we know about Him, as we have emphasised, from conscience. There are "the starry heavens above and the moral law within". And above all we know about Him from the Bible. We see His hand in the history of His people. But all of these ways bring us only half-way. We are in the train; but, instead of going on to the terminus, we get out in a field. God says, not only "Hear the Word of the Lord", but also "Come unto Me". Knowledge of God, as contrasted with knowledge about God, involves two factors:

(1) Being like-minded with Him. To understand truth, a man must be truthful. To understand purity, a man must be pure. To understand love, he must be loving. Religious knowledge is possible only to those who make the venture; but, also, it is a venture which is continually being justified. That is natural. If religious truth is the truth that belongs to God, it will sufficiently answer for itself.

(2) Communion with Him; the cultivation of His acquaintance. This feature of true religious knowledge has been brought out forcibly by Francis Thompson in a memorable passage of his essay "Sanctify and Song". "To most, even good people, God is a belief. To the saints He is an embrace. They have felt the wind of His locks, His heart has beaten against their side. They do not believe in Him, for they know Him."

KNOWLEDGE OF HEARSAY NOT TO BE DESPISED BUT NOT TO PUFF UP

I wish to make it plain that we must not despise the first kind of knowledge. There is the knowledge of hearsay and there is the knowledge of the heart. There is the soaring, airy head-knowledge, and there is the saving heart-knowledge. The fault is not having the hearsay knowledge or having the head-knowledge, but being contented with it, even conceited about it; taking pride in it as if it were enough; as if it were our own doing; as if it absolved us from the duty of decision. The really grievous fault is that of using the knowledge of hearsay as a way of escape from the challenge of the Living God.

NATURAL AND REVEALED RELIGION

The debate concerning natural and revealed religion will go on down the centuries. Meantime, a useful comment is made by Clement Webb. In his book *Religious Experience*, he proposes to maintain a distinction which has weathered the centuries and to use it in this fashion—On one side is that knowledge of God which comes through a common experience, perhaps from the observance of design and purpose in nature, or through processes of reasoning concerning the necessary grounds of change and the like; and on the other side is that knowledge of God which is historically mediated, and this would include private history, divine guidance seen in the circumstances of our own life (p. 32). I agree that we cannot dismiss as worthless the knowledge about God which comes from nature, conscience, society; since God can use and does manifestly use these to lead men to knowledge *of* Him. And we have to remember that the Bible itself may give soaring, airy head-knowledge only, unless the Spirit interprets it to the reader. The conclusion must surely be that none of these sources is to be despised; that some are demonstrably less adequate than others; but that with God all things are possible. The prime necessity for the coming of faith is confrontation, meeting, encounter, *Begegnung*; the coming of God with a challenge and a summons. In that, there is involved obedience, which follows acceptance of the challenge: it means decision for this rather than for that.

We dare not deny the richness of response to the divine approach which can be seen even among those for whom what we call "general Revelation" is alone available. We cannot dismiss this as merely error, ignorance, sin. We must learn from it—and often be humbled by it. Hence, as we have seen (p. 181), many of our best missionaries, insist that it is not sufficient to go to the non-Christian peoples simply as iconoclasts. We have to learn as well as teach. We find always that the Master has been there before any of His missionaries. Indeed the next stage is frequently that in which we discover that the Gospel, preached to these people, evokes a variety in response which is a new enrichment of our understanding of the Christian faith; and this enrichment of response would never have come without the preparation which some despise. The mistake of looking upon all other faiths as idolatry is part of the same mistake which looks on all labour as secular and profane. The Christian faith does not annul any sphere of human life except that which is sinful: on the contrary it fulfils it; illumines it; satisfies it. It is indeed perpetually necessary to be on guard against any tendency to reduce religion to human discovery, for there is always an overplus of mystery; but it is important to remember that mystery does not annul rational intelligibility: it enriches it. The Christian faith is not identical with intellectual agnosticism.

THE INNER LIGHT AND SCRIPTURE

According to the teaching of Robert Barclay, the object of faith is *Deus Loquens,* God speaking. Revelation may come by dreams and visions but we cannot just accept any vision.

As the prophets before us, so we give credit to visions because of the secret testimony of God's Spirit in our hearts. It follows, according to Barclay, that true revelations will agree with Scripture and with Reason. Where this is not so, it is, presumably, because of a faulty response on the part of the recipient. Mistakes are to be ascribed to the weakness or the wickedness of man and not to the Holy Spirit.

Of special interest for us is, of course, the relation of these revelations to Scripture. Barclay proves his points repeatedly by Scripture—which seems odd, as if he were proving by Scripture that Scripture has not the last word in proof; but this is another instance of his profound reverence for the Bible. It has the second place, inferior only to the Spirit. It is not a case of every man setting forth a new Gospel, but of new revelations of the good old Gospel. What he is affirming, I think, is that God is before both Scripture and Church. And indeed no one will quarrel with him on that.

This gifted man, the theologian of the Friends, was a gentle, modest soul—in spite of the fulminations of that other gentle soul, John Brown of Wamphray. Such is the heat of controversy that Brown could speak of " Quakerism the Pathway to Paganism " and denounce this " devil in Samuel's mantle " and his "serpentine venome sugared over with fair speeches ".

According to Barclay, as we saw, the Scriptures are not the source of truth but only the product of the truth, the precipitate laid down by inner revelations vouchsafed to the writers. Spirit and light precede the Scriptures.

IN CRITICISM : THE INNER LIGHT DEPENDS ON LIGHT ALREADY GIVEN

I insert here a brief criticism, for it is also true that, when once one part of Scripture is there, the conditions are changed. The light which produces subsequent Scriptures is dependent on the Scriptures which are already there. (Hence the odd and significant feature in the way in which Barclay seeks to prove his contention from Scripture—even using Scripture to prove that Scripture is not essential for revelation.) The Inner Light depends, then, on light already vouchsafed to others.

PROPHETIC VISION WAS CONCERNED WITH A SITUATION

There is a second point to be made. The revelation which came, for example, to the prophets is not necessarily the result of a direct and unmediated contact with God. It most frequently emerged from a situation with which prophet and people were confronted. The prophet's gift was that of clear insight into the religious significance of an event, a situation. He did not first receive, in contemplation, a message from God and then come forth to discover it providentially adapted to the situation confronting his nation. On the contrary, he penetrated into the heart of the events and saw their religious meaning. The light may be called inward, not in the sense that it comes by looking away from the outward, but in the sense that, when the outward is rightly seen, its significance becomes inwardly clear. Margaret Kennedy wrote, in *The Constant Nymph,* of a young girl who felt that " if she could ever see but one thing properly she might quite easily see God ". It was in the process of events that the prophet saw God and declared Him. " The revelation is in the fact, or it is nowhere. But the fact requires an eye to see it. And only if the eye that sees it is single, is the body full of light—Inner Light." [1]

There are two other points which require elucidation in connection with all doctrines of this type.

To whom are " openings " granted? Who are the recipients of inward illuminations? The Society of Friends gives an important place to the Christian congregation. It is the object of a special care and bounty of the Spirit. Illumination and utterance are given to *all* the worshippers. In other schools of the same type of belief the tendency has often been to hold a monopoly of illumination for a few chosen and privileged spirits.

How are the revelations conveyed? Among those who emphasise individual inspiration, there are two theories on this matter. The one believes that light comes only under abnormal circumstances, when the ordinary functions of the mind are temporarily suspended. In the early history of Israel it was in the trance and in ecstasy that people saw the credentials of the true prophet. Paul had to correct the view of the Corinthian Church that ecstatic utterances were more valuable than sober meditations. And nearer our own time it is touching to read that " Edward Irving would pause in the midst of a sublime discourse, in which genius met with holiness, and would keep reverent silence while some ecstatic brother or sister interrupted the preacher with contributions in an unknown and unknowable

[1] See article by J. B. Russell, *Expository Times,* October 1933.

tongue ".[1] The other theory holds that revelation comes through the normal channels, the ordinary processes of thought and will. There is, of course, no doubt of the *fact* of individual inspiration. It is undoubtedly true that most people have acquired convictions on religious and moral questions which no argument could ever shake; against which the pleasures and terrors of the world are powerless. Their convictions shine by an inner light of their own. Arguments cannot shake them, because they are not reached by argument. But clearly, not every " opening " is a divine revelation: not every light is a light from Heaven. The substantial content of the doctrine of the Inner Light is this, that truth authenticates itself to the sincere and obedient soul. The bare theory of individual inspiration could result in making each Christian who believes himself inspired into "his own church and his own Bible ".[2] We must allow a place to the individual—the prophet; yet must also hold that the Spirit authenticates religion to the individual *within the community*. Even the prophet claims that he is right because he represents the *true* community.

Involved in Quakerism at the outset was a marked depreciation of the intellect. This arose, in part, from the disparagement of human reason, and the suspicion that the mind of man might be a possible hindrance to the work of the Spirit, and this defect largely accounts for the stagnation of the Society of Friends during the whole of the eighteenth century. " Depreciation of the part which the intellect plays in religion has always been characteristic of mysticism. The inner experience of religion does undoubtedly result in a new illumination, but that illumination is not the whole of knowledge. An interpretation of religion which may seem to justify men in putting a premium on ignorance can never hold the field for long." But happily this does not necessarily belong to the Quaker position. That is evidenced by their recent history. "The combination of spiritual insight with intellectual and social passion which they present in modern times is a remarkable contribution to the religious life of our time."[3]

1 *Vide* W. P. Paterson, *Rule of Faith*, p. 82.
2 Inge, *Faith and its Psychology*, p. 90.
3 See W. B. Selbie, *Nonconformity*, pp. 106-107.

IDENTIFICATION OF THE TRUTH

In every age there is some recrudescence of Montanism with its theory of private illumination and short-cuts to truth. Illumination there will always be, but, if it is to make any real contribution to faith, it must be authenticated, not only in the two ways already indicated, (1) by the Word of God, (2) by the Church ; but also, more broadly, by that which prevents the growth of idiosyncrasy. Rationality is the criterion applied by the mind : Experiment is the scrutiny applied by life and facts. The obvious disadvantages of the Inner Light are two : (1) that it is not consistent. It may vary from individual to individual ; and (2) it is not permanent and adaptable. There is no organic growth and development of this type of revelation. It is individual, unitary, and atomic. We need therefore to consider two methods by which these weaknesses are overcome, namely, Reason and Experiment as avenues to religious knowledge.

1. THE CRITERION OF REASON

You find that the individual experiences are not consistent with one another. Reason must enter. Certainty, it has been said, comes to the soul in immediate experience, but this certainty has two drawbacks. "The experience from which it is derived does not last, and the knowledge that it brings cannot be shared."[1] Now, if what is given in such an experience is *truth*, then it must be objective and communicable, that is, it must exist in itself, apart from the experience in which it is apprehended, and it must be there for the experience of others to apprehend. It is legitimate, therefore, to invite the scrutiny of Reason. One function of Reason is to find whether intuitions will stand the test of consistency—and that in two ways. They must have inner coherence (they must not contradict one another). And they must have outer coherence. (They must be compatible with what is otherwise confidently believed of the world, man, and God.) The achievement of the intuition is not to give new facts but to convey a luminous interpretation of what is already known or given. The ascent here ceases to be gradual : there is a vertical leap of insight.

[1] Adams Brown, *Pathways to Certainty*, p. 225.

2. THE CONFIRMATION OF EXPERIMENT

It is legitimate also—and necessary—to seek the confirmation of Experiment. For it may be discovered that the inner experience is static, and not adaptable to changing circumstances. If that which is given in the inner revelation is *truth,* then it will stand the strain of life. Faith can come only by the way of experiment—an experiment, Dean Inge calls it [1] (in a phrase which is suggestive, though by itself inadequate), which ends in an experience. So another writer says, paradoxically, "No man has a right to more faith than he has earned; and the only way to earn faith is to act upon it before it comes".[2]

Here we recur (see ch. vi) to the doctrine of the inner witness of the Holy Spirit, *testimonium Spiritus Sancti internum.* It is very clearly stated in the Westminster Confession: "The authority of the holy scripture, for which it ought to be believed and obeyed, dependeth not upon the testimony of any man or church, but wholly upon God (who is truth itself), the author thereof; and therefore it is to be received, because it is the word of God." "Our full persuasion and assurance of the infallible truth, and divine authority thereof, is from the inward work of the Holy Spirit, bearing witness by and with the word in our hearts." "The whole counsel of God, concerning all things necessary for his own glory, man's salvation, faith and life, is either expressly set down in Scripture or by good and necessary consequence may be deduced from Scripture: unto which nothing at any time is to be added, whether by new revelations of the Spirit, or traditions of men. Nevertheless, we acknowledge the inward illumination of the Spirit of God to be necessary for the saving understanding of such things as are revealed in the word." "The supreme Judge, by which all controversies of religion are to be determined, and all decrees of councils, opinions of ancient writers, doctrines of men, and private spirits, are to be examined, and in whose sentence we are to rest, can be no other but the Holy Spirit speaking in the Scripture."[3]

Or we hark back to Calvin[4]: "If then we would consult most effectually for our consciences, and save them from being

---

[1] *Christian Mysticism,* p. 50.
[2] Quoted from Clutton-Brock by Edward Grubb, *Authority in Religion,* p. 38.   [3] Ch. i, *passim.*   [4] *Institutes,* bk. I, ch. vii, §4.

driven about in a whirl of uncertainty, from wavering, and even stumbling at the smallest obstacle, our conviction of the truth of Scripture must be derived from a higher source than human conjectures, judgments, or reasons ; namely the secret testimony of the Spirit."[1] The Spirit which spoke to the writers must speak to the readers. "Let it therefore be held as fixed. that those who are inwardly taught by the Holy Spirit[2] acquiesce implicitly in Scripture ; that Scripture, carrying its own evidence along with it (αὐτόπιστος) deigns not to submit to proofs and arguments, but owes the full conviction with which we ought to receive it to the testimony of the Spirit."[3] We are brought face to face with the question, Does God ever by-pass Scripture and the Church? Has the Quaker emphasised something which, though possibly very unusual, is nevertheless actual? Just as the Westminster Confession is careful to say concerning the Church that it is "the kingdom of the Lord Jesus Christ, the house and family of God, out of which there is no ordinary possibility of salvation", must we be careful to say, concerning knowledge of God, that outside the Bible there is no ordinary means of revelation, yet add in all humility of heart that with God all things are possible?

Emil Brunner, in the first chapter of *The Scandal of Christianity* ("Historical Revelation") condemns the desire for *religious immediacy*. Those who want it are particularly averse to the connection of Christianity with history, with a personality and with the happenings of a distant age, and conceive of truth as timeless and supra-historical. They agree with Fichte in saying that it is not the historical but only the metaphysical that saves and with Lessing in detecting an impassable gulf between historical facts and eternal truth. Thus Brunner is led to indicate the nature of history and its central place in the Christian faith. Human sin is an irrational intrusion into the created world ; and the irrational givenness of the historical event bears an exact correspondence with this irrational fact of sin (p. 15). One is bound to wonder whether there is any need to suppose with Brunner that one irrationality should be matched by another ; and whether it is ever helpful to speak of any work of God as irrational. The assumption is made—is

---

[1] *Arcano testimonio Spiritus.*   [2] *Quos Spiritus sanctus intus docuit.*
[3] Bk. i, ch. vii, § 5 ; cf. also bk. iii, ch. ii, § 34.

there evidence to support it?—that God can speak only in the historical events of the outer world, happenings in the field of public world-history. But God speaks also in the events of the human soul; in man's private encounter with God. These events also must belong to the sphere of special revelation.

RELIGIOUS IMMEDIACY

Let a new plea be entered for religious immediacy. It *is* there, and it is acknowledged, in the experience of the orthodox Christian believer, for only the inner witness of the Holy Spirit can enable him to apprehend the revelation aright. This immediacy is not to be set up as able to stand alone for ever in isolation from the Word and the fellowship: it cannot do that; but it represents the fact that God can speak direct to a man's heart. We must not lose this essential feature of religion because there are often spurious and dangerous forms of it. Indeed the difference between the apprehension of the same revelation by one Christian and that by a brother Christian may be so great that we could not say that the witness of the Holy Spirit spoke in both. The gulf between these two may be greater than that between a Christian believer and an adherent of a pagan religion. We might be compelled to say that the Spirit has spoken in the latter more surely than in the (possibly orthodox) Christian. The one thing of which we must be quite sure in our approach to these matters is this, that God speaks in no magical fashion, whether by inner illumination or by Scripture; but He speaks to the human conditions and through the faculties which He has given to human beings. These faculties will be transformed by divine grace, till they are as new organs of apprehension (as it were a new eye, says Calvin—*Institutes*, bk. III, ch. ii, § 34); but it is these faculties and no others which are transformed. Particularly we must note the place of Reason and of Duty. The weakness of many theological systems is evident here. Revelation, it is said, is infallible; but when we seek to know confidently how revelation can be recognised, the answer is confusion. The Barthian is notoriously open to this difficulty. Revelation is *autopistos*; and, when one asks, How is man to recognise that it is the Word of God that confronts him and not any other word? The reply usually is that this is a question that cannot be answered because it should never be asked. Brunner puts this point, and his reason for making it, perhaps better than anyone else. "That this revelation is a reality, that it is really God who speaks and not a voice of man's own psyche or spirit, falsely interpreted as a revelation —this of course cannot be proved. Why not? Because proving is exactly, by definition, what human thought handles in its own capacity and competence. What is capable of proof is by definition immanent in thought, just as revelation, by definition, transcends thought and is therefore incapable of proof. Faith as it understands itself is a real encounter in which something happens that cannot happen within man's own thought-life."[1] The awkwardness of his statement is that it presents another religious immediacy. It seems that here we have to choose. Either we open the door to complete irrationalism or we open the door to verification. We are beginning to realise that the second must be the choice. Does the divine light shine by itself and shed light on all else?—that is a question that we are not only entitled to ask, but in sincerity are *obliged* to ask. Brunner has said a very sensible thing in his *Revelation and Reason*[2]—"God has granted to man the gift of knowledge. There are some things—in spite of all that can be said from the theological point of view about the absolute darkening of the faculty of reason—that we *know*."

It is to the human faculties with which He has Himself endowed mankind that God addresses His Word; but not to leave these faculties as they are. God speaks to Reason to say what is above Reason; and He speaks through Duty to say what is beyond Duty. This "above" and this "beyond" can be revealed only to those who are faithful to that which is not yet "above" and not yet "beyond".

And this is no alien principle for the Christian who is using his Bible wisely and interpreting his Bible aright. He knows that God speaks in Scripture to say that which transcends Scripture.

[1] *Op. cit.* p. 36.   [2] P. 204 of the English edition.

CHAPTER VIII

GIVENNESS AND GROWTH: CRISIS AND THE NEW LIFE

WE have reached the point indicated in the metaphor by the third stage. After fuel and match, the moment of ignition. We have seen that there may be discontinuity in the process, as it appears to human observation. Nothing apparently new is added, but the whole situation is changed. We arrive in what Heim describes as a new dimension; and the characteristic of a new dimension is that it is recognised, not by additional knowledge, but by a new insight into what is already known. Out of three sounds there is created, not a fourth sound, but a star.

DISCONTINUITY AND PARADOX

Discontinuity is the key-word of Kierkegaard's theology and with it goes the concept of paradox. Insisting on the infinite qualitative difference between the eternal and the temporal, he found that paradox was essential to indicate, first, the profundity of faith; for like Sir Thomas Browne, he longed for an *O Altitudo!*[1] and to indicate, second, the limits of human reason; since he realised that the System, against which he constantly inveighed (the philosophy of Hegel), misses both the terror and the glory of the Christian Gospel. Thus he presents the paradox of despair, which is the "gift of God" and yet "the most dangerous illness of all".[2] (I recall a soldier of the British Army of the Rhine who sent home to his sweetheart an attractive box of innocent-looking candies, bearing the label GIFT. It made all the difference in the world whether the language used was English or German. It was, in fact, German, but the mistake was discovered in time to send a cable to overtake the poison.) Above all, says Kierkegaard, there is the paradox of Christ, "which history can never digest or convert into a common

---

[1] *Religio Medici, sub init.*   [2] *Sickness unto Death.*

syllogism ". Though He entered history, Christ is "an extremely unhistorical person ": He is the contemporary of us all.[1]

Christianity must deal in paradox, as is evident in its affirmation of the Eternal in time; of the spirit incarnate; of the God-man; of the Beyond that is akin: and it may be that in contrast with philosophy the believer is prepared to rest content with this opaqueness of vision so long as he is on his earthly pilgrimage. Paradox is constantly found in the sayings of Jesus —for example " Whosoever will save his life shall lose it " (Matt. xvi. 25); " the last shall be first" (Matt. xx. 16); "having eyes, see ye not? " (Mark viii. 18): "if it die it bringeth forth much fruit " (John xiii. 24);—and in Paul—" the foolishness of God is wiser than men " (1 Cor. i. 25); "having nothing, and yet possessing all things " (2 Cor. vi. 9-10); " when I am weak, then am I strong" (2 Cor. xii. 10); "work out your own salvation, for it is God which worketh in you " (Phil. ii. 12-13); "I live, yet not I, but Christ liveth in me " (Gal. ii. 20).

Kierkegaard undoubtedly carried paradox too far, and left it questionable whether even the divine self-revelation in Christ can bring light. God is, in consequence, described mostly in negative terms.[2] We need to distinguish between those paradoxes which are significant and those which are not, and to realise that the special contribution of paradox in Christianity has been to indicate the endless *wonder* of the Gospel; and to affirm that the Cross must always appear to the eyes of the world as an *offence*. But it is of extreme importance to remember that God is not fully described as the hidden abyss: He is also the hidden home of His people. We worship a God Who has revealed Himself. Of a *deus absconditus* we ought in strictness to say nothing, not even that He is, because we know nothing; and the concept may be more misleading than helpful. It is more important to say that, though God is unfathomable, His own revelation has taught mankind to believe that there is no portion of the whole universe, or of His own unfathomable nature, which is not determined by His redeeming love in Jesus. Truth must appear as paradox to those who are as yet blind to the dimension in which it lies, and it may be that the real paradox of Christianity is not that discontinuity which

Kierkegaard stresses, but the fact that regeneration means a creature marvellously renewed, rather than a new creature— καινὴ κτίσις, (not νέα); that God is able to make use of the old, sinful personality. The converted man has put off the old man, but not human nature. It is not the substance of man that is renewed, but his qualities. He keeps the old human nature, but he gains qualities that are utterly new.[1]

GIVENNESS

In these two contrasted pairs, givenness and growth; crisis and the new life, *givenness* cannot be ignored, for we must all be conscious of finitude, creatureliness, mortality; but we can and often do reject the thought of these limitations on human life. Pride rules our will. We want to owe nothing to any outside agency; to win what we can win by our own bow and spear, or at least to think that we have so won it. But that is not the real danger for theology. It is too obvious to cause worry. The real danger may well be a misunderstanding. The Hebrews were determined to hold on to their tradition of temple ritual and their sacrificial system, and to do so on the grounds that these were part of the divine revelation, that nothing but these could possibly be the will of Yahweh; that they were a sacred part of the Word of the Lord. The Babylonian exile taught a bitter lesson. If faith were to continue it must be free from its anchorage in the familiar and sacred cultus. Faith survived, but the misunderstanding survived also. We still suffer from the corresponding error, whether in doctrines of the verbal inerrancy of Scripture, in new legalisms, in magical views of the sacraments, in unspiritual orthodoxy, or in the exaltation of a particular church to a monopoly of divine favour and of revelation.

GROWTH

On the other hand, to ignore or reject the fact of *growth* is to deny the work of the Spirit. Theological liberalism made an excellent contribution in this sphere, beginning with Lessing

---

[1] See Bernard Citron, *The New Birth*, pp. 21-22.

and his metaphor of the education of the human race. He distinguished religion from the religious canon ; faith from the record of it. All the records might perish, he thought, and the faith still persist, being permanently there apart from its records. He moved the seat of authority from the Bible to the religious consciousness. Reimarus had said that the Old Testament could not be intended as a religious revelation, because of the historical, non-religious elements in it, and because of the absence of such doctrines as that of life hereafter ; but, if we accept the presuppositions of a divine education of the human race, then this negative conclusion is vitiated. The primer must have many childish features and must omit very much which can be assimilated only at a later stage. On the other hand, Lessing erred through the misunderstanding of his own metaphor. He wrote as if education were no more than instruction through the medium of revelation. But education is far more than the passing on of knowledge. On Lessing's own principles the mere transference of a body of truth is unimportant. "Not the truth which a man possesses or believes himself to possess, but the sincere attempt which he has made to reach the truth, constitutes his worth. . . . If God held in His right hand all truth, and in His left only the ever-active impulse to search for truth, even with the condition that I must for ever err, and said to me 'Choose! ' I should humbly bow before His left hand and say, 'Father, give! Pure truth belongs to Thee alone'." [1] It is in the discovery of truth that the full personality is trained and developed. On Lessing's narrow interpretation it was inevitable that history and religion should fall apart. All that was needed was the transference to men of eternal *truths* ; there need be no place for historical *facts*. "Accidental truths of history can never be evidence for necessary truths of reason." [2] This famous difficulty arises for Lessing because of his inadequate view of the divine plan of human education. Christianity is not a body of truth to be conveyed automatically to men. It is bound up with events, persons, institutions, in a word with history. Mankind learns about God, not solely through God teaching, but through God at work, through God entering on the stage of human history.

[1] Lessing, ed. Lachmann and Maltzahn, xi (2), 401.
[2] Lessing, *Werke*, ed. Lachmann and Maltzahn, vol. x. *Ueber den Beweis des Geistes und der Kraft.*

Once the reality of growth was established, it was possible to misinterpret its nature in either of two ways. It might be viewed as the unaided achievement of man's own efforts; and the truth has often been sadly obscured that growth is as much dependent on the divine working as is creation itself; that each stage is a miracle beyond the power of man to compass. But the process is no less misunderstood if the contribution of man's response is denied. This is an ever-present tendency in the loyal religious mind. All is of God: man can do nothing. In supposed loyalty and humility it could become dangerous heresy, and could present even the Person of Jesus docetically, forgetting His boyhood, His developing mind, His soul maturing in conflict; His disappointments, His temptations; His growth in grace. It is the same tendency which today seeks mistakenly to exalt the Old Testament to a position it was never meant to occupy; to speak as if the promise of the Messiah found there in anticipation is on the same plane of revelation as the acknowledgment of a Messiah Who has come, since—so the argument runs—the recollection of Christian people is no less frail and faulty than the anticipation proper to the Hebrew people. In this school of thought, the Advent becomes almost unimportant. In contrast, we must proclaim again and again that between the Old Testament's expectation and the Church's remembrance something happened: Christ came. This Crisis must not be obscured; as it sometimes is in the Theology of Crisis.

Crisis and the new life are best considered together. Comparable with the rejection of the unseen force which lies behind growth and the attribution of all upward movement to human striving alone, is the error of seeing in *crisis* only the natural outcome of the growth, of explaining conversion in psychological terms; of seeing in the Old Testament prophets the inevitable product of the age and circumstances; of seeing in Jesus only a religious man of genius.

The new life may also be misinterpreted in several ways. Even Christians may fall into the mistake of acknowledging their calling yet avoiding the responsibilities of it; taking the privilege and rejecting or ignoring the duty.

Some hold that in conversion there is a complete break with the past; that there remains scarcely even identity with the old self; but this would obscure the actual process, which is not substitution of one thing for another, but conversion of the first into the second. We are not even dissociated from our past sins: what happens to them is that they are forgiven, and so may be remembered to God's glory more than to our shame. We are in fact confronted here with the more wonderful achievement, not the creation of a new person but the remaking of the old. The divine grace has preserved the soul from destruction. We see a parallel phenomenon in the beginnings of Christianity. The Christian Church is continuous with the community of the Old Testament because divine grace ensured the perpetuation, in the midst of disloyalty and disobedience, of a Remnant which, though often a sharer in the disloyalty and disobedience, nevertheless held to its course by virtue of one thing, its belief in God's promise. Here is the response that was called for. The response also is of God: it is God and none other who keeps the hope alive: yet the faithful were summoned to give themselves to the purposes of God and by the way of trust and penitence to bear witness to their belief in the final victory of God which would bring them succour.[1]

The opposite misunderstanding of the New Life is that which suggests that there has been no real break with the past. We need not linger over this view: it is put out of court most manifestly by the testimony of converted people, who proclaim with impressive unanimity that the burden *is* lifted; the power of the past *is* shattered.

Once again, the New Life is not for privilege, nor is it for one portion of the Christian community. That is a grievous error which so elevates the earthly church as to allow it to come between man and God and even to be a substitute for the Church's Lord. It is to the penitent, humble, learning church, and to her penitent, humble, learning members, that victory is promised and power is manifested. We live "between the times", between ὁ αἰὼν οὗτος and ὁ αἰὼν ὁ ἐρχόμενος,

---

[1] A. C. Welch writes in *Kings and Prophets of Israel*, pp. 228-229, "The past contributes to the future: it contributes the remnant who are to be the foundation of the future. Yahweh can use them and He will use them for His own ends. This, of course, means some form of evolution as over against cataclysm. . . . Each new stage then, in its history, since it was a fresh stage in His self-manifestation, brought with it the fullness of the past, lost nothing real out of the great past, but preserved its contribution to the greater thing which was to come."

עוֹלָם הַזֶּה and עוֹלָם הַבָּא within the context of an inaugurated eschatology. The Church is central, but she must never claim to take, or seek to take, the place of the Holy Spirit, though she is used by the Spirit to challenge the world.

These features of givenness and growth, of crisis and the new life, cannot, however, be adequately studied in the abstract. We need a concrete case. Out of many possibilities let us take that of St. Augustine and try to illustrate the essential factors by reference to his experience, vividly described by himself in the *Confessions* and in his letters.

THE WITNESS OF AUGUSTINE

As a child, he had learned to speak the name of Jesus with awe and reverence and wistful longing, thus falling under the spell of the name, before he understood the meaning of it. Those who taught him as a child did not know how great was to be the result of this simple lesson. They were working, though they did not know it, for the long result, and that name came to his rescue at the very moment when he was in greatest need. Augustine was not a believer yet, but the day was coming when that name was to be the rock on which he should build, his shield and hiding-place. Teachers and mothers of children may take heart from this; for even when they seem to have made little headway with their religious instruction, they have already accomplished something very important if they have given a child a wistful reverence for the name of Jesus. Looking back on his youth, Augustine once used that memorable phrase, " And Thou wast at the helm, though very secretly ".

The other sign that God was at the helm is to be found in the account of Augustine's mother, Monica. There is an old Hebrew saying that " God could not be everywhere, so He made mothers ". It was proved true in this case. Monica's one desire and ambition for her son was not that he should have a brilliant career, but that he should become a Christian. She was to see him for many years involved and involved again in darkness and sin. but she never ceased to pray for him and to weep for him, so that the bishop could assure her that it was not possible for a son of so many tears to perish.

The *growth* is dramatically recorded by himself. At the

age of nineteen we find him in Carthage, studying with great
eagerness, but leading a vicious life. He was a close ally of
what we might call today the "fast set". They called themselves "the wreckers". His career, like his soul, was threatened
by the impurity into which he fell back time after time. Looking back on those years long afterwards, he wrote his *Confessions,*
in humility and shame remembering before God the sins and
faults of youth. Sending a copy to a friend, he said that the
book would remind people of what he had once been, and prevent them from holding him in honour which he did not deserve.

In the second period of his life we see the time of the
struggle between light and darkness. As the motto written
across his pagan youth might have been his later words, "God
was at the helm, though very secretly", so the motto for this
period might be the words of his own prayer, surely the most
pathetic prayer in all the history of the human spirit, "O God,
make me pure, but not yet". He longed now to be pure in
soul and body, but he could not bear to give up the secret
delights of impurity. So he kept putting off the day when he
would have to face the call and challenge of Christ. He pretended to himself and to others that he had intellectual doubts
that kept him back, when all the time he knew that his sins
were the only hindrance. They were too precious to give up—
yet. His favourite indulgences and temptations muttered behind
him, and plucked furtively at his garments, so that he might
turn and look at them again when he felt inclined to answer
the call which he heard. Rooted habits, that had long been
very sweet, cried out to him "Dost thou think that thou canst
live without us?"

Then came the decisive hour, the hour of his conversion.
And here we step into a country which must always be
mysterious, because it is the country of God Himself. It is a
mysterious thing when a soul is suddenly changed from evil
to good; plucked out of the darkness and made immortal. "I
had destroyed myself" Augustine wrote later, "but He who
created me created me anew". The story of that hour can
be told only in his own words. The tumult in his breast had
driven him out into the solitude of the garden. "I knew what
evil thing I was; what good thing I was soon to be I knew
not." "I flung myself down under a fig-tree, and gave my tears

free course. . . . And I cried unto Thee incessantly. . . . How long, O Lord; wilt Thou be angry for ever? O remember not our iniquities of old times. For I felt that I was held fast by them, and I went on wailing, 'How long, how long? to-morrow and tomorrow? Why not now? Why not this hour make an end of my vileness?' Thus I spoke, weeping in bitter contrition of heart, when lo! I heard a voice from the neighbouring house. It seemed as if some boy or girl . . . was repeating in a chant the words, 'Take and read, take and read'. Immediately, with changed countenance, I began to think intently whether there was any kind of game in which children sang these words; but I could not recollect that I had ever heard them. I stemmed the rush of tears, and rose to my feet; for I could not think but that it was a divine command to open the Bible and read the first passage I lighted upon. . . . I caught it up, opened it, and read in silence the passage on which my eyes first fell, 'Not in rioting and drunkenness, not in chambering and wantonness, not in strife and envying: But put ye on the Lord Jesus Christ, and make not provision for the flesh to fulfil the lusts thereof'. No further would I read, nor was it necessary. As I reached the end of the sentence, the light of peace seemed to be shed upon my heart, and every shadow of doubt melted away."

Through the long darkness of his night, that name had been sounding like some church-bell to guide lost wayfarers. Again and again it had recalled him from perilous quicksands and now, after many years, it had led him safely from the dimness of things seen to the clearness of things unseen. Here was a foretaste of that time when at the name of Jesus every knee shall bow, of things in heaven and things in earth, and every tongue shall confess that Jesus Christ is Lord.

No figure in history could give a clearer example of the word "transformed"; no life a clearer illustration of the difference that Christ makes. "All men know" Augustine wrote in a letter "that I went to Italy one man, and returned another." In the interval, Jesus had entered his life.

We see the end of old desires and the coming of the new. He uses a significant phrase himself, referring to his conversion as the hour "when I ceased to desire those things". **Never again was he swayed by the old passions which had** disfigured his youth. He was not even stirred by them; the break was complete and final. Only in dreams was he sometimes haunted by memories, but they were dreams which kindled no longings, and "upon waking, I returned to peace of conscience". He had no longer any evil desires, because he was filled with the desires which were God's.

We see also how he changed his mind about sin. He had not worried very much about it before, being like those very modern men of whom Sir Oliver Lodge once spoke—"The higher man is not troubling about his sins." Augustine had got rid of his worries on this score by joining a school of philosophers, the Manichees, who said that sin was not your own fault. It was just an evil kind of nature that you could not help, and you were not to imagine that you were responsible. (It makes us reflect whether it may sometimes be wishful thinking that leads us to choose the school of philosophy to which we join ourselves.) But now Augustine saw sin as a thing of terror; hated it and loathed it; and knew very well that there was no one in heaven or earth to take the blame, but only himself. It is strange that a man does not know how terrible sin is, until he has become a good man. But Augustine never thought of himself as a good man again. When he knew that he was dying he called in his servants and had them write seven psalms on the white walls of his bedroom, and the ones which he chose were the " Penitential Psalms "—" Against Thee, Thee only, have I sinned"; "Cast me not away". In our own age, which tends to think of the language of penitence as extravagant, we have to remember that there are slumbering fires in the soul of man which may break out again at any moment. The angel has us by the hand, and the serpent by the heart. We have read of those higher men who are not troubled about their sins; but they are not in the company of the saints. We read of them in the Gospels. They crucified Jesus.

Augustine has recorded also that he gained a new view of death. Just as his sins began to be a terror to him in his conversion, so death ceased to be a terror. It had once been that. In his earlier days he passed through a bitter sorrow, losing his dearest friend, a companion whose fellowship, he says, was " sweet to me above all sweetness of my life". There was then

for him no God of Love to Whom he might turn for comfort.
His heart was utterly darkened. His eyes sought his friend
everywhere and he hated all places, because *he* was not there.
We think of our own Andrew Lang's

> Twilight and Tweed and Eildon Hill,
>   Fair and thrice fair you be:
> You tell me that the voice is still,
>   That should have welcomed me.

Augustine found himself thinking that his friend was absent
only for a little while. He found himself saying, "He is coming: he will soon be here" and then remembering that he
would come no more. At that time he was unable to say, "He
shall not return to me; but I shall go to him". He saw the
whole world as one dark cemetery. Now compare his words
some years later, and we see what the company of Christ has
done for him in this darkness. A deeper sorrow had fallen
on him, the death of his own son at the age of fifteen. He
can speak with tranquillity of him. "I now remember him
without anxiety, fearing nothing for him." He had not vanished into forgetfulness but simply passed, a little sooner, to the
presence of his Master.

The transformation in the man's daily life can be read from
his own records. On one side is a picture of himself before his
conversion. He had decided to seek his fortune in Rome. His
mother was against it. She saw in this step the destruction of
all her hopes for her son and the fulfilment of all her fears.
Nevertheless he persisted. That might have been pardonable,
but the manner of his escape was not. He persuaded her to
spend the night before the departure in a chapel near the quay,
promising that she would accompany him to Rome. During
the night he sailed away secretly. The other picture is this.
His mother is dead. He stands in her room, remembering how
she had turned to him in her illness and called him "her good
son", and said with great emotion that she had never heard from
his lips an angry word. "But yet", he says, "O my God and
Creator, what comparison can there be between my respect for
my mother and my mother's drudgery for me?" The remembrance of that dishonesty was bitter to him in that hour.

Along with evil passions, the outstanding sin of his early

years was pride. He loved to hear the praises of men. **For these** he worked and planned. Afterwards we find this proud man, who loved to bask in the admiration of the crowds, flinging up a brilliant career simply because he found that he could not serve his Master in it. He would have hidden himself away altogether. It was only with great difficulty that he was persuaded to become a priest in the African town of Hippo. "I have to take the place at the rudder", he says, "when I cannot even manage an oar." Still more reluctantly he accepted the office of bishop in the same place. Beyond that he would not go. Till his death he remained one of a very large number of very undistinguished African bishops. Pride and ambition were dead, because his new life was consecrated to God.

Finally, there is the contrast between former unrest and present peace. Augustine had spent all his youth, as young people tend to do, searching for happiness. He was troubled once, in Milan; for on the way to one of his oratorical triumphs, in which he hoped to find happiness in the applause of the crowd, he passed through the streets and happened to catch sight of a beggar, joking and laughing and blissfully content. Augustine realised that this poverty-stricken man was supremely happy. He had already reached that contentment which so many others were striving after and would probably never attain. In his conversion, the seeker became the finder. He had known dimly, all along, that it was really for God that he was searching. On the first page of the *Confessions* he sets down that famous sentence, "Thou hast made us for Thyself and our hearts are restless until they find their rest in Thee". At last he had found that which he had been dimly groping after; and he knew that happiness was to be found there and only there. Out of all his writings this is perhaps still the most fruitful message. He wrote it again and again as a benediction at the end of his letters, "God make thee more and more happy in Christ, my son."

NON-REDEMPTIVE KNOWLEDGE OF GOD

Here we must look at one of the prominent topics of contemporary theology—Can any knowledge of God be non-redemptive?

The most recent contribution to this discussion from the side of Calvinistic theology is in the debate between Karl Barth and Emil Brunner.[1]   Barth sought to draw a distinction between "natural theology" and "Christian natural theology"; between a doctrine of revelation through Creation which can be gathered from mere observation of the created world and one which can be gathered only from the Scriptures.   Scriptures, Barth now says, bear witness to the revelation in Creation; and this witness is not separated from that of the historical revelation.   This revelation in Creation found in the Scriptures also reveals to man an original truth about himself, and this is an integral element of the message of Christ.

At this point, says Brunner, Barth makes a mistake.   He confuses the *principium cognoscendi* with the *principium essendi*.   He keeps on thinking that the recognition of a revelation in the Creation must imply the recognition of a natural knowledge of God.   He takes the true statement "Only through the historical revelation of the Old and New Testaments is sinful man able to recognise the original revelation of Creation, which is concealed from him by sin" and he turns it into an erroneous statement, "There is only one revelation, the historical revelation in Christ".   Similarly he turns the correct statement "Only through the historical revelation in Christ can man perceive his sin" into the false statement, "Only in the light of the revelation in Christ—namely in the rejection of it—does man become a sinner".   The same confusion of the *ratio cognoscendi* and the *ratio essendi* affects, according to Brunner, the arguments of Barth on the *analogia entis*.   God *has* impressed the stamp of His Spirit upon the world.   Created things *do* bear this stamp within themselves; they do not first have to acquire it through the historical revelation in Christ.   It is of course true that we cannot see the truth of these analogies without the historical revelation in Christ and the faith which it creates.   Barth is defending an important element in Reformed theology against Thomism: the *analogia entis* does not give a sound basis for the construction of a natural theology; for when man is left alone with these analogies he will certainly interpret them wrongly, and in a pantheistic sense.   But it is foolish to go further and say that the analogies only *exist*

[1] Barth in *Dogmatics*, II, i, and Brunner in *Revelation and Reason*.

because of faith. What Barth should have said, and what we are entitled to say, is that they become visible only to faith.[1]

NATURAL THEOLOGY IN A FALLEN WORLD

We are bound to raise the question of "natural theology", because it is in a *fallen* world that we live. Can such a world be a similitude of God's being, and, supposing that it can, is it likely that sinful man would be able to interpret it? Must we not go, for insight into the nature of God, to the revelation through which God undertook the work of restoring the fallen world and redeeming sinful man? Must we not go, in fact, to the history of Israel, the Scriptures, the life and death and resurrection of Jesus? The revelation in Creation, Brunner would seem to say[2] can reveal man's sin but cannot remove it. The Revealer is the same, but the method of His revelation varies. Brunner's distinction between the material and the formal *imago Dei* is a little difficult, but the main contention seems to be that fallen man remains a responsible person ; one who can be addressed by others and by God ; possessing this capacity to hear the Word, yet not the capacity to obey it, but only to disobey. Dr. Brunner is, of course, seeking to avoid the two errors—one, as in the eighteenth century, asserting that natural theology is sufficient and all else redundant ; the other, as in the Roman Catholic theology, holding that there is a natural theology distinct from Christian theology, and capable of providing a rational basis for doctrine. Barclay had his clear answer here. It was that the Inner Light makes it quite plain, for example, to the Mohammedan that Mohammed is an impostor! Perhaps today we are in danger of a similar absurdity, of supposing that revelation makes it clear that Laotse, Plato, Marcus Aurelius, and others like them have nothing whatever of the divine truth. A plausible case could no doubt be made for that assertion ; but it is very doubtful whether the case is founded on revelation alone. Nowhere does it seem to be made plain by the Holy Spirit that in the "good pagan" there is only darkness and error. We ought to be careful that we do not fall into the old pit which yawned at the feet of our

[1] Brunner, *Revelation and Reason*, pp. 77 ff.
[2] *Vide Revelation and Reason*, pp. 66, 76, etc.

forefathers when they made an absolute opposition between Moses and Darwin, and so slowed down the Christian's proper appreciation of both.

SAVING KNOWLEDGE

Of Saving Knowledge,[1] Calvin says that it is not for the heathen. "Though in old time there were many who boasted that they worshipped the Supreme Deity, the Maker of heaven and earth, yet as they had no Mediator, it was impossible for them truly to enjoy the mercy of God, so as to feel persuaded that he was their Father. Not holding the head, that is, Christ, their knowledge of God was evanescent."

The term is one which invites re-examination. Knowledge does not save. To say that it did would be Greek or Indian philosophy and not Christian truth. The basis of the phrase is found in Romans i.19 ff. There is a natural knowledge of God (cf. Acts xiv. 17) but the knowledge that can bring salvation is only by God's Spirit (1 Cor. ii). The term must signify knowledge of God *acted upon,* and that is in fact its connotation in the Johannine writings. It involves correct response and obedience and faith. To know God and to be *in Him* are the same thing.

Inevitably the word "knowledge" is itself open to many and varied interpretations. In the beginning of Genesis, for instance, the knowledge that attracted Adam and Eve has the connotation of intelligence, with a derogatory nuance; knowing one's way about; knowing what's what; the kind of knowledge that is scorned in the book of Ecclesiastes. In Genesis it meant losing the knowledge of God and getting a knowledge of sin. But throughout the Old Testament, *knowledge of God* is almost the equivalent of true religion. It is never merely an opinion; never an otiose conviction, but always a certainty which arises out of an experience of salvation. In the New Testament, ἐπίγνωσις τοῦ θεοῦ stands for knowledge of the Christian revelation together with deeper insight into the obligations which it brings. It leads in turn to a Christian interpretation of the whole world. In Philippians iii. 8 we read, not of saving knowledge, but simply of the knowledge of Christ. And that

---

[1] Salvifica Dei cognitio, *Institutes,* bk. ii, ch. vi, §4.

knowledge means the discovery that men are accepted for the sake of Christ; that they can become by grace what He is by nature; that God sees His children in His Son.[1]

In 1 Corinthians xvi. 22 we come clearly within sight of the fact that it is *love* for Christ that alone matters. Obedience is impossible in our own strength; correct response in conduct or in worship to divine revelation lies quite beyond our unaided powers. So does true love towards God; but in this task of the Christian's life special grace is promised. It was so with those who in Israel continued to be faithful. They were in no way better than many others who were rejected. They differed only in this, that they held fast to the promises of the Lord when others faltered and fell away. They knew that Israel had proved unfaithful to her covenant with Yahweh; but they knew also that Yahweh would never prove unfaithful to His part in it. Attached to such people, the few, the Remnant, almost as a technical phrase of description are the words " they that love the Lord." [2]

THE LIGHT OF NATURE

To speak of " saving knowledge " implies that there is a kind of knowledge of God which is not to be so qualified; and the Westminster Confession of Faith puts this matter quite clearly (i.1): " Although the light of nature, and the works of creation and providence, do so far manifest the goodness, wisdom, and power of God, as to leave men inexcusable; yet they are not sufficient to give that knowledge of God and of His will, which is necessary unto salvation "; and follows it up (xxxi. 1) with the implications in worship, " The light of nature showeth that there is a God, who hath lordship and sovereignty over all. . . . But the acceptable way of worshipping the true God is instituted by Himself."

[1] Cf. Barth, *The Knowledge of God and the Service of God*, p. 74.

[2] See Deuteronomy, vi. 5, " Thou shalt love the Lord thy God with all thy heart . . ."; " He keepeth covenant with them that love Him " (Deut. vii. 9); Joshua xxii. 5, " Take heed to love the Lord your God "; Nehemiah i. 5, " God keepeth mercy for them that love Him "; and frequently in the Psalms, as v. 11, " Let them that love Thy name be joyful in Thee "; xcviii. 10, " Ye that love the Lord hate evil ". Cf. Isaiah lvi. 6, " To serve and love the name of the Lord "; and the divine response " I will love them freely, for Mine anger is turned away " (Hosea xiv. 4).

This raises at once and acutely the problem of the good pagan who has honestly faced the choice and in all sincerity cannot believe as Christians believe ; the problem of the philosopher who has sought to arrive at truth by the application of the only methods which he considers to be unbiased, and who cannot conscientiously bring himself to substitute any others for them ; the problem of the follower of an alien creed who has given to that creed all the fidelity of which he is capable ; the problem of the good man before the Christian era, who lived up to the best that was offered to him in belief and worship and conduct. They are inexcusable and without hope—that is all this doctrine can say about them, even about those of them who had no opportunity to hear of Christ. If this is the truth, then the phenomenon of differentiation, by which some are born to circumstances in which they can hear the Christian Gospel and others not, becomes an insoluble mystery. No doubt that phenomenon will never become transparent to our mortal eyes, but we ought not to deepen and darken its mystery beyond that to which we are compelled.

Brunner has stated his case with admirable clarity in *The Scandal of Christianity* (p. 16). Sin implies that a new situation has been created, an irrational situation concerning which nothing whatever can be deduced from the original order. If there is some immediate, timeless revelation of God, it will presumably have given man knowledge of reality, but "that primeval knowledge which is related to the primeval situation does not give us any light" in the dark and perilous situation which is present and actual, for now man's condition, because of man's sin, is broken and desperate. Conscience may, indeed, tell us what is God's request, what we ought to do, but it can never tell us what is now God's relation to those who have disobeyed His commandment.

Thus the term "saving knowledge" in this context will stand for the knowledge of the way in which God acts in saving mankind ; and this is the meaning also, it is to be presumed, of the phrase in the Westminster Confession (II. vi) "the saving understanding of such things as are revealed in the Word".

There is thus one point which is commonly ignored in this connection. Just as knowledge does not save, and understanding does not save, so it is equally true that salvation must not be

inseparably bound to knowledge or understanding or right
opinion or correct dogma. Inadequate conceptions of God, even
wrong conceptions of Him, do not prevent Him accomplishing
His saving work. Brunner (p. 27) is prepared to maintain that
we are not living in a democracy in this world, but in an
absolute monarchy, since there is between man and God no other
equality except that which He bestows on us by His free gift as
His image. The term "absolute monarchy" is perhaps an unfortunate one, since the bestowal of the divine image on man
seems to indicate that the response which is expected from him
is not that of servile acknowledgment but of loving obedience
to One whose service is perfect freedom ; but it is in the present
reference that the concept of absolute monarchy has whatever
justification may attach to it. The words are less dangerous in
this context, since they represent a truth (though not the conclusion for which Brunner is contending), that God does not
need to wait for correct opinion on man's part before His saving
work can begin. It is the same God who is knocking at the
closed door, though the door may be a thick one and the
residents asleep, or deaf, or careless, or ignorant. There were
conceptions and practices which Jesus condemned outright, but
the search for God made by the sincere Gentiles was never one
of them. If we apply that to our own day it will mean that the
fact that philosophy may often ignore the Christian revelation
—even despise it—need not make the Christian despise and condemn the philosopher or say that his philosophy is utterly
devoid of revelation. The philosopher, no less than other men,
needs the appeal of Christian patience. Intolerance seldom
advances a cause : where there is sincerity on both sides, only
the intolerant is condemned.

If we learn at all from the teaching of Jesus we learn that,
wherever God judges, He also offers salvation if man turn to
Him in penitence and need. The extreme doctrine at this point
falls into error by condemning those whom God has not condemned. We must believe that God, having appointed men
to their lot, has given them the opportunity of saving faith.
Otherwise they are not only inexcusable ; they are inescapably
doomed. It is hard, perhaps it is impossible, for us who live
within the dispensation of the Gospel of Jesus Christ to imagine
how salvation can come to any who are outside, since that would

suggest that it can come otherwise than through His incarnation, death and resurrection ; but we know also that with God all things are possible. Sin and grace should never be thought of in separation, and therefore we ought never to speak of sin as if it were the last word. Man could not know the darkness and the desperation of man's life unless the light of revelation had broken through the darkness and illumined the despair.

It is the same God Who seeks the heathen through the works of His hands or through His own private speech to them, and Who has sought us through His Son. Encounter with this God must have saving significance, if it is real encounter, however it occur. Brunner would join issue here, for he argues[1] that the essence of religion is that which Christianity has ; while that which is possessed by Christianity in common with other faiths is non-essential. It is difficult to accept this view of the essence of religion, for it seems that if God meets with a man at all, there is nothing non-essential in His self-communication. Instead of agreeing with Brunner that general revelation does not give saving knowledge, we should ask, *Can* God impinge at all on the life of a man and not do so savingly?

The better term is "saving faith", as in the admirable chapter with that title in the Westminster Confession of Faith (xiv) ; and it is quite clear that, if we cannot join with that Confession in its anathema "Others not elected, although they may be called by the ministry of the word, and may have some common operations of the Spirit, yet they never truly come unto Christ, and therefore cannot be saved ; much less can men not professing the Christian religion be saved in any other way whatsoever, be they ever so diligent to frame their lives according to the light of nature, and the law of that religion they do profess ; and to assert and maintain that they may, is very pernicious, and to be detested" (x. iv)—if we cannot take part in that anathema, then we escape one perplexity, that of believing that God left the greater portion of His children to gloom, despair, and final condemnation, only to fall into another, that of justifying our urgent call to evangelise the world. If we are not prepared to take the extreme view and to hold that there is no hope for any one born outside the reach of the Gospel, then we may be challenged to defend our sense of a world-wide

[1] *Revelation and Reason,* p. 220.

mission. It is to be noted at once that those who cannot share
the extreme view are no less urgent in their sense of the obligation laid upon them to carry the name of Jesus to the ends of the
earth. Many of them are to be found among the ranks of
devoted missionaries in far-off lands, giving all their lives to the
service of Christ because of their belief that there is none other
name than His whereby men must be saved; yet knowing in
their hearts that they never yet entered an alien country or
spoke to a pagan household without discovering that God had
been there before them. They know well that man—pagan and
Christian alike—is a compound of angel and demon; that
nothing can make him a son of God but the Gospel of Jesus
Christ. There seems to be paradox here. In Matthew xi. 25 we
have the declaration of Jesus Himself " All things are delivered
unto Me of My Father: and no man knoweth the Son, but the
Father; neither knoweth any man the Father, save the Son,
and he to whomsoever the Son will reveal Him ". Dr. Kraemer
maintains [1] that we cannot use the word "fulfilment" concerning
the Gospel in its relation to the ethnic faiths; that they are not
to be regarded as in any way a *praeparatio evangelica*; but I
think he ignores another possibility. Christ both judges and
fulfils the genuine non-Christian faith as He does both judge and
fulfil the Christianity that is sincere but inadequate. The
relation of Jesus to the Old Testament gives us the pattern of
a fulfilment which is also a judgment. There is no incom-
patibility in these two processes. In the matter of the ethnic
faiths also, though the way of God is not transparent to us and
perhaps can never be, we can trace the tension of continuity
and discontinuity, of the three sounds and the star. We may
express the truth either way—(1) There is continuity, but nevertheless something that is absolutely new comes into being; or
(2) There is discontinuity, yet the good that was in the old is
not annihilated but fulfilled.

No blame can attach to the people to whom the light of the
Evangel has never yet been brought nor, so far as human
judgment can be relied upon, even to those who have turned
from the light in honest disagreement. The blameworthy
attitude is to see the light and, recognising it as the truth,
nevertheless to reject it. Admittedly, we must all acknowledge

[1] *Op. cit.* p. 123.

the perversion of our own hearts and confess that much "honest disagreement" has within it a root of sin. The unbeliever who is eloquent about his unbelief—the loud mocker in the roaring street—is often betraying the insecurity of his own guilty conscience. The agnostic who makes a show of intellectual superiority may be merely superficial, but there is at least a strong possibility that the spiritual pride which is in all of us like a core of sin has all unknown to him asserted itself in an ingrained habit of evasiveness.

What should be the response of the Christian to the challenge of the non-Christian faith which may seek to "absorb the values of Christianity" and what should be the attitude of converts to Christianity towards their own sacred scriptures? Hinduism offers the clearest instance of these difficulties. The Hindu may point to the long controversy recorded in the New Testament concerning circumcision and the burden of the Jewish law; and to the wise and providential decision of the Apostolic Church that these were not to be imposed on Gentile converts; and may go on to argue that the same kind of decision should now be made in respect of the Old Testament documents. Even as we have now ceased to assume that Western civilisation should necessarily accompany the spread of Christianity, so, it might be affirmed, we should pass from insistence on the prescription of the Old Testament as "required reading" for the Eastern catechumen. Ought not the Hindu to be allowed to offer the Upanishads as an alternative?

Certainly, we are not to put a stumbling-block where none should be. And we may perhaps believe that in the Old Testament we see not simply particularity of revelation, but also uniqueness of response; that the duty of obeying and keeping the Covenant was always a condition of continuing as God's people (Exodus xix. 3-6); and that the human response to the Word in its turn becomes the Word of God. It is true that we must also go further and acknowledge that without the grace of God that unique response could not have been made; but nevertheless the distinction between revelation and response is sound and important. We may realise also that Israel had to learn in harsh experience that many things which once appeared to be part of the indispensable essence of religious worship and practice, as for instance the temple ritual and the sacrificial cult, though they were accepted as owing their institution to God's direct decree, could nevertheless be taken away without bringing Israel's religion to an end; and we may go on to wonder whether the lesson learned by Israel in the bitterness of Exile may be one which God is impressing on us by the experiences of missionary enterprise today. But we notice that the proposal, that the scriptures of the Vedas should take the place of the Old Testament for Indian converts to Christianity, is generally put forward by the non-Christian Hindus; and we may suspect that there is more of nationalism in it than is at first apparent. Most of all we must indicate the obvious danger, that, in return for a tolerant recognition of the claims of the New Testament, a *quid pro quo* may be expected whereby the Christian would make a corresponding affirmation concerning the value of the Vedas, and that this is simply one more expression of the all-absorbing catholicity of Hinduism. Deep down lies its belief that all faiths are equally true—and all equally false. When Gandhi writes, in the interests of toleration, that "Everybody is right from his own standpoint, but it is not impossible that everybody is wrong" he indicates unwittingly the fundamental weakness of Hinduism, and the impossibility of its being allied with Christianity. The two differ theologically in the region which matters most. Where Christianity believes in the redemptive action of God the Creator of the world, the Father of Jesus Christ and our Father, Hinduism believes in "a supra-rational, supra-personal unitary Reality", which according to some not only transcends in its own nature everything known in experience or apprehended in thought, but which even annuls all such in its unitary integrity.[1] On the theme of Incarnation the two present, it may be, a superficial similarity, but in fact they diverge vitally. The Hindu scriptures deal with ideal truth, not with historical event. The most plausible case can probably be made out for that supreme flowering of Hinduism which is found in Bhakti. In this emotional attachment which is distinct from knowledge or action, man recognises that if he does not love and worship he becomes confined within the prison of his own egoism. When rightly regulated, this way leads to the perception of the Supreme. According to the Bhagavadgita, Bhakti, or true

[1] Vinjamuri E. Devadutt in *Biblical Authority for Today*, p. 63.

devotion, is to believe in God, to love Him, to be devoted to Him and to enter into Him. It is its own reward.[1] In this approach to God there is profound insight, but it does not escape the touch of profoundest pathos, for there is nothing *in fact* which Hinduism can offer to its vision and its longing. The avatars are the militant gods struggling against sin and death, evil and destruction. Quoting the familiar words of Vishnu, "Whensoever righteousness languishes and unrighteousness is on the ascendant, I create myself. I am born age after age, for the protection of the good, for the destruction of the evildoers and the establishment of the law" the same author adds "It is an eloquent expression of the law of the spiritual world. If God is looked upon as the saviour of man, He must manifest Himself whenever the forces of evil threaten to destroy human values." But the succeeding words give the other aspect. This is Hindu *mythology*.[2] Hinduism thus offers either a way which is false and must be rejected since it leads to an idea of God which is in contradiction of Christian truth, or a way which raises longings for a saviour which it cannot satisfy. If it is said that the Old Testament also looked forward to a Messiah and that the Messiah who came was very different from the expectation, it is still true that the Hindu convert will not be helped towards an understanding of Jesus by a more intensive study of his own former scriptures, but rather hindered. Jesus fulfilled the prophecies of the Old Testament, and He cannot be understood as the Christ without a knowledge of the Old Testament. He did not fulfil the Vedas or the Upanishads. Without denying what is lofty in them, we need to point to the Old Testament as the historical preparation for the New; and to commend it, not as a burden, but as the Book of Jesus Himself, knowing that those who wish to understand Him will wish to know His Book.

Furthermore, there is that which we do not have in ethnic faiths. We do not find the *event*, the coming of Christ into history; and therefore we do not have the message of salvation which the event declared; for Christ not only brought the message: He also *is* the message. We must therefore listen to the warning notes, such as that spoken by Jesus Himself in Matthew

[1] See Sir Sarvapalli Radhakrishnan, *Indian Philosophy*, vol. I, pp. 558 ff.
[2] *Op. cit.* p. 545.

xxi. 37 : "Last of all he sent unto them his son, saying, They will reverence my son." God sets a limit, "Last of all ". Beyond that He has nothing more. If that does not win men, they have exhausted even God's resources. Nor do we infallibly know when the limit has been reached. We may be near the verge, and beneath there may be the precipice. Another step in the wrong direction, and we have gone too far. Hence the tragedy of last-minute repentances. The soul goes out on its dark journey and no man can tell whether it has been accepted on the far side. All the world is judged by the God of all the world ; and, in the nature of God's dealing with mankind, it is those who have received the full revelation who will be most harshly judged in failure. Of those to whom the Gospel has not been preached we cannot say more than this, that they will be judged by a God Who is all-righteous and all-merciful. The warning note which is sounded throughout the New Testament might drive men to despair, were it not that side by side with the warning goes the promise. The parable of the Husband-men declares God's infinite patience. After all the contempt and cruelty which he had been shown, God still held His hand. Instead of punishing, He sent one more embassy. The Son was sent not to destroy, but to ask, and to ask only what was His by right. There is thus more than infinite patience ; there is infinite love behind the patience. God mustered *all* His resources and placed them without reserve at the disposal of men, and all the reserves of God's love are called up to save every soul. It was natural for the human father in the parable to think that they would reverence his son. He had no fore-knowledge of the future. What of God, who knows the hearts of men? One by one the prophets had been spurned and killed ; yet in spite of all, He entrusted His Son to the same race of men. We know the tragic outcome. "They will reverence my Son " ? They did not reverence Him till it was too late, and He was crucified. Man's unfaithfulness seemed to be finally and for ever sealed in that act. Nevertheless the outcome is not tragic, since it is still in the hands of God. God goes on loving when the worst has happened. He might have left the world to its own ways ; might have withdrawn His sustaining power, which men had rejected along with Himself, and might have allowed the earth to grow cold and all life to perish. It seemed that

His experiment of making men had failed. Man himself had shattered His hopes. Somewhere else—perhaps on some remote planet—it might be tried again with more likely material. Yet this was not the end, for it was still God who was concerned. Even after all that had happened He trusted men. In the Resurrection, Jesus came back to the earth that had rejected Him; in the coming of the Holy Spirit at Pentecost men were declared still to be the recipients of the supreme divine gifts.

JESUS AND HISTORY

Not altogether dissimilar from the position of the loyal and sincere Hindu in respect of his ancient scriptures is that of the earnest philosopher genuinely seeking to interpret the Christian witness by the categories with which he is familiar in the exercise of reason and the study of history.

Jesus is *in* history, yet not *of* history. He willed to enter history; no *man* does that; and because He entered it of His own choice He is not controlled by history. He is Lord here also. Faith confronts the same event as unbelief and indifference and materialism confront, but faith discovers a new dimension in the event. When St. Paul, in 1 Corinthians ii, says "I came to you not with excellency of speech or of wisdom, declaring unto you the testimony of God. For I determined not to know any thing among you, save Jesus Christ, and him crucified", he is witnessing that he has discovered in that event of history the significance of an eternal redemption; but he is not to be interpreted as repudiating the whole of human reason. When Luther quotes the same passage and says that the Christian "should know only Christ and Him crucified, for in such knowledge alone is justification of faith" he proceeds at once to add that, apart from justification, when a Christian is disputing with others concerning the power, wisdom, and majesty of God, he should employ all his wit and industry to that end and be as profound and subtle a disputer as he can, since then he is "in another vein".[1] The believer is bound in honesty to become the philosopher. "One of the most devastating of life's ironies", says Professor Urban,[2] "is the seeming fatality which drives the believer to join with the unbeliever in attempting to

---

[1] *Commentary on Galatians*, i. 3.   [2] *Humanity and Deity*, p. 41.

demolish all attempts made by reason to justify his belief ". And if the believer is bound in honesty to become the philosopher, we ask, May not the philosopher, through his honesty, become the believer? The knowledge which he acquires by sincere devotion to truth is knowledge of God and of God's world.

Again there is a real similarity in the case of the earnest moralist. He is in pursuit of truth. It is not impossible, indeed, that our purest feelings should conspire to deceive us, but, as Lotze asserted, it would be intolerable. The theory that what presents itself as a necessity of ethical thought may nevertheless prove to be misleading or at the least uninformative concerning the ultimate nature of things is as unreasonable and as incredible as any other kind of ultimate scepticism.[1] Plato believed that if we live as we ought to live we shall see things as they are (and the Christian has learned that obedience is a condition of the grasp of divine truth); and went on to argue that if we see things as they are, we shall live as we ought. The second is, unfortunately, not true since man lost his innocence; but it is always true that the two are inseparably connected. It is the pure in heart who shall see God. We may say with truth that conscience dawned in man as a result of man's fall. In a state of innocence he would not need to await the command of the Beloved One: he would anticipate His wishes.

THE RESPONSIBILITY OF WITNESS

The aim of the evangelist is to confront others with Jesus Christ, the Way, the Truth, and the Life, and to do so in the full knowledge that this will involve those others in that judgment which inevitably follows on failure to close with Christ when confronted by Him. It is a dilemma that runs through much of Scripture, which tells of those who are blinded by the light, made deaf by the hearing of the Word; whose hearts are hardened by the advent of the Gospel, so that it brings not health but condemnation upon them. As scholars in His school we have a responsibility to God's other children; and, as in all education, training, or proclamation of the truth, we introduce a danger for them that was not present before. Just as every sermon is a crisis—lest the Word be heard and not re-

[1] See Hastings Rashdall, *Theory of Good and Evil*, II, p. 230.

ceived, and so turn to judgment and not to blessing—so every missionary act is two-edged.   But it must also be said that the challenge presented to the non-Christian will continue to elicit, as it has done again and again in the past, responses to the Christian Gospel which have never come hitherto from Christian circles.   The contribution of the young Christian churches to the understanding of the Gospel is profound and far-reaching.

There is urgency in the call to go into all the world preaching the Gospel, and humble Christians acknowledge that in the day of judgment the member of an alien race and a strange faith may go in to the Kingdom before them, if it is their failure in evangelism that has prevented him from encounter-tering Christ as his Saviour and Lord.

Dr. Alan Richardson is very clear and constructive on the matter of *saving knowledge*.   "As we have said that all revela-tion is from God, so we must now add that all revelation is *saving* revelation.   The knowledge of God is always saving knowledge.   We cannot for one moment entertain the view which, in the imagined interests of the Gospel, is ready to argue that only the biblical-Christian knowledge of God, or special revelation, is redemptive, and that general revelation falls out-side the sphere of saving grace." [1]   He would therefore prefer to speak of "general revelation" rather than of "natural knowledge of God".   And he goes on to say "There is indeed a sense in which the noblest insights of the humanist are ful-filled in Christ, but there is also a sense in which they are judged and transcended by him" (p. 129).   "Thus special revelation is not a concrete illustration of general revelation, but a correction and transvaluation of it."   I believe that he is here sounding a note of warning which should be taken to heart.   (1) It can be real Bibliolatry to say that God cannot speak outside the Bible ; it may even be blasphemy.   (2) The knowledge of God that comes from elsewhere is not to be dis-missed as "natural".   It is not "natural" but revealed, as all knowledge of God must be.   No more than Biblical knowledge of God will it come to any but the sincere and the obedient. (3) Revelation in Christ can give that which is utterly new without decrying or destroying that which has gone before.   To

[1] *Christian Apologetics*, p. 127.

use the imagery from Abt Vogler again, the star is not out of all relation with the three sounds, because sounds and star are all alike from God. The hybris lies in imagining that man can pass from sounds to star, or produce any of them, by his own creaturely skill.

Recall Calvin on this (*Institutes*, bk. i, ch. vi, §1): "Therefore, though the effulgence which is presented to every eye both in the heavens and on the earth, leaves the ingratitude of man without excuse, since God, in order to bring the whole human race under the same condemnation, holds forth to all, without exception, a mirror of His Deity in His works, another and better help must be given to guide us properly to God as a Creator. Not in vain, therefore, has He added the Light of His Word (*verbi sui lumen addidit*) in order that He might make Himself known unto salvation (*quo innotesceret in salutem*) and bestowed the privilege on those whom He was pleased to bring into nearer and more familiar relation to Himself."

We begin perhaps to feel that the absoluteness of this distinction—between condemnatory knowledge of God in the mirror of His works, and saving knowledge of God through His Word—is precarious. *God* cannot be known at all without a saving significance. (And "adding the Word" is surely the wrong phrase. The revelation is a unity. We are wrong to think of a time-schedule of operations.) There is faith in all knowledge of God, even in that obtained by the contemplation of the world. Without faith, that would not be knowledge of *God*. And if it is knowledge of God, it is saving knowledge. It is customary, I suppose, to say that we have here sufficient at the most to drive home the need of salvation, but not to point to its reality. The true distinction is probably between the general and the particular; and the chief feature of the second is that we have to do something about it: it is a challenge to decision. The requisite caution is that we should not dogmatically rule out the possibility that *some* are challenged to this decision by the first way; though we may be very well aware that in the first there is far greater danger of misinterpretation, of going wrong through human blindness and error. By the grace of God, conviction is both enlightenment and enablement. Were it the first only, without the second, the consequences would be despair. We need both simultaneously. Moreover, only when we are enabled to do the will, can we know of the doctrine. The knowledge comes by action.

We seem, therefore, to be directed to this position:—There is redemptive significance in all of these—the decision of the good man (even the good pagan) to do what is right though the heavens fall; the loyalty of the pious Moslem to his own faith, in the belief that it is the true one; the devotion of scientists to the austerity of disciplined research; the rationalist's intellectual persistence and his sense of the inherent sinfulness of apathy and indifference when the solemn questions of life are placed before him. When decision is made for the best that a man knows, there is redemptive significance in the choice. God is present, using the situation and its challenge towards the saving of the man's soul. "Glory, honour and peace ($\epsilon i\rho\eta\nu\eta$, שָׁלוֹם—that is *salvation, eternal life;* for the Hebrew word of which $\epsilon i\rho\eta\nu\eta$ is the regular translation, has this profound meaning) to every man that worketh good, to the Jew first, and also to the Greek" (Rom. ii. 10). This is one of the few passages in which St. Paul makes generous acknowledgment of man's natural endowment. Normally he refers to it for the sole purpose of indicating that all men are without excuse (Rom. i. 20). The urgency of man's need of redemption through Christ is so overwhelmingly present in his mind that he makes small allowance for the place and function of conscience. Where the Gentiles have the guidance of conscience, it is not by intuition but as a consequence of their natural knowledge of God. Natural religion indicates that God is omnipotent, a lover of order and not of confusion; purposive, well-disposed towards men; and men ought in their own lives to imitate these qualities, of orderliness and benevolence. St. Paul did not develop this view and therefore has nowhere given a thorough examination of the difficulty that arises too clearly from it. The difficulty is this —if the moral sense of the Gentile is derived solely from his observation of the created world and from his reflections on it and his consequent conception of God, then there is nothing to prevent him from including within his idea of God, and seeking to emulate in his own conduct, those features of tragedy, of cruelty and indifference which cannot be separated from the contemplation of nature. If therefore the Gentile is truly endowed with a moral sense which is sufficient to make him inexcusable, it must have another source than that of the panorama of the created universe. He has found elsewhere the right to deplore the apparent cruelty and indifference of nature. The proper distinction here seems to be that which we have already made. Clearly, knowledge *about* God, knowledge of hearsay, can be utterly non-redemptive; may be little more than science or philosophy; may call for no decision, bring home no responsibility: knowledge *of* God is necessarily redemptive, in the sense that it brings a man into the critical situation. If it leads to confrontation, the recognition of the divine Person challenging a man, the decision which results must have redemptive significance, for the man is either accepting or rejecting. He will never be the same again.

Robert Barclay[1] has his own special, very definite and dogmatic opinion on all this. (1) There is, for *every man*, a day of visitation. (2) There is a measure of light in all men. (3) If the light is received and is not resisted, God's salvation is wrought in all, even in those ignorant of the death and sufferings of Christ.

The substratum of truth in his contribution is, I think, this, —that it is certainly no part of the defence of the Christian Gospel to decry human reason which God has created and implanted; and no consequence of the revelation of God in Christ that we should decry His action in history and in the mind of man.

Religious knowledge as little demands the sacrifice of Reason as the religious life demands the ascetic renunciation of the normal activities of human life. (Some of the mystics tried this way, and there was a nemesis of eroticism in their thoughts and writings. The corresponding nemesis that may follow upon the rejection of Reason is seen in excessive dogmatism and barren scholasticism.) Further, the divine act of revelation is not confined to the birth, life, death, and resurrection of Jesus. It includes the Old Testament history. It must be widened out at least as far as that; and, since the history of the Jewish people has ramifications far beyond the pages of the Old Testament, there is no *a priori* and obvious reason why the sphere of revelation should exclude the actions of God in nature and in secular history. God has spoken to the heathen through the works of

1 Prop. V, vi, §xi.

His hands; and God is at work in secular history, not simply to negate it, but to turn it to the divine purpose. Professor William Manson has noted[1] that the Jewish "Similitudes of Enoch" present a Son of Man, the representative of the people of God, who is exalted and glorious indeed, but not a redeemer. "He does not stoop to earth, nor integrate himself with history. He bears no sins or sorrows. He lays no transforming law of love on a reclaimed humanity. He merely waits in heaven to receive an elect who come to him at the end of days when he shall reign among them. It is another mystery altogether which is unfolded to us in the Gospel. It is *the mystery of a transfigured apocalyptic which takes history up into its process, which indeed apocalyptises history.*" Nevertheless the paradox remains, and the danger of interpreting some one event or some one period prematurely as final and determinative. "The Second Advent", Professor Manson continues, "*is never allowed to become identified with any contingency in contemporary events, however earth-shaking and portentous these may be.*" But we are not yet clear of the problem—a problem perhaps in the same category as that of universalism—if the improving of common grace may be sufficient for salvation, what becomes of the urgency of world-evangelism? If God will have all men at the last, what becomes of the urgency of the Gospel? I have sought to answer this by saying that, just as we cannot dogmatise about the soul of a child and his place in the economy of God (as our forefathers were inclined to dogmatise), so we cannot set limits to God's grace; but we dare not slacken our efforts to carry His Gospel to all the world, and to proclaim the Incarnation, the death and resurrection and eternal reign of Christ, our Lord and Saviour.

If I were to sum up the conclusion to which I have been carried, it would best be done in the admirable phrase of Whichcote, the Cambridge Platonist. He is answering Tuckney, who had complained of " a vein of doctrine, in which reason hath too much given to it in the mysteries of faith ". Whichcote answered "I oppose not rational to spiritual, for spiritual is most rational". And I might develop the thought in five propositions. (1) Revelation does not act by discarding or dismissing the normal faculties. (2) Reason is not discarded by revelation,

[1] In *The Scottish Journal of Theology*, June 1952, p. 119.

but illumined. (3) The moral consciousness is not left behind by revelation, but is enabled. (4) Historical events are not negatived by revelation, but are turned to the divine purpose. (5) Man's individual disobediences are caught up by grace to man's own good. God takes the human situation, together with all the complications which man's sin has introduced into it, and deals with it, still in love.

What is the place of reason in the final conviction of a religious man? It is right, as we have seen, to seek confirmation, by every means at our disposal, not because the Christian is seeking a compromise between faith and reason, for the sake of peace and quiet, but because he aims at the integration of faith and reason in the name of truth. (It would be easy to make out a case for St. Thomas, commonly called the Doubter. He wished to be as sure as it was permitted him to be, in a matter which was of the utmost significance for his own eternal destiny.) But it is wrong to suppose that confirmation is all. The means of confirmation can examine Browning's "three sounds": they cannot produce the "star". They cannot even comprehend it when it appears. Revelation is not discovery: it is the self-communication of a loving, personal God. All that is true and fundamental. But it is important also to realise that God's self-communication does not come by magical ways. The divine Spirit speaks through man's natural faculties to illumine and to transform the soul. It seems to employ ways which are certainly mysterious but nevertheless familiar. It operates through the avenues of man's thought and man's action. Therefore the verdict of Reason and the confirmation of Experiment are valuable elements and genuine factors in religious conviction.

Finally, we should keep in mind that there are five respects in which we must ask how the Inner Light or the *Testimonium Spiritus Sancti* is to be regarded.

Relation to the Bible. In the case of the *Testimonium Spiritus Sancti*, the answer is simple; for it is to the Bible that the witness is borne. The only religious authority is the Holy Spirit speaking in the Scriptures and speaking, therefore, of Christ of Whom all Scripture tells. The doctrine of the Inner Light is equally clear, but allows vast uncertainty as to the Scriptures. The divine and inward revelations, says Barclay

(Prop. II) can neither at any time contradict the Scripture's testimony—as they cannot contradict the testimony of sound reason. If it is true that the same God is speaking through them all, clearly there is a pre-established harmony in what is said and revealed. But the Scripture is not a good nor certain rule. See, he says, how the different denominations of the Christian Church are continually buffetting one another with Scripture. Nevertheless, he affirms (Prop. III) that they provide, after the Spirit, the secondary rule. "We do look upon them as the only fit outward judge of controversies among Christians." So perhaps Barclay could be pressed to admit that the controversies arising between Christians of different denominations are due, not to any error or opaqueness of the Scripture, but to faulty or obstinate readings of it. It would be very hard for him to prove that the Inner Light had been any more successful in removing occasions of controversy among Christians. There is no need to illustrate by recalling instances of contradictory findings claiming the support of immediate revelation. Of the two, immediate revelation and Scripture, it is fairly clear that the less liable to faulty interpretation is the Scripture; whereas the two when combined, as is visualised in Reformed teaching, provide us with the nearest approach to ultimate certainty that is available in our human pilgrimage.

Relation to the Church. In the case of both the Inner Light and the *testimonium Spiritus Sancti* it is necessary to say that private interpretation must always be dangerous; that religious knowledge comes by way of the worshipping community; yet we must certainly allow that truth is given also to the lone worshipper. Once that has been clearly stated, however, we are forced to go on to say that the lone worshipper has learned from the Church of the past, and it is frequently his part in the corporate Church of the present which (possibly now only by aftereffect but just as truly) keeps him sane and wise and balanced. Of the Church, Barclay holds that, just as it is the life of Christianity taking place in the heart that makes a Christian, so it is a number of such, being alive, joined together in the life of Christianity, that make a Church of Christ (Prop. X). The Church consists of "such as God hath called out of the world, and worldly spirit, to walk in his Light and Life . . . it comprehends all that are thus called and gathered truly by

God, both such as are yet in this inferior world, and such as having already laid down the earthly tabernacle, are passed into their heavenly mansions, which together do make up one Catholic Church, concerning which there is so much controversy. Out of which Church we freely acknowledge there can be no salvation; because under this Church and its denomination are comprehended all, and as many . . . as become sanctified by it, and cleansed from the evil of their ways." Compare the passage from the Westminster Confession, "The visible church . . . consists of all those throughout the world that profess the true religion, together with their children; and is the kingdom of the Lord Jesus Christ, the house and family of God, out of which there is no ordinary possibility of salvation", all going back to Cyprian, "He who has not the church as his mother has not God as his Father".[1] Perhaps our forefathers were thinking of Cyprian in terms to which Gwatkin once gave frank expression: "Saint he is and martyr; and the Christian Church is justly proud of him; yet his general conception of religion is much more heathen than Christian."[2] They were exercising a right and proper caution; guarding against the idea that the Church is indispensable, or that it necessarily secures salvation, and also against the idea that God regards His own appointed means of grace as of slight importance. With God all things are possible; but God has provided this, His chosen way—that of the Word and of the Spirit. The Church is the servant of the Word and it is the servant of the Spirit; yet we declare that it is the *divine* servant whom God Himself has chosen.

Relation to the creatureliness of man. Finitum non capax infiniti. The Inner Light can mislead; can be supposed to be present when that which is confronting us is really an upsurge of the unconscious. The question of the reliability of the immediate illumination must be raised. Is this applicable also to the belief that we have the *testimonium Spiritus Sancti internum?* Religious conviction, when wrong, has led to such terrible results that we are under the most profound obligation to be humble. There are two errors to be avoided. On one extreme, we recognise man's dignity and ignore his corruption, and so fall into pride. On the other extreme, we realise man's

1 De Catholicae Ecclesiae Unitate, v. 6.   2 *Knowledge of God*, ii. 167.

infirmity but forget his value, and so become a prey to despair. Christianity, as Pascal said, has alone been able to cure both these vices, pride and despair, "not by expelling one through means of the other, according to the wisdom of the world, but by expelling both according to the simplicity of the Gospel ".[1]

Relation to the sinfulness of the recipient. This is a much more vital matter. *Homo peccator non capax Verbi Divini.* Is it conceivable that we should feel free to transfer to our knowledge of God even the loftiest thoughts and even the purest principles that are appropriate in speaking of our knowledge of the created world, of the events of history, of the demands made on us by duty, of our converse with other selves? How. we ask, is it possible to do this when we are involved in the contrast between Creator and creature ; between the Infinite and the finite ; between the Holy One and the sinner? In answer we are bound to affirm that man was not meant to be for ever creaturely, finite, and sinful. Within him he has that which is creative ; those longings which are part of the infinite ; that love which is the foreshadowing of a life in which sin has no dominance. Repentance implies the acknowledgment that these creative impulses, these infinite longings, these foretastes of a holy life are not our own achievement, but come from God alone. Redemption means that the fulfilment of these creative impulses, these infinite longings, these foretastes of a holy life, is already on the way. The testimony of the Holy Spirit and the radiance of the Inner Light are disclosed as redemptive activities, with power to remove the sinfulness which is the barrier to knowledge of God ; both to illumine and to enable. Where these things are happening we have the surest indications that it is God Himself at work. Where mysticism ignores the gulf between sinful man and the Holy and Redeeming God, it proclaims itself as inferior.

Relation to history. (Even to geography? An old Quaker woman once said: "Jerusalem? It has not yet been revealed to me that there is such a place.") (1) We must remember the influence of other revelations and interpretations which have preceded us. Christian theology cannot be immune (and should not be) from influences coming out of other worthy ways of thought and worship. (We think perhaps of the influence of Zoroastrianism on the ideas of later Judaism or of Greek influence in

---

[1] *Pensées,* 435.

the early Christian Church.) These ways of thought and worship are to be corrected and judged by Christianity; but they are not to be ignored nor despised. (2) We recognise the relation between immediate illumination and historical event. We realise that there are times when and people to whom illumination may come most of all by inspired interpretation of what is happening in the world. (3) We place first the relation of immediate illumination to the events of the Incarnation, the Cross, the Resurrection. Once again, that mysticism marks itself as inferior which is out of relation with these events; which makes history irrelevant.

When Karl Barth argues for a " Christian natural theology" he employs a phrase which is misleading, for the answers to the questions posed are, of course, drawn by him from Christ and from the Bible, not from nature. It is right to guard against belief in a natural capacity of man to discern and to test revelation; but we ought also to raise the question whether Christian theology is infallible. May not "Natural Theology" have worthy corrections to make? But once again, we are probably wiser to employ the term "General Revelation" and not "Natural Theology". Ultimately, indeed, the apprehension of religious truth is through repentance and faith. Yet there are many strange ways by which man is moved to repentance, and many unreal obstacles which can be taken away in order to allow faith to enter in and to expand; and for this both reason and experiment have their proper place in the divine plan. Assuredly it is only too easy to place excessive reliance on the results of speculation and of experiment. Scientists too can be pontifical and will often accord to a favourite hypothesis of the day "a more than credal inerrancy"; but this, says Professor C. E. Raven, "is all a normal, lovable, and entirely human procedure which only invites criticism when its devotees imitate the behaviour of other priesthoods and claim a pontifical authority for their theories".[1] From the opposite side, Buber quotes Luther and Calvin with their belief that "the Word of God has so descended among men that it can be clearly known and must therefore be exclusively advocated" and he adds in comment "I do not believe that; the Word of God crosses my vision like a falling star to whose fire the meteorite will bear

[1] *Science, Religion and the Future*, p. 88.

witness without making it light up for me, and I myself can only bear witness to the light but not produce the stone and say 'This is it '".[2] The truth surely lies between these two extremes. It is not that all the Word of God is plainly comprehended by the Christian, so that he can be completely intransigent towards others; nor is it that religious illumination is the momentary trace of a meteorite from which we can only seek to record the centre of radiation and to deduce the nature of the light which is now invisible. Reading the parables of Jesus, one cannot believe that Jesus meant to convey the irrationalism which characterises some theologies in our day.

A study of the factors involved in revelation and personal conviction indicates on the one hand the relation of faith to certainty and on the other the relation of faith to love. It is not always a contradiction to speak of " faith as certainty ". Faith may be contrasted, at the one extreme with dread, despair, anguish; but at the other extreme with vision. In contrast with the first it partakes of certainty; in contrast with the second it seems to lack the final touch of assurance. What we discover is, in fact, that there is certainty sufficient to assure us that salvation is offered, but not certainty sufficient to satisfy our speculative curiosity. We discover, moreover, that the distinctive feature of love (*Agape*) is not that it is directed to that which is unlovely, nor that it is spontaneous, though both may be true, but rather that it is a love which chooses. It is not merely emotional: it sees with clarity and it counts the cost. In man, it is response, as Nygren rightly insists; but that fact does not make it identical with faith.

There is a knowledge of God which is hearsay, and there is a knowledge of God which is of the heart. There is airy soaring head-knowledge; and there is saving heart-knowledge. And the fault is not having the knowledge of hearsay, but resting in it; the fault is not in the airy, soaring head-knowledge, but in the using of it to evade the challenge of God. The saints do not believe in God: they know Him. Here it is not mental accomplishment that counts. A child could understand: indeed *only* the child in heart could understand. That can scarcely be said of much of the transcendent theology of our time which has sought to displace theological liberalism and has succeeded in

1 *Between Man and Man*, p. 7.

obscuring many of the values of liberalism. Thus I am pleading for humility among theologians. Not humility before men only, though that also is commendable when it is not truth that is at stake but the theologian's own cherished theory; but humility before God; readiness to recognise that His thoughts are higher than ours; that His voice may be heard by others when our ears are not in tune. It is only when we are humble before God that we can be valiant for God.

EPILOGUE

"THIS then is the message which we have heard of Him, and declare unto you, that God is Light, and in Him is no darkness at all. If we say that we have fellowship with Him, and walk in darkness, we lie and do not the truth: but if we walk in the light, as He is in the light, we have fellowship one with another, and the blood of Jesus Christ His Son cleanseth us from all sin. If we say that we have no sin, we deceive ourselves, and the truth is not in us.

"If we confess our sins, He is faithful and just to forgive us our sins, and to cleanse us from all unrighteousness."

This first chapter of St. John's First Epistle, with its theme, God is Light, may have been present to the mind of Beethoven when he composed a striking passage of his opera *Fidelio,* the *Hymn to the Open Sky.* The hymn is sung by a crowd of prisoners. They have spent many years in the darkest of dungeons, without a glimpse of sunshine; then, for one brief spell, they are brought up into the courtyard of the castle. They come stumbling out of dark stairways, white-faced, worn by starvation and stunted for lack of sunshine. They stand for a moment bewildered and dazzled. Then, raising their hands to the blue heaven, they join in the noble hymn of praise to the open sky and the sunlight and the fresh breeze blowing in their faces. Down there in the dungeons, they had forgotten what light was. Their only fellowship was amongst themselves, and they had begun to believe that this was the highest reach of human life still available to them. Now they are face to face again with God in the splendour of His sunshine and His fair world.

> O welche Lust! in freier Luft,
> Den Athem leicht zu heben!
> O welche Lust! nur hier, nur hier ist Leben,
> Der Kerker eine Gruft.

Wir wollen mit Vertrauen
Auf Gottes Hülfe bauen.
Die Hoffnung flüstert sanft mir zu,
Wir werden frei, wir finden Ruh'.

From the beginning of religious writings the term " darkness ", it has been found, has been the most appropriate word to
describe human sin, that which shuts out the light and glory
of the world. It is more than all else a kind of prison, where a
man is bound and fettered by his own passions ; where, after a
time, he loses his own will and is compelled to do the sinful
things he would not.

There is the dungeon, but there is also—and this is the
wonderful feature—*the secret stair* out of the prison, the stairway of confession. " If we confess our sins . . .". Stumbling
in the gloom of his cell, the prisoner finds this way leading
upwards. It needs courage and faith to follow it. It may be
only a trap taking him into a more rigorous captivity, taunting
him with the "torture of hope", or luring him out to some
dangerous ledge of the castle-rock ; but then it comes into his
mind that this secret stair has been opened for him by his friend,
who is outside the castle, planning and working for his escape,
even at the risk of his own life. Somewhere up there he will be
waiting for him. The secret stairway of confession is God's plan
for man's escape. He is waiting above for man to come to Him.

Our prisoner takes that way, believing that it has been uncovered for him by his friend ; and, at the top of it he finds *an
open door*. His friend has been faithful: he has kept his word.
" If we confess our sins, He is faithful." Take that secret stairway and you find the open door. How grim if it were not so ;
if the door were locked and barred ; if the prisoner, exalted by
hope, were forced to turn back again to the dungeon. There
have been genuine doubts on this matter ; but since the life
and death and resurrection of Jesus we have the words of promise
and assurance, " Behold I have set before thee an open door,
and no man can shut it."

The prisoner slips through the open door, and now he is
done with darkness. About him are *the wide spaces*, the sunshine and the fresh air. He bursts forth with the hymn to the
open sky. Yet these prisoners of the opera—they go back again
when their short spell of exercise is over. They return to the

same dark and hopeless dungeon, and their captivity is all the more hideous for this memory of sunlight and liberty. But we remain. " If we confess our sins . . ."—that is the secret stair. " He is faithful and just to forgive us our sins "—that is the open door. " And to cleanse us from all unrighteousness "— that tells of the wide spaces of a new life in God's love. *We* are done with darkness.

The Secret Stair. Acknowledgment of sin. " If we confess." There is an " if ": there is doubt about it ; for perhaps the most difficult thing that a proud human being has to do is to admit that he has been wrong and grievously wrong. Especially is it hard to acknowledge, in this greatest of all matters, that he has been wrong ; that he has known the love of God in Jesus and has brought shame on it. It is easy to make a good case for ourselves ; it is tempting, when we have wronged a friend, to keep out of his way, to avoid meeting with him, to seek any company rather than his—and even to end by working up a grievance because he is no longer the constant companion he once was. But the only secret stair out of the darkness is this of confession. It would be easier if we were called upon only to acknowledge in general terms that we are sinful ; human beings and therefore sinners. That admission costs little. We could almost feel in making it that we were apologising for the manner in which we had been created. But the words are " If we confess our *sins* "—the particular things we have been guilty of ; and such confession costs a great deal : it is a guarantee of sincerity. Confession in such particular terms is a personal and searching discipline. For, consider what sin is. It is godlessness, the desire that there should be no God at all ; that we might live in a world where no divine hand could reach us. And consider what confession involves. It means acknowledging definite sins ; and it carries the admission that the defiance of God was our own act ; that we take on ourselves the responsibility of it to the end of time ; that we are prepared to acknowledge that once we deliberately accepted this as part of us. Sin that remains unconfessed may work like a poison in the soul ; may make necessary a whole system of pretence and lies ; but the sincere confession of it sweeps away for ever this false hope, and the soul recovers its simplicity. As a child stands before his father, having told everything, the soul stands before God.

The Open Door. Before the Gospel came into the world, men could never quite be clear in their own minds whether their confessions did not go into the empty air. Just as an enemy may spurn our apology, so God might turn from our confession. The secret stair might end at a locked door. But Christ has lived and died and risen again. " If we confess our sins, He is faithful and just to forgive us our sins." The prayer for help is answered. Our turning home is not the only thing that has been happening. In the parable of the Prodigal Son, Jesus meant His hearers to see that the chief character is not even the younger son; for, if the father had died, the wanderer might have returned to find the door shut, the home deserted and the possibility of forgiveness lost for ever. But the father lived and loved and waited. (See H. R. Mackintosh, *The Christian Experience of Forgiveness*, pp. 13, 100), God is faithful, and the abiding proof of His faithfulness is the life and death and rising again of Jesus. The guarantee of God's forgiving love is His Cross. It is that which has replaced the intimacy of actual touch with Jesus in the days of His Flesh.

"Faithful" the verse says; but it adds " and just ". There is the thread of a more sombre colour running through the pattern. There is a note of sadness which makes itself heard in passing. God is just, too. Our sins cannot be glossed over and ignored, for they meant the Cross for Jesus and they still mean that. There is the Open Door, but there remains also, till memory sleeps, the recollection of that dungeon. A bitter memory, yet still a memory that makes the new life the sweeter.

From the dungeon the prisoner comes first by the secret stair to the open door, and then emerges into *The Wide Spaces.* Forgiven! And now a joyous life to live, for God will cleanse him from all unrighteousness. The significance of this new liberty is well illustrated by a story not now available in print ("The Solitary", by George W. Cable in *Strong Hearts,* Hodder and Stoughton, 1899). At the close of the American Civil War a young Confederate officer, caught in the reaction that followed the excitement of campaigning, had fallen deeper and deeper into intemperance, till, in the shame of it, all his friends passed him in the street. He lost heart; he lost hope. Only one friend was loyal to him; and to him he confessed that he still had occasional spasms of virtue but they were of no value to him, because he lacked all strength and depth of character. His friend suggested that these spasms of virtue might be used to cure himself completely. The man was roused by the suggestion and acted on it with novel vigour. He sailed off alone in a small yacht to a deserted island in the Mississippi Sound, taking with him only his food and a parcel of books. Landing there, he deliberately burned his boat and so cut off all hope of escape. He knew that the lighthouse patrol-boat would pass that way in a month's time, and till then he must live without alcohol. The craving did not come till the middle of the second week. He drowned his thirst in water; but soon the craving began to seem better than the stream's brief cure of it. He formed the habit of running up to the hill-top to look for a sail, though he knew there was no chance of seeing one. He broke under the strain. He pledged creation and its Creator that on the day of his return he would drink the cup of madness, and would continue with it till he died. Then a saner moment came. He began to discipline himself. For one hour he would stay where he was without going to look for a sail. He found he could lengthen the period. Then, one day, a sail appeared; and he went mad, shouting and waving. But the ship had already turned about. In a frenzy he began to build a raft. He would escape even at the risk of his life. He was to set off the following morning; but that night a storm rose and destroyed the raft. The storm saved him. There was no escape now. He became resigned. He almost fell in love with his prison. Peace was restored to his heart. He began to read the books he had brought. One of them, slipped into his bag by the wife of his friend, was a copy of the Psalms. There was one which caught his attention, a very long one. (It was the 119th). It was in the evening, after a most marvellous sunset, and he read on to the last verse in the fading light and closed the book.

Let my soul live, and it shall praise Thee; and let Thy judgments help me. I have gone astray like a lost sheep; seek Thy servant; for I do not forget Thy commandments.

Then he sat in the nearly motionless air, gazing at the ripples of the lagoon as, now singly and now by twos and threes, they glided up the beach tinged with the colours of departing day

as with a grace of resignation, and sank into the grateful sands
like the lines of this last verse sinking into his heart; now singly
—"I have gone astray like a lost sheep"; and now by two—
"I have gone astray like a lost sheep; seek Thy servant"; and
now by three—"I have gone astray like a lost sheep; seek Thy
servant; for I do not forget Thy commandments." When the
patrol-boat rescued him, he was a changed man.

"This is it that we declare", writes St. Augustine in his
Homily on the First Epistle of St. John "that 'God is Light,
and there is no darkness in Him at all'. Who would dare to
say that there is darkness in God? Or what is the light? Or
what darkness? Lest haply he speaks of such things as pertain
to these eyes of ours. 'God is Light'. Saith some man, 'The Sun
also is light, and the moon also is light, and a candle is light.'
It ought to be something far greater than these, far more excellent, and far more surpassing. How much God is distant from
the creature, how much the Maker from the making, how much
Wisdom from that which is made by Wisdom, far beyond all
things must this Light needs be. And haply we shall be near
to it, if we get to know what this Light is, and apply ourselves
unto it, that by it we may be enlightened; because in ourselves
we are darkness, and only when enlightened by it can we become
light, and not be put to confusion by it, being put to confusion
by ourselves. Who is he that is put to confusion by himself?
He that knows himself to be a sinner. Who is he that by it is
not put to confusion? He who by it is enlightened. What is
it to be enlightened by it? He that now sees himself to be
darkened by sins, and desires to be enlightened by it, draws near
to it: whence the Psalm saith, 'Draw near unto Him, and be ye
enlightened; and your faces shall not be ashamed'.... If 'God
be Light, and in Him is no darkness at all, and we *must* have
fellowship with Him' then from us also must the darkness be
driven away, that there may be light created in us, for darkness
cannot have fellowship with light."

———

"Then spake Jesus unto them saying,
I AM THE LIGHT OF THE WORLD,
HE THAT FOLLOWETH ME SHALL NOT WALK IN
DARKNESS,
BUT SHALL HAVE THE LIGHT OF LIFE."

INDEX

INDEX OF BIBLICAL REFERENCES

Date Due

MAY 9 '73			
MAR 15 '73			
MAR 29 '73			
MAY 7 '73			
NOV 21 '73			
OCT 31 '75			